HIGH & MIGHTY

When Samuel Spencer and Elizabeth Hill Johnson "retired" from aspects of Salem public life in May of 1979, many gestures and gifts were made. The several hundred present in the special pavilion raised for the occasion must have judged it among the more hilarious evenings of recent times. But at the same happening some of us decided that a lasting gift should be made.

It was my assignment to come up with something appropriate. As yet there is nothing in this fragmented age so lasting as print. Then State Representative Rick Gustafson and I at last decided that a special book about some aspect of Oregon history would be most suitable. My eventual determination was that we commission a number of special papers from persons who in some way share the very personal commitment the Johnsons have for so long given to central Oregon, and the Deschutes and Metolius rivers in particular.

It was a great pleasure to work with the estimable persons whose observations follow, and with Bruce Taylor Hamilton who determined all aspects of the format of this book. Thanks should go also to those who assisted financially the publication of this commemorative volume: Judge Owen Panner of Bend and Portland, Robert F. Wallace and Leland Johnson at First National (now First Interstate) Bank of Oregon, Frank Gilchrist of Gilchrist, Phil Dahl in Redmond, Harold Barclay of Sisters, Robert Chandler, editor of the Bend Bulletin, *Al Becker at Pacific Northwest Bell, Gerald Frank of Salem, John McGehey of Boise Cascade, Bill Moshofsky at Georgia Pacific and Donald Frisbee at Pacific Power and Light Company, Portland.*

As it happens, Sam and Becky never retired at all. He gave up his long-held seat in the House of Representatives in the Oregon Legislature only to begin immediate service as Mayor of Redmond and President of the Oregon Historical Society among many duties. Becky left her distinguished service on the Oregon Board of Higher Education only to join the Educational Coordinating Committee, to name but one of her demanding assignments.

Good citizens are the greatest of the many wonders in Oregon.

Thomas Vaughan
Executive Director
Oregon Historical Society

DEDICATION

These select sketches, gathered by their friends to honor Samuel S. and Elizabeth Hill Johnson, are published in recognition of the Johnsons' long and inspired public service and generous benefactions to Oregon and the Deschutes country.

HIGH & MIGHTY

Select Sketches about the Deschutes Country

Edited by

Thomas Vaughan

Oregon Historical Society
1981

Frontis: Mid-1850s view of Black Butte and Mt. Jefferson, a rendering published as part of the *Pacific Railroad Reports*. The Metolius River flows from the opposite flank of Black Butte. A century after this artist's interpretation was done, Samuel S. Johnson donated the headwaters of the Metolius to the state of Oregon for a park (OHS Coll.).

Cover and dustjacket art work by Bruce Taylor Hamilton and Sidney Howard Wildesmith.

Library of Congress Cataloging in Publication Data

Main entry under title:
High & mighty
    Includes bibliographical references and index.
    1. Deschutes River (Or.)—History.   2. Deschutes Valley (Or.)—History.   3. Deschutes River (Or.)—Description and travel.   4. Deschutes Valley (Or.)—Description and travel. I. Vaughan, Thomas, 1924-   . II. Title: High and mighty.
F882.D45H53   979.5′6   80-84482
ISBN 0-87595-066-3   AACR2
ISBN 0-87595-103-1 (pbk.)

Printed in the United States of America

CONTENTS

ILLUSTRATIONS & MAPS

[All illustrations from the collections of the Oregon Historical Society, unless otherwise noted]

INTRODUCTION

In the late 1940s I had the good luck to camp several times on a bank above the Deschutes River mouth. I was going back and forth to school on the East Coast and I never felt that I was getting to my own stamping ground until I had seen legendary *Spilyai* the coyote slinking down the hillside above Celilo Falls and heard the wondrous sound of the autumnal cataracts of the Columbia. But the arid Deschutes scene was different. It burbled down from a cleft in the southern hills, cool and green, bringing a wonderful torrent of fish-filled water into the Columbia, a then less harnessed, less hardworking and more interesting stream.

In those pre-pool days I had no thought or special knowledge of where the Deschutes waters came from. The broad uplands, the arroyos and twining canyons winding down from the Cascades and their lupine covered foothills rising to masses of firs and pines were unknown to me. I was captivated by the sun and moon and the winds eddying through the Deschutes gorge. It was apparent from the simplest nudge of a toe in the river sand that native Americans had lived near the Deschutes mouth for many centuries, although this archaeological record is now engulfed by impounded water as are so many rich and evocative sites. And what had occurred upriver on the Oregon plateau cut through by the Deschutes

Thomas Vaughan

I could scarcely tell. It was obviously a very high and mighty stretch of country. Nor could it be of such an even disposition as the beautiful central stream suggested. It seemed never to rise or fall. Dreams of those hot and windy evenings at the high end of the magnificent Columbia River Gorge are only transcended by memories of an occasional moon-filled night of sublime memory. Permanent intruders in the Gorge may thoughtlessly deface this magnificent landscape even more than it has been by our last two generations. We do not as yet understand our obligations to Nature and Time.

In the mid-1950s as Director of the Oregon Historical Society I soon had remarkable opportunities to look into the life of the Deschutes basin and to observe through the eyes of its oldest settlers some of its arcane secrets—not all of them contrived by Nature.

First, however, I read some of the earliest reports, astonishingly accurate and comprehensive for their time. Especially those from John Frémont in the mid-1840s, who headed south from my camp built on one site of his own campfires, and even more those in the Pacific Railroad survey reports of the mid-1850s. Not only were those observations broad and useful, but so also were the stylized and in some degree whimsical drawings. More particularly did I respond to the romantic content in style and tone—most unlike the federal reports of today.

In his "Geological Report" of 1856 for the Pacific Railroad survey John S. Newberry begins to rhapsodize, as well he might:

Standing on the summits of the passes, we saw the main crest of the range crowned by several peaks of considerable altitude, but particularly marked by the lofty and snow covered cones of Mount Jefferson and Mount Hood, trending away nearly due north. . . . This mountain system seems like some grand fortification, as though Nature, when the broad plateau, which reaches inland from its base, was redeemed from the sea, had built along its western margin a wall of such altitude as should forever bid defiance to the waves, and at all the salient or re-entering angles had planted towers which should strengthen and command the whole. . . . The series of principal peaks marks the line of fracture in the earth's crust, along which the greatest exhibition of volcanic forces would naturally be displayed. Toward the east, the great plateau preserves its general horizontality, only broken by subordinate hills and mountains, which mark the cracks and fissures formed in the convulsions by which it has been shaken.[1]

Strong and meaty fare, but hardly an exaggeration. There is vastness, magnificent scale, grandeur. Newberry and his companions also exclaim over the region south of the Three Sisters, "abounding in lakes, mountain meadows green and fresh, and forests of fir and pine, of different species from those occupying the plain below. The soil in many places was fertile, the scenery as picturesque as can be found in any part of the world." How true. But especially so in summer. Winter has its own extremes, at least for some observers. The entire landscape has a fierce and intimate beauty, from the broken skyline familiar to hikers, horsemen and motorists to the darkest canyons known to native fishermen, botanists and poachers. And certainly with the cataclysmic blast from St. Helens peak off to the north, only a year ago, one's historical perceptions of the landscape are heightened and intensified. Mountains are not, after all, imperishable. The noble Roman phrasing of Ovid comes to mind:

I have seen land made from the sea: and far away from the ocean the sea-shells lay, and old anchors were found there on the tops of the mountains. That which was a plain, a current of water has made into a valley, and by a flood the mountain has been levelled into a plain. The heavens, and whatever there is beneath them, and the earth, and whatever is upon it, change their form.

And all along the eastern slopes of the Oregon Cascades appear more and more man-made changes. The long vistas which Newberry so well described, the empty meadows, some so deceptively boggy, are filling up in the 1960s, 70s and 80s as more and more thousands are attracted, one way or another, to what Israel C. Russell in his *Preliminary Report* of 1905 described as "the seemingly boundless plains." It may be the cerulean sky or the winy aroma of the air laced with juniper berries—slightly crushed but not stirred. The climber standing on the lunar-like summit of Smith Rock, the shunpiker driving along in the dust- or ice-covered back roads soon comes upon palpable reminders of man's occupation of this landscape—ancient and not so long ago.

fig. 1

Black Butte & Mt Jefferson
Central Oregon

No 2897
Copyrighted by
B.B.Bakowski

fig. 2

xiv

fig. 3

Fig. 1: Looking north across a meadow near present Sisters, dark and symetrical Black Butte and rugged, snow-capped Mt. Jefferson, Oregon's second highest peak, rise in striking contrast. Compare this photograph with the mid-1850s view (p. iv) reproduced as the frontispiece of this book (OHS Coll.).

Fig. 2: Beef cattle graze in the Cascade foothills, with the striking silhouette of Three-Fingered Jack rising in the background. The animals and the peak represent two major features of the Deschutes country—livestock and rugged scenery (Dept. of Trans., OHS Coll.).

Fig. 3: A solitary horseman poses for this Benjamin A. Gifford photograph of the falls on the Deschutes River just above Sherars Bridge. Originally used by Indians as a crossing and fishing site, and later forded by fur traders and pioneers, the site was used by John Y. Todd to build the first bridge in 1860 (Gifford photo, OHS Coll.). (Best known for his many early photographs of the Columbia Gorge, the remarkable photographer Benjamin Gifford left a treasure of evocative images of the Deschutes country, many of which are reproduced in this volume.)

fig. 4

fig. 5

xvi

fig. 6

Fig. 4: Somewhere northwest of Bend, Benjamin Gifford used two companions to set the scale for this turn-of-the-century photograph of (from left) Broken Top, South Sister and the shared bulk of the Middle and the North Sister (Gifford photo, OHS Coll.).

Fig. 5: Three early women hikers clamber on one of the lava formations in the Three Sisters area, probably near McKenzie Pass (OHS Coll.).
Fig. 6: Early climbing party begins its ascent of either the North or Middle Sister (background). The group is on the shoulder of the mountains near the present location of Sunshine Shelter (OHS Coll.).

fig. 7

fig. 8

Fig. 7: Deschutes County's Benham Falls. Located about ten miles south-southwest of Bend, this Deschutes River cataract occupies the attention of the spear-fishing gentleman (Gifford photo, OHS Coll.).

Fig. 8: Redmond's Main Street in the 1910s (possibly a holiday; the American flag flies midway down the street). Sharing this scene with other land-sales agents are the B. S. Cook & Co. and the Redmond Town Site Co. in the building to the right, offering, "farm and city property," "800,000 acres in Central Oregon, large and small tracts, cheap lands, easy terms" (OHS Coll.).

Native Americans learned the harsh and unrelenting aspects of life in central Oregon, and through countless generations, found the means to mother a spartan existence there. But one also sees in decreasing numbers each year the rude and modest pioneer shacks, homes and barns of broken dreams. Flapping and shuddering in the hoary blasts of winter, cracking and sagging in the blazing sun, these are the vanishing homesites of those tireless dreamers who attempted to live without water or power other than their draft animals, including their exhausted and too trusting wives and children.

Let us look at the view with Essie Maguire, who has just come over from the Willamette Valley to be a school teacher, living with a homesteading family on a small ranch with no well and no water—except that hauled by the husband. In a series of letters she wrote to her family in Portland, she expressed:

It is cold again—dry and cold. . . . During the day it ranges around twenty. Last week for a day or two it was perfectly beautiful—not warm by any means—but just pretty. There was a heavy fog nearly all week and it froze all over everything . . . every tiny needle on the junipers and every little leaf on the sage brush was four or five times its natural size with frost . . . and every barb of the . . . fencing looked like a huge chrysanthemum. . . . It just looked like an ice and snow world. I have never seen anything like it before—but I am told that it is quite common here. (25 January 1915)

Last Wednesday we had the worst wind storm of any since I have been here. For about two hours in the afternoon . . . the whole country was one cloud of dust. Lots of time we couldn't see the wood pile or the fence around the school yard—and they are only about fifty feet from the building. . . . I am sure that one couldn't have walked along the road facing it [the wood] . . . .it is that awful, awful dust. Mrs. Nichols says that real estate is changing hands when the wind blows like that—and it surely does. Some poor fellows find half of their homesteads and all of their seed scattered over their neighbors' fields the next day. (23 March 1915)

I wish you could see McGregor's place [the only one irrigated].
*It consists of about two hundred acres—all under cultivation and
as level as a floor—with just here and there a juniper tree out
in the big fields. I thought to-day that I had never seen a more
beautiful picture than the immense field of alfalfa in which we
played ball. The alfalfa is up about four inches and it looks like
an enormous green lawn. . . . All the stock was turned on it. Away
back near the other end of it were the horses—about ten I guess;
then scattered over the whole thing were pigs and chickens and
great white geese and some turkeys . . . and then the water ran
through the irrigation ditches, and the sky was blue and the sun
shone brightly over the whole thing. You can't imagine how pretty
it was.* (25 April 1915)[2]

Miss Maguire kept a useful and revealing diary, but let's be factual;
not every questing emigrant to America is a natural farmer, rancher or
economist. Too many learned the hard way—as did our native-born, as
will other questers in the future.

One of my friends of long ago who knew the far-ranging country
so well was Maida Bailey of Sisters. Sitting in her beautifully constructed,
low-sloping ranch house (now burned), we regarded the sunset illuminating the alpine immensity to the west. "Yes," she stated,

*we had our good times. We would all come together at a house
or barn like ours. The wagons and the horses would arrive. A
few would walk. The men would get together for a smoke. There
would so some jugs. A number of the women would cry for a
while. Life was so hard. Then we would dance all night long. Until
breakfast time and daylight. Then everyone would go along home.
They were great times.*

With the arrival of railroads, roads, improved wagons and then automobiles, especially with irrigation ditches, dams and electric power, everything changed. The long dark nights were pierced. Loneliness was amelior-
ated. Who would believe how much aspects of life could change, or that
certain grim examples might go relatively unheeded in the face of a high
technology economy. Life that was once hard, brutish, but relatively sim-

ple, based on the necessities of life, has become much more complicated and interdependent, based on a series of probabilities that "the earth and whatever is upon it" might in several ways change form. It does not necessarily follow that the change of form will manifest itself as progress or improvement. The vastness of the West has through the decades been spotted with long-forgotten towns. But the men and women who have been attracted to Oregon's high and mighty country have been an energetic and ingenious crowd, and their eyes have been opened to more than one main change.

When Orrie Johnson for one came up the tree line years ago, responding to a treed horizon that promised so much, he was building for himself and his family to follow him. This remains the vision of Samuel and Elizabeth Johnson and hundreds of others who have established and moulded the very finest tranditions of high and mighty central Oregon—the Deschutes country. To the Johnsons who have contributed so generously to the public service traditions of the Deschutes country and the Pacific Northwest we respectfully dedicate these essays.

HIGH & MIGHTY

HIGH
&
MIGHTY

High were the mountains shoved into the sky long ago to help create central Oregon's grand scenery, and mighty were the forces that twisted seabeds into domes and peaks, while giant volcanoes were taking shape to the west. Over a span of millions of years, the earth-warping forces and pressures lifted old marine beds from bays to peaks, warped thick lavas into folded mountains and reshaped shores of continents.

New in the field of geology, this continental drift concept is called by geologists "plate tectonics." It is one that will give new meaning to central Oregon's high country. Dr. Ewart M. Baldwin, University of Oregon professor of geology, writes: "Recent evidence indicates that the crustal margin of the Pacific is being shoved under the continent, resulting in a series of thrust plates off shore. This plate tectonics concept should be kept in mind when considering the geologic history of the region. This shoving movement has affected the old formations."

Faulting like this has created in south-central Oregon, land of fault-block mountains, some of the most spectacular scenery in the West. Lava, pouring from volcanoes and fissures and spilling from vents like those girdling Newberry Crater, has smoothed some of the faults and giant cracks in the earth.

A kindly minister-geologist, Thomas Condon, with Bible in pocket

Phil F. Brogan

and pick in hand, first probed into the grand story of Oregon's high interior country. He opened new chapters that attracted the attention of savants at eastern colleges and museums. It was Condon, Oregon's first state geologist, who "caught a first glimpse of lands as they rose from the ocean bed and saw her first strange mammals feeding upon her old lake shores."

Actually, the study of Oregon dates to the epoch of sea exploration when ships' captains scanned rugged headlands to note a "range of high hills," or to observe, as did Lt. William R. Broughton from his boat in the Columbia River on October 29, 1792: "A very distant high snowy mountain now appeared beautifully conspicuous." The mountain was, of course, majestic Mt. Hood.

Peter Skene Ogden, trapper, trader and explorer, also got some fine views of the "high country"—central Oregon—when he penetrated the upper Deschutes country in 1825-26, on his first trip into the rugged region. "A grand and noble sight," was Ogden's description of the Cascades from a viewpoint on Tygh Ridge. The close-up view inspired Ogden to make special mention of the country through which he was passing. To the south was bulky Mt. Jefferson. In the distance beyond Jefferson were three white peaks later known as the Three Sisters. Ogden said they were in the shape of sugar loaves. There was little geology in his description of the peaks, but in later years they were to receive full geological attention.

John C. Frémont, in his 1843 passage through the Deschutes basin, made some geological notes mentioning especially the Cascade Mountains. He made the first recorded mention of the diatomite deposits at Lower Bridge in Deschutes County and described the Metolius Gorge.

Many warm oceans pounded against the cornerstones of ancient Oregon, especially the inland country, but few left more spectacular records than did Mowich, named by early-day geologists Dr. Earl L. Packard and R.L. Luper. It was a primordial sea, rich in marine life, whose ooze, silts and sandstones were pressed and folded into one of the region's great ancient mountain ranges. The Mowich beds are found not far from the geographic center of the state, in the highlands that shoulder up between the head of the Crooked River to the Ochoco summits.

Pressed and altered into durable cliffs, possibly by continent-building plate tectonics, stony silts of the old Mowich sea mark the ramparts of a long-vanished mountain range. In the rocks are found fossils representative of lower Jurassic times, a division of a long era, the Mesozoic, when giant reptiles ruled the oceans. There is evidence that some of these seas swept in from the south, possibly spreading over the present Deschutes country.

Most frequently mentioned mammals of the pre-Columbia lava days are the three-toed ponies that scampered over the Oregon landscape long before men lived on earth. Camels, some sheep-like, and others with giraffe-like necks, have received attention, and rhinos and their kin shared the Oregon scene with animals known on other continents. But beyond this select group, others that lived in Oregon in prehistoric times receive only slight mention. It was an age when mammals faced tough conditions; Cascade volcanoes were drifting ash east over the Deschutes basin, and lava flooded the valleys. Volcanic gases poisoned springs, streams and rivers.

But there were animals in the land—many of them. More than 100 different kinds of mammals have been described from the Deschutes and John Day basins, world-famous for their fine record of ancient life. It was these animals that attracted attention when interest in marine life faded. The long list of animals includes flesh eaters (cats, exemplified by the true and saber-toothed cats, and a great variety of dogs) and herb eaters. Horses fed on lush meadows and camels kept their trails well marked with fossils.

One of the best-known horses from Oregon's high ranges of yesterday was the Hypohippus, the "animal akin to the horse." This animal shared its verdant Oregon range with the rhinos (and that unbelievable creature given the name Chalicothere), and it has been called a clawed horse. Scientists were hard put to explain evolutionary processes when this creature's bones emerged in 1899.

Prodding through the John Day beds, holding world-famous fossils, students found proof that the John Day ash beds, in their three blazing colors, were deposited on top of old seabeds. These were the beds of the Cretaceous seas of the final era of the Age of Reptiles. Apparently over the ages, ash drifted east from the growing Cascades in great clouds, settling in swampy basins, covering forests, obliterating rivers and their canyons and hiding the expansive marine beds deposited through the Mesozoic eons. Geologists say the colored strata of the John Day possibly can be attributed to conditions under which the ash was deposited and the magmatic reservoirs from which the pumice was ejected. Some of the ash fell into swampy basins, with vegetation gases intermingling with those of the various minerals brought in by the ash.

What was the role of this great accumulation of volcanic ash in the survival, or disappearance, of mammal life of the region? Some geologists are inclined to believe that the bones were scattered over the basin before the ash fell. Some believe the ash was carried in by torrential floods. Adding to the mystery of fossil distribution in the central Oregon country is the fact that few creatures are found with their bones fully articulated— that is, fully assembled.

In the Midwest, some articulated fossils have been found, where creatures suffocated in a group when overwhelmed by desert conditions. Most notable discovery of the "cast" of a mammal in the Pacific Northwest, was in the Blue Lake area, near the Columbia in Washington. There, a rhino of the Pliocene apparently was overwhelmed by lava, forming a small encasement that looked like a cave. Possibly killed by gases before the Columbia lava rolled into place, this animal left its form in the lava, and some of its bones in the "cave." These fossil bones of the Blue Lake mammal revealed that it was a rhinoceros, of a species common in ancient Oregon. Remains of this creature, a rhino given the name Teleoceras, were found in the high country of Oregon, near Gateway northwest of Madras.

Columbia lavas, which spread over some 200,000 square miles of the Pacific Northwest, did not always remain where they cooled. The lava flood poured into valleys, filled lake beds, obliterated topographic features of the Tertiary landscape and, in the Picture Gorge area, spread over a downwarp, a syncline.

Blocked by the lava barrier, the John Day formed a large, long lake upstream. But this lava barrier was to be only temporary. Slowly through the years, the river sawed its way through the warped lavas. Then the river went to work to sweep out much of the sediment that had massed upstream through the eons.

Here in the central Oregon high country certainly are fine examples of the plate tectonics theory. There is evidence that oceans advanced and receded as the world aged and Permian life succeeded the Pennsylvanian creatures of the deep. Each advance of an old Oregon sea left a new record of changing life.

Time has been careful with its ageless records, preserving in sealed rocks the story of the oceans that beat against Oregon headlands long ago. Atop the Paleozoic formation in the Suplee region of central Oregon, through which Highway 395 slashes in the Seneca country, are records of another world, the Mesozoic, that era when mighty reptiles dominated the earth and dinosaurs wallowed in the swamplands of ancient Utah and Colorado. Remains of land creatures such as the ambling saurians have not been found in Oregon formations, although the Mesozoic record with its fine marine fossils is outstanding in some areas. Most spectacular of the marine records are the acres of clam reefs, whose individuals once lived in an embayment over which frowned Triassic cliffs.

The discovery of old marine records in central Oregon was made a century ago, but it was the fine field work of recent years that revealed the extensive sections of Paleozoic rocks and the more recent formations of the Age of Reptiles. Soldiers of Captain John Drake, patrolling the "Indian Country" on the trails into the eastern Oregon and Idaho gold fields, made the first discovery of ocean shells in the Oregon highlands, over which Snow Mountain looms across streams that drain into Crooked River, and thence to the Deschutes River.

Returning to Fort Dalles for supplies, the soldiers took some of their specimens to Dr. Condon. The find amazed the kindly pastor. He told the soldiers they had found evidence that long ago an ocean covered the sagelands through which led Indian trails. The fossils given to Condon were shells typical of a Cretaceous ocean. Interest of the soldiers increased when they learned of the importance of their discovery, and soon their headquarters on upper Crooked River became a geological cabinet.

Soon the word spread to eastern colleges that much of the Oregon Country was a natural cabinet holding time markers of eons. Condon commented: "How strangely out of place a score of palm trees, a hundred yew trees or even a bank of ferns would seem here now," ferns with an ancestry dating dating back millions of years when members of the group dominated lush lands of central Oregon.

One of the two new species of primitive Oregon ferns has been named *Osmundites chandleri* in recognition of A. K. Chandler, Portland, who discovered the fern fossils on the slope of a barren Jefferson County hill, nine miles east of Ashwood. The other species, discovered by Cecil C. Moore, Bend, has been named *Osmundites oregonesis*. The two new ferns, which grew in the Oregon Country millions of years ago, eons before the Cascades were built by volcanism on the north-south skyline, were described by Dr. Chester A. Arnold, University of Michigan paleobotanist (the discovery report was published in Stuttgart, Germany). Dr. Arnold noted in the discovery notice that the fern family probably originated in the world's age of fishes, the Paleozoic. Before their discovery in Oregon, the Osmundites were found only in Arizona and the Queen Charlotte Islands in North America, but were well known in other parts of the world, especially Russia. Dr. Arnold noted that the Oregon ferns constituted a noteworthy addition to our knowledge of the history of this cosmopolitan group of ferns, because none of them grow in the western part of the continent at present.

Dr. Ralph W. Chaney said the Clarno forests of millions of years ago were widely distributed in Oregon east of the Cascades in dawn-age times. Even stumps of giant redwoods have been found in eroded hills of the high desert. Near Prineville in early days was the so-called Brink Fossil Forest, long ago stripped of the last vestige of fossil wood. This "forest" apparently had been under volcanic ash.

One of the stops made by the migrating redwoods of early Tertiary times apparently was in the spectacular Smith Rock country of the Deschutes basin, where the Crooked River cuts into volcanic tuffs, to leave spires and pinnacles on high cliffs. Redwood traces were found in the Crooked River shales, facing Smith Rock.

The Smith Rock cliffs, grotesquely eroded, sharply tilted and carved into fantastic figures by the storms of centuries and the ever-eroding Crooked River, were long presumed to be of Eocene age (the dawn age of Tertiary time), but discovery of the redwood flora indicates that Smith Rock, now a popular state park, is of more recent age than Clarno.

Paleobotanists believe that some 50 million years ago the Clarno locality may have been at the mouth of a river system. This river washed debris into the low country and built deltas that nourished a varied flora. In this area, temperate plants from the highlands were buried with those from the tropic low country. Over this debris, Clarno volcanoes spread their ash.

Drills, dynamite, bulldozers and picks played a part in the unearthing of a forest buried in volcanic debris on the Vanora grade leading to the Deschutes River and the Warm Springs Indian Reservation from Madras. Grade excavation work brought to light some evidence that a Tertiary forest, growing on a mountain slope near the edge of a lake, was deeply buried by volcanic ash.

Chaney visited the locality, discovered by L. H. Irving of Madras. In his studies, Dr. Chaney found a new species of cherry, to which he gave the name *Prunus irvingi*. There is evidence that this tree and its associated species grew in the shadow of a volcano that once loomed over the country occupied by the gorge of the Deschutes. Eruption of the volcano apparently resulted in a heavy fall of ash followed by a mudflow. Buried under the ash and mud of the Vanora volcano were trunks, branches and leaves of the old forest.

Coarse volcanic conglomerates fell on top of the mudflow as the prehistoric volcano hurled showers of debris into the central Oregon sky. Then, following a long period of quiet, lava, some 50 feet thick and in places shaped into palisades, spilled over the plain. This is the formation known as the Madras rim lava.

For innumerable thousands of years, the Pliocene forest of the Deschutes was entombed. Over the eons, geologists say, the region lowered more than 1,000 feet. Today, rocky slabs bearing leaf imprints can be found at roadside.

Probing into marine formations uplifted into highlands of central Oregon, earth scientists have interpreted a new story from the ageless records of the rocks—a story of a clam that grew on a stem and left reefs that cover over 80 square miles south of the Ochoco Range. This strange clam was new to the world of science. Studies of the creature have continued through the years, since that summer half a century ago when E. L. Packard found it.

The name given the clam by Dr. Packard was Plicatostylidae—a word new in the study of ancient marine life and difficult for Packard's summer camp students to pronounce. The fossils were found in a rocky rim, with Snow Mountain of the Ochocos off in the distance. Packard said the word is not difficult to remember or pronounce when it is defined as "plicated," or folded stylus. Anchored to rocks in the embayment of the Mowich sea of Jurassic times, these clams formed extensive reefs. Outgrowing their older valves, the creatures apparently moved into new penthouse homes and grew to surprising heights.

The development of a column, capped by a simple upper shell, would permit such a clam to keep abreast of rapidly accumulating sediments. Fossils from the central Oregon high ridges indicate that the creature grew in crowded conditions, in restricted space off the rocky platform facing the primordial headlands. Nothing is known of the antiquity of the creature, which millions of years ago battled for space in that part of Oregon near the head of Crooked River.

Massive clouds that billow into the sky and trace their icy "anvils" over great thunderheads have played an important role in shaping the landscape in rugged lands east of the Oregon Cascades. From these everchanging clouds, which weathermen call cumulo-nimbus, come the brief but destructive torrential rains that send floods roaring down narrow canyons to move boulders weighing tons and spread rocky debris over foothill aprons. Geologists say that without mountain-scouring flash floods, fossil hunters would have learned little about the intriguing, interesting story of the old Oregon Country.

A pioneer geologist, Dr. John C. Merriam, then of the Carnegie Institution of Washington, D.C., on a field trip in 1899 into Wheeler County, encountered one of these sudden and short-lasting storms characteristic of semi-arid regions with steep slopes. He reported: "As we entered the devastated region that has been hit by the storm, evidences of water were encountered at every turn. From the mouths of gulches, great streams and fans of large rocks were spread over the flats, sometimes being carried for considerable distances across the level ground. In one valley, an alfalfa field a mile long was completely destroyed. The storm was accompanied by heavy hailstones, of large size. Some measured a circumference of six inches. Noise is characteristic of these storms that carry floods roaring through gorges."

Geologists looked on the results of these floods with considerable interest. In places, entire hillsides, generally of the John Day formation, were exposed by the floods, creating ideal conditions for fossil hunters.

The story of ancient Oregon is a huge volume bound in basalt and illustrated with fossils from ancient seas, mammal beds and varied forests. Primarily this rocky binding was provided by dawn age volcanoes that blazed along the line on which was developed the ancestral Cascades and by the great floods of lava known as the Columbia basalts.

Between the bindings of this multi-million-year-old story of the Oregon Country are other lava flows, but, geologists concede, none is as spectacular as the Columbia basalts. The great Columbia basalt plateau, covering parts of five states, embraces some 200,000 square miles, rivaling in size the great flow that mantles northwest India.

Long before the outpouring of the Columbia flood, Oregon was a land of volcanic violence. But, despite the blasts of the flaming volcanoes and the eastward drift of ash, mammals lived in the area in great numbers. Jungle-like areas covered the lowlands and redwoods spread over the low hills. And long before giant volcanoes bulged in the west, redwoods were shedding seeds in the region. Most of the inland region was a gently rolling plain, or a low, hilly region, dissected by rivers and streams.

Then came the first flow of liquid rock that marked the start of the lava flood that was to change entirely the Pacific Northwest landscape and erase from the landscape the redwoods that left their fossils in the Brothers area of Deschutes County.

Tall Thielsen on the southern Cascade skyline was reduced to pinnacles of rocky splinters, a natural rod for lightning bolts. Once-massive Mt. Washington, overlooking the Santiam divide from the south, lost most of its bulk, and its dome was cut into lava needles that now sway in the winter winds. Immediately east of the Three Sisters, a huge glacier covered most of the area and left its trails in many places that are now well below the spring snowlines. Broken Top suffered most from the cutting action of the Cascade glaciers. The alpine ice masses virtually ate into the heart of this now-pinnacled mountain of the Three Sisters family.

By tracing the glacial trails and similar ice grooves in rocks from Hood to Crater Lake, geologists have been able to picture the Cascades as they appeared in that not remote age when alpine field ice pushed moraines into the low country, where they are now cut by highways and exposed in stream gorges.

The late Dr. Edwin T. Hodge, Oregon geologist, told of the vast flows of ice such as those that cut the Zigzag and other canyons into the Mt. Hood area. Similar deep canyons were slashed in the aprons of Mt. Jefferson. These huge glacial gorges are spectacularly visible from the Metolius River country, where lava later followed the ice into the lower country through which the white river now cuts its way. Least glaciated mountain of the Cascades is the South Sister, which only yesterday, geologically, pulled its ice sheets back into the high country.

The Deschutes country, slashed by the spring-born stream that gives this inland area its name, is fenced by a spectacular "corral of mountains." In the west are the Cascades with the sisterly peaks, mighty Jefferson, strikingly-profiled Mt. Washington, Bachelor of ski-slope fame, Three-Fingered Jack and the fine cones to the south that have Theilsen, close to Crater Lake, as their anchor.

The southern part of the mountain corral is Newberry Crater, which mirrors Paulina Peak in both its East and Paulina lakes. Off to the east are desert peaks, weathered domes of glassy lava origin that yield semi-precious stones, and to the east-northeast are some very old mountains, the Blues, and Smith Rock, backed by Gray Butte and Jefferson County's slightly tilted Juniper Butte.

Within this corral of mountains is much of geologic interest, from Smith Rock, cut through by Crooked River, to the jagged rim of Newberry Crater, where astronauts trained, preparing for their trips to the moon. The astronauts got a close-up look at the moon-like Newberry Crater, named for a scientist of pioneer days, Dr. John S. Newberry, physician, botanist and zoologist with a Pacific Railroad survey party in 1855. The survey party never visited the crater, but it did make a wide sweep through central Oregon, adding to information about the region.

Newberry Crater has developed into a laboratory for students of volcanism. Geologists have found that Newberry Crater and its mothering Newberry Mountain have stories similar to fiery, lava-belching Kilauea of the Hawaiian Islands.

The most recent grand story of central Oregon geology came to an earth-shaking end 6,000 years ago, the approximate time that mighty Mazama, ancestral mountain to Crater Lake, lost its top in an ash-billowing eruption that covered forests with ash, choked valleys with lava and undoubtedly smothered animal life with swift-moving glowing avalanches.

Geologists believe the eruption occurred in winter, with pumice skidding across the ice of Diamond Lake. The first drift of pumice was before a westerly wind. Later the wind shifted to the southwest. A heavy blanket of pumice fell under the drifting clouds. The ash shifted well into the northeast, with about six inches the estimated fall in the area of present Bend. The fall of ash has been traced into Washington and western Canada. Near the vast, steaming crater, the fall was heavy. Pine trees have been found under it near Chemult. Much of northern central Oregon was covered. Lava Butte, 10 miles south of the Bend site, escaped, since the fissure eruption which brought it into being occurred a little later, but older Pilot Butte was dusted with pumice.

The "morning after" scene at the Mazama site must have been even more fantastically devastated than that created during the recent St. Helens experience. Now, centuries later, the ash can be traced in the area, on top of older lavas. Nothing so world-shaking has occurred in central Oregon since: it was a mighty blast, and its plume was high.

PIONEERS OF DESCHUTES COUNTRY

We would therefore say to every invalid in Oregon, instead of converting your stomach into an apothecary shop, secure a pleasant companion or two, mount a good pony, and take to the mountains; scale their lofty heights; drink from their pure fountains, and breathe their balmy air, and in due season you will return restored and strong.[1]

The people woven through the tapestry of central Oregon—the "high and mighty" country of the Deschutes drainage—bring the rich and varied threads of their antecedents. There are trappers and explorers, immigrants and gold seekers, bad men, bankers, doctors, stockmen, merchants and homesteaders. There are those who brought water to arid lands.

Before them all, of course, were the Native Americans. There was Simtustus who supported the treaty of 1855 but who saw his wife and daughter abducted by Snake Indian raiders.[2] There was Stockietly (Stock Whitley) who bitterly opposed signing the treaty but who died from wounds he received fighting to preserve the body of young Lt. Stephen Watson from Snake mutilations.[3] And there was Billy Chinook who accompanied Frémont on his 1843-44 exploration to California and Sutter's

Keith & Donna Clark

Fort, and on to Washington, D.C., who was still with Frémont during the fighting which followed the Bear Flag Revolt in 1846.[4]

People came here to satisfy needs they had—for living space, for wealth, even for recreation. Some traveled here for health, some to avoid an arrest warrant back on their trail. Some came to make homes at the edge of the desert. Hot summer days made cool nights an enjoyment, especially for settlers who remembered the humid summer nights in Missouri and Illinois, Kansas and Nebraska. And everyone enjoyed the air, particularly in the crisp October days when it was laced with the tang of brush fires in the various foothills.

It is difficult to realize now, but it was quiet then—no automobiles, trucks, jets, motorcycles or locomotives. There was some clatter around the ranch houses or in the towns where the activities of the day went forward, but there were not enough people really to disturb the quiet. In 1895 the population of Crook County was 3,202 for an area of about 8,600 square miles. Three years later the same area (still including later Deschutes and Jefferson counties) had 5,000 people.[5]

And so we wove a fabric, of burlap and binder twine, of cowhide and potato vines, of mint and wild roses, of sage and juniper and pine, of peace and violence, of dreams and reality. Our fabric portrays settlement in central Oregon—not minutely, but with feeling.

Native Americans

Articles of agreement and convention made and concluded at Wasco near the Dalles of the Columbia River, in Oregon Territory, by Joel Palmer, superintendent of Indian affairs, on the part of the United States, and the following-named chiefs and head-men of the confederated tribes and bands of Indians, residing in Middle Oregon, they being duly authorized thereto by their respective bands to wit: Symtustus, Locks-quis-sa, Shick-a-me, and Kuck-up, chiefs of the Taih or Upper De Chutes band of Walla-Wallas; Stocket-ly and Iso, chiefs of the Wyam or Lower De Chutes band of Walla-Wallas; Alexis and Talkish, chiefs of the Tenino band of Walla-Wallas; Yise, chief of the Dock-Spus or John Day's River

14

band of Walla-Wallas; Mark, William Chenook, and Cush-Kella, chiefs of the Dalles band of the Wascoes; Toh-simph, chief of the Ki-gal-twal-la band of Wascoes; and Wal-la-chin, chief of the Dog River band of Wascoes.[6]

When Que-pe-ma, Taih chief, thumbed his nose at Indian Bureau officials and left the Warm Springs Reservation for whatever better hunting grounds he pleased, he was following the philosophy of the Indian as it had been in the beginning: to go with the natural food supply. The idea that he must be confined to one parcel of land was contrary to that philosophy.

Adjusting to the white man's "civilization" was not easy for Que-pe-ma, a rebel for several years after the 1855 Treaty with the Confederated Tribes of Middle Oregon. In 1862 James Hamil, superintendent of farming at Warm Springs, wrote: "The Tigh Indians, under the influence of the chief, Quepe-ma, will listen to no propositions to engage in farming; and seventy acres of land, which has been enclosed and broke for them, remain untilled. Quepe-ma rarely visits the agency, and seems to be more desirous of obtaining arms and ammunition for his men than agricultural implements and seed."[7] Similar reports came to Oregon Superintendent of Indian Affairs J. W. Perit Huntington, in late 1865: M. Reaves at The Dalles wrote that "Quepema has taken away about half of the Warm Springs indians and a good many of the dechutes indians have gone across the [Columbia] river to Simcoe"; and James H. Wilbur, Indian Agent at Fort Simcoe, reported that "Que-pe-ma" was with "Smo-ho-lay's" band of "Drummers," doing much to create dissatisfaction among the Indians on the Yakima Reservation.[8]

In August of 1866, the Taih chief and his followers returned to Warm Springs Reservation, and John Smith observed that they had no farms under cultivation, "but they appear to be undergoing a change, as they express a willingness and a desire to cultivate farms. Their unsuccessfulness in hunting last season has caused them to search for a different source from which to derive the means of subsistence—They have witnessed the success attending the Indian farmers and have decided that they will do likewise. Previous to this year, they have always refused to receive Annuity Goods or any presents from the Agent."[9]

15

Four years later Que-pe-ma and his people were reported to be away from their farms again, visiting at Umatilla Agency, Pendleton, and "preparing roots and other provisions" in order to leave, either for the buffalo country or to join the Snakes, "declaring how they would do as they pleased hereafter or die."[10] But Que-pe-ma did not die during any of his flights and he lived a peaceful, respectable life on the Warm Springs Reservation from 1880 to his death in 1901 or 1902.[11]

The first human inhabitants of central Oregon were here a long time ago, over 13,000 years, according to Cressman's research on the High Desert. Carbon dating of relics found there during his excavations, sagebrush sandals, push human occupancy back that far.[12] Occasionally, from springs or badger holes deep in the central Oregon pumice, delicate, chipped projectile points (usually obsidian) find their way to the surface. Excavations for basements here have unearthed caches of knife and spear points buried so deep that the overlay is additional evidence of the antiquity of occupancy.[13]

Que-pe-ma's ancestors hunted the sage plains, the juniper ridges, the canyons, the lava rims, the forests and the grasslands now known as Deschutes country. And they fished in the turbulent Deschutes River and its tributaries for salmon, for trout, for eels and other fishes. Then "no trespassing" signs had not yet been posted.

Early Travelers

Mr. McKay with four Men joined us he informed me Mr. McDonald was at a short distance from this anxiously waiting my arrival their Success in Beaver [h]as not been great only 460... I must endeavour to reach Beaver ere I make a halt.[14]

So Peter Skene Ogden wrote on December 8, 1825, one of the first white people who came to or through the Deschutes country for furs. The white trappers and traders exhausted the resource and moved elsewhere, a use-pattern deeply engrained. Generally they came in late fall and winter, confining their observations about the country to seasonal successes, although Nathaniel Wyeth introspectively recorded on January 11, 1835: "Last night grew cold and set in for a hard snow storm...

the cracking of the falling trees and the howling of the blast was more grand than comfortable   it makes two individuals feel their insignificance in the creation to be seated under a blankett with a fire in front and 3½ feet of snow about them and more coming and no telling when it will stop."[15]

Another trapper who discovered the central Oregon scene was independent: Joseph Gervais, native of Quebec and once voyageur with Wilson Price Hunt. Settled at French Prairie with his family, after summer harvest Gervais would cross the Cascades by way of the Santiam to hunt and trap until the fall rains. Returning home he would turn his pelts over to a Hudson's Bay Company trader, then go to Fort Vancouver for his money. John Minto implies that Gervais passed a number of such golden, recreational autumns in this manner between 1832 and 1846.[16]

In the latter part of 1843 John Charles Frémont entered central Oregon from the north, noting that "the country is abundantly watered with large streams, which pour down from the neighboring range. These streams are characterized by the narrow and chasm-like valleys in which they run, generally sunk a thousand feet below the plain. . . . The road across the country, which would otherwise be very good, is rendered impracticable for wagons by these streams.[17] Charles Preuss, Frémont's cartographer, traveling past Benham Falls on the Deschutes, commented on the "nice waterfall. I believe there is hardly a country where one sees as many as here. As soon as we pitch our camp at a river, we hear the din of some larger or smaller waterfall."[18]

After Frémont's party, immigrant wagons from the States passed, attempting to find shorter routes to the Willamette Valley from the Oregon Trail at Vale—first in 1845, then in 1853 and 1854. To W. A. Goulder, an 1845 drover, "The new route [across central Oregon] was a trackless waste, covered, for the most part, by immense fields of sage-brush that grew tall, strong, and dense. Through these sage-fields we were obliged to force the oxen, the teams taking turns, day about, in breaking their way."[19]

Traveling that trackless waste produced powerful thirsts, and the Deschutes River was a lifesaver. In 1853 J. Marion Gale described the immigrants' relief: "That day about 150 wagons, with almost famished teams and immigrants, camped on the banks of the rapid, sparkling river and drank of its waters, more delicious than wine, to our satisfaction; and never in my life have I seen a day so intensely enjoyed in drinking as was that to us and our poor beasts."[20] Another immigrant, Hanks Hill, said: "The water was too cold to do us any good, so we carried some up in our hats and cups, built a fire and warmed it before we were satisfied."[21] And Benjamin F. Owen, of the 1853 rescue party, noted that "it was all that I could do to drink what that Cup would hold once. I couldn't forbear a feeling of displeasure at the thought of so much good water going to waste after Suffering So much for it."[22] An 1854 immigrant who took the central Oregon route, James H. Rinehart, wrote: "I reached the other camp. . . after twelve hour ridge. . . at midnight three men started on the back trail with canteens full of fresh cool water from the Deschutes River for the dry and weary people in our train."[23]

Some of these men were farmers, and though their travel through the land was hastened by nightly frosts and new snow on the elevations, some, like James F. McClure in 1853, remarked on the grazing: "[came to] Fall River, a beautiful stream fifty yards wide. The desert we have just crossed is covered with the finest kind of bunch grass."[24] Others responded variously to the rugged terrain. James Field remarked: "Had a long hard pull. . . to ascend the hill. . . but once up we felt amply repaid the trouble of climbing by the prospect which lay before us. There were the Cascade mountains stretching along the western horizon, apparently not more than forty miles distant, forming a dark outline, varied by an occasional snow-peak, which would rise lofty and spire-like, as if it were a monument to departed greatness."[25] In 1849 Betsy Bayley wrote that in 1845, "in this mountainous wilderness we had to remain for five days. At last we concluded to take a northwesterly direction. . . . The mountains looked like volcanoes and the appearance that one day there had been an awful thundering of volcanoes and a burning world. The valleys were all covered with a white crust and looked like a salaratus. Some of the company used it to raise their bread."[26] While Samuel Parker, a captain of 1845, simply stated: "Swareing without end."[27]

18   At least one group of 1845 immigrants is known to have found gold, a discovery which, at the time, bore small significance. Later, after the

big rush in California, the prospects of another golden cornucopia drew men from the Willamette Valley, Idaho and California to search the interior of the state—often through or in the Deschutes country—trying to trace, by 1855 and afterward, the dim tracks of the 1845 Stephen Meek train.

The story of the Blue Bucket passed into legend when repeated expeditions found none of the elusive nuggets. In 1858, one mining party included A. S. McClure, also a member of the 1853 wagon train, who wrote: "This is a barren God-forsaken country, fit for nothing but to receive the footprints of the savage and his universal associate, the cayote."[28] But gold was discovered in eastern Oregon, in Griffin Gulch and other places in Baker County in 1861, and at Canyon Creek in Grant County.[29] And tied to mining developments was a constant market for beef cows. Stockmen in the Willamette Valley with herds large enough to market looked to the market of the mines; their route was across the Deschutes drainage.

Stockmen

This was, certainly, as fine a country then as a stock man could wish to see. The bottoms were covered with wild rye, clover, pea vines, wild flax and meadow grass that was waist high on horseback. The hills were clothed with a mat of bunch grass that seemed inexhaustible. It appeared a veritable paradise for stock.[30]

As early as 1857 some cows had been driven east over the Cascades. In 1862 Felix Scott, Jr., with his brother, Marion, drove 900 head by the McKenzie Pass; they spent the winter in a cave on Hay Creek near Madras.[31] The size of that herd reflects two things about pioneer economy in that time. Some Oregonians had purchased cows in Missouri and Illinois with California gold. Those and local bovines had multiplied on the rich grass of the Willamette Valley bottoms to the point that finding graze was a problem. Furthermore, grazing land might now be put to growing wheat. When the first stockmen came into the Deschutes country they looked at the graze with speculative eyes, for what they found was bunch grass on which cows grew fat quickly.

19

George Barnes, born in Missouri in 1849, grew up in Linn County, Oregon. In 1868 he came to the Ochoco Valley in company with William Elkins, Ewen Johnson, "and one other." Elisha Barnes, father to George, had come to the area the previous fall with Wayne Claypool, William Smith, Captain White, and Raymond and George Burkhart. They returned to the Valley in early spring, some to bring their families over. Young Barnes took a homestead near Prineville, raised stock, later studied law and was admitted to the bar in 1880. His stories of that first summer are memorable, for among other adventures they were burned out by the Indians. In his words:

Four days after our arrival here Elkins and the forgotten man left us, leaving three people in all this country, Johnson, White and myself. Johnson and myself were employed in making a trip to the timber each day. We were stopping at the Claypool place. Captain White worked the garden and did the cooking. On the sixth day as usual Johnson and I went to the timber, and while loading the wagons we noticed a huge smoke down the valley; but as the captain was almost daily engaged in burning the heavy crops of wild rye that covered the bottom, we thought but little of it. But when fifteen minutes later we saw the captain coming up the bottom, hat off, and as if he had half a notion of breaking into a run, we knew something was wrong. When we got within yelling distance he shouted, "Boys, the Indians have broke out and killed every d——d one of us and burnt the house," we knew exactly what was the trouble. And when the captain came up and gave us the particulars, how, while he was absent from the house they had taken all our guns, blankets and provisions, and what they could not carry off they had burned, leaving us desitute, we felt lonesome. That morning Johnson and I both, contrary to our usual custom, had omitted to bring our guns with us. We had only an old six-shooter of the cap and ball style, and this we had emptied at a bunch of sage hens, and as we had not brought any ammunition, it was about as valuable as a knot-hole. We held a council of war and then and there organized the first militia company ever organized in this county. We each got us a willow stick six feet

20

long, which we shouldered as guns and marched down to where our house had stood. In fact they had burned up everything we had which they did not carry away. We were completely stripped and it looked to us that evening that the next bite we would get to eat would be found somewhere on the west side of the Cascade mountains. As we were afoot and would have thirty or forty miles of snow to wade through, the prospect did not seem very cheerfull; in fact, to attempt to cross the mountains seemed so hopeless that we finally concluded to attempt to find the Canyon City road which we knew lay somewhere to the north of us. How far it was we did not know. In fact our ignorance was so dense that it seems foolishness now. So we gathered together a few traps, such as were not burned, hitched up our oxen and started for "grub."

> *Not a drum was heard, not a bugle note,*
> *As our course down stream we worried;*
> *But like a boy caught in a melon patch,*
> *We whopped, and humped and hurried.*[32]

The little squad wandered to the Warm Springs Agency, was guided by an Indian to Cache Creek from where it moved through snow to the Santiam River. Fortunately, the men (now out of provisions) met Captain James Blakely of Linn County, who was bringing a herd of cows across the mountains. According to Barnes's recollections, Jim gave them supper and breakfast, "for which I am certain the pack horse was ever after thankful, for we certainly lightened his load." They reached home safely the next day. Barnes continued:

Even now I look back with feelings of pride and longing regret to those bright sunny mornings when we arose with the lark and sage tick and joyously ambled down to the spring branch, bathed our expansive brows, scoured our pitch-covered hands and with appetites that passed all understanding, did ample justice to the ability of our cook, and blythly took our way to the rail patch with an ox gad in one hand, a trusty United States gun on one shoulder, and two Colt's revolvers swung to our belts, and let our fine soprano voices ring out on the morning air. Bull-whacking is not work; it is only recreation.[!]

21

Sundays we washed and patched our clothes, and right here I want to say that along toward spring our wardrobes got to be very threadbare; we thought we had come with clothes enough for a year, but three months' ranting around over the rimrocks and through the juniper trees after the mule deer had left us barefooted and naked. There were no stores that we could possibly reach where we could obtain a new supply and toward spring we were the nakedest lot of white men in Oregon. The makeshifts we utilized to hide our skins from the biting winds—we didn't care a cent for the public gaze—was but another illustration that "Necessity is the Mother of Invention." Newt Bostwick capped the climax in the footwear line by soling a pair of moccasins with a piece of bacon rind. We all wore moccasins and before spring buckskin breeches and shirts.[33]

After 1868, when fear of Paulina and his Snake (Paiute) raids had subsided, population grew steadily. Settlement then meant ranches, cattle mostly, for most sheep ranchers were content to graze the natural pastures of northern Wasco County from Antelope north and east. Some had permits for grass on the Warm Springs Reservation.

So stockmen decided to stay, to build cabins on the river and creek bottoms, to winter cows here and drive them to markets. Howard Maupin, who had operated a ferry on the Deschutes at the site of Maupin, settled on Trout Creek in 1867. On Hay Creek, Ochoco Creek, Mill Creek, ranches began in 1868-69. Samuel Hindman and Jerome LaFollette took land on Squaw Creek. Willow Creek attracted Linn County residents James Blakely, Perry Read and others, while McKay Creek appealed to B. F. Allen, "Jake" Guilliford, George Millican, John Latta and Andrew Lytle.[34]

In the southern and southeastern section, on Camp and Beaver creeks, settled James and Charles W. Elkins, William Noble, John Jaggi, William Adams, John Davis and Abram Hackleman. Hackleman first came to Deschutes country about 1868 when he drove 300 herd of cows to the rich grazing lands. His early ranch was on upper Camp Creek where he eventually took land totaling some 3,000 acres, and raised cows and horses.[35]

With rich grazing, herds brought from the Valley multiplied—both cattle and sheep. Mining camps were, by 1870, not so isolated that they could not be supplied locally. Consequently, ranchers in central and eastern Oregon had two choices: they could drive herds to railhead at Winnemucca, Nevada, or they could drive to eastern markets. A surprising number of sheep and cattle were thus trailed in a procession that sometimes took six months. Such was the enterprise in which John Y. Todd, Joseph Teal and Henry Coleman engaged—a financial disaster. In 1880, Todd and Coleman drove 3,000 head of cattle to Cheyenne, stock belonging to the trio and a number of other ranchers. Todd's son, John C., explained in 1922:

Blackleg attacked the herd, and other misfortune caused the drive to be a financial disaster, but it created a market for small stock owners where none had existed before. Todd was forced to sell all of the stock under his brand on the range adjacent to Farewell Bend, and also the Farewell Bend ranch, in order to pay for cattle turned into this drive. The cattle went to Breyman & Summerville of Prineville for $15,000, and the ranch, now worth many times as much, to John Sisemore for $1,500.[36]

John Y. Todd, Missourian and acquaintance of Marshall Awbrey, first brought cows east of the Cascades in 1857. He established a home ranch in Tygh Valley, built a bridge across the Deschutes (later Sherars), took pack trains to the mines at Canyon City. In 1877 he acquired Springer's ranch at Farewell Bend (later Bend), grazed cows in the Deschutes basin near Squaw Creek, and west to the Metolius.[37]

Cortley D. Allen first came to the Deschutes country when he was 14, in 1872, but not until 1877 did he return to settle on the land of the Big Meadows where ultimately he took 680 acres:

People think we first settlers should all be rich. Our trouble was lack of transportation. I have sold cattle to be driven to Cheyenne, and others to be driven to California. Men with capital would buy calves at $2.50 a head, and let them out to us on shares. We gave them half of the selling price, and that way we would get a start. Some years we would make money, and other years conditions would be bad and we would be cleaned out again. . . . Those who did make a success of the cattle business found it a

23

rough life. They camped under the juniper trees at all seasons of the year, no matter what the weather, sometimes with few blankets. Almost every day was spent in the saddle. . . . It was a rough life, but we liked it.[38]

Near neighbors were W. P. Vandevert and family who settled on the "Old Homestead" about 1891, after a remove from Powell Buttes. Claude Vandevert remembered, "mostly cattle. That's what they came here for: the good pasture in the summer time. Most up-river cattle ranchers sold their cows on the ground to Sid Stearns and others. They did not drive long distances, kept 50-75 head."[39]

The 1880s a new wave of settlement washed across the Cascades to the Deschutes, and beyond. One of those who came was John Sisemore in 1881 when he purchased the John Todd ranch. His cows ranged the meadows of the upper Deschutes with those of Pelton and Brown. After 1882, Sisemore's interest in Farewell Bend led to extensive real estate holdings, though he kept his ranch until 1905. He got his start in the cattle business with $32,000 in gold dust from his placer mine at South Humbug Creek in California.[40]

Sidney Stearns brought his new bride, Frances, to Farewell Bend in 1887, where they lived on a homestead in a one-room log house, 18 × 25 feet, with a fireplace in the north end, two four-pane windows, a door, and running water in the Deschutes just outside. Nearest neighbors were Sam and Mary Collins (sister of William H. Staats) about three miles north of Bend where they planted an apple orchard, of which one tree remains yet at Sawyer Park.

Later the Stearnses moved to Crooked River, eventually owned ranches at both Prineville and La Pine. Frances Day Stearns remembered that "the Deschutes river was literally full of fish of all sizes. We could stand on the log and throw fish from the river into the frying pan. . . . I also remember the first time I went to look at the Crooked river ranch, I told Sid he'd have to hog-tie me to take me to such a God-forsaken place where the sun never shone except at noon, and full of rattlesnakes and dens in the rim rocks."[41]

24

In the spring of 1870, Thomas Jefferson Logan came to Crooked River. His son Sanders helped drive a starting herd of cattle. Logans were the first to run cows on Bear Creek, and in 1873 they moved their stock to the South Fork of Crooked River, establishing the 96 Ranch near Logan Butte. They drove herds south from here to the Winnemucca railhead. Sanders Logan said: "Cattlemen in the early day really believed in branding their stock. Many of them went to the extreme, branding them in every conceivable place, and put the same iron on several places on the same animal. The iron used by the Logans became known all over the cattle ranges of the state and the ranch is even yet spoken of as 'The 96 Ranch' by old cattlemen."[42]

W. E. Claypool came to the Sisters area in 1878. In 1883, when he was seven, one of the most severe winters on record in central Oregon almost cleared the ranges of livestock. In places horses and cattle had taken shelter under trees; here the stock tramped out circles but were imprisoned by the walls of snow. Some, found in time, were rescued. Starving horses had eaten manes and tails; cows and horses had girdled the bark on trees. But the long cold spell crusted the snow so that rescued stock could walk on top to safety.[43] John Fryrear, too, remembered the big snow of 1883-84, when "just before Christmas two feet of snow fell, which melted back to 18 inches. Then it snowed again two days and two nights altogether, without stopping."[44] There were 72 inches of snow on the level, which stayed until March, 1884.

To the north, on Agency Plains, veteran sheepman A.W. Boyce remembered the winter of 1884-85. It started snowing on December 13,

and kept on snowing day after day until there was fully five feet of snow on the ground. We had no hay, and at that time a great many stockmen did not. . . . When spring opened my brother and I had about 400 head of sheep left from the 2600 we started the winter with. We herded these in lambing time. . .going every few days to our home cabin to get food supplies, and one of these times I went there to get food for our camp I found our cabin burned to the ground, but still smoking. Someone had stolen our supplies and burned the cabin to hide the robbery.[45]

Another big blizzard, in 1887, remains in memory: "We didn't have Simmons mattresses in those days, and perhaps it's just as well, for there is no nourishment for a starving calf in a modern day mattress." The

25

men carried the straw ticks out on the range to save as many cattle as possible."[46]

Sheepmen were contemporaries of cowmen in this country. William C. McKay's Snake War diary records his meeting James Small and a band of sheep in the Trout Creek bottom in 1867.[47] Sheep herds multiplied rapidly. Some, however, also encountered a local disease. George Barnes described the situation in 1868:

That summer James McKay brought out a band of cattle, and E. Barnes, E. Johnson and W. H. Marks each [had] a small band of sheep. . .I have a painful recollection that the sheep had the doubtful honor of having the first case of scab in the settlement, though at that time we did not know what it was. We thought it was the mange, the same disease that the hogs have in the Willamette valley, and we lost all our wool and nearly all our sheep before we learned what ailed them. Greasing the measly things with a bacon rind did not cure them, and some of us retired from the business with disgust. Why, the scab is a native of this section. I have seen the coyotes perfectly naked with it; the rim rocks had it; the sage brush had it; it was in the grass, in the rocks, in the air and our sheep caught it and caught it bad.[48]

Dr. David Baldwin of Oakland, California, established the Baldwin Sheep and Land Company on Hay Creek in 1873. John Edwards became half owner of that spread in 1898, and made it the greatest Merino breeding station in the world, with an annual market of 250 tons of wool, with an annual production of 2,500 tons of alfalfa, with 70,000 acres of land. Here, indeed was a sheep empire.[49]

Morrow and Keenan had a home ranch on Willow Creek, 15 miles from Prineville. Some other early Deschutes country sheepmen were Steve Yancey, James Faught, Columbus Friend, Thomas Hamilton, Thomas Lafollette, and Charles and John Palmehn who homesteaded the basin where Madras stands, giving their name to the original townsite (Palmain).[50]

John Knox remembered in 1934 how in 1894 he had participated in one of the big sheep drives of early days, trailing 25,000 head. Though

26

destined for Nebraska, the drive ended in Idaho with feed cheaply obtainable there (hay was $3.50 a ton). Four years later he took a band from Crooked River to Nebraska. Knox, with 10 other men, took six months, not out of the saddle a whole day during that time.[51]

Walter McCoin, who was born in 1886 in the "Old Culver" area, earned his first "very own" dollar at about nine years of age: "I used to herd horses for sheep-shearers. The sheep-shearers would ride from herd to herd during the shearing season, and they hired a boy to care for their horses."[52]

Mrs. Eva Doak came from Springfield to Hay Creek in 1884 where her father, Amos Dunham, had acquired three ranches: "My father bought sheep and had sheep for several years. I used to go to The Dalles with him to sell his wool, and it was quite an enjoyable trip for me, although it was a long, hard ride with the wagon and team."[53]

Knox Huston, educated at Cornell in 1858, came to Lane County in 1862, and taught school there until 1878. In that year he took savings, purchased a band of sheep, and drove them to the Ochoco. He brought his wife and family to the frontier, continued in stock raising until 1890. Then his formal education found use as a county surveyor and civil engineer; in the latter capacity he laid out the majority of irrigation lines in Crook County.[54]

The list of stockmen is long, among them Richard Breese (1889), Ralph Porfily (1889), and J. I. "Dad" West (1892), but space limits extensive discussion.[55] The undisputed leader in stock raising—cattle, sheep and horses—was Bill Brown who came to Wagontire in 1882 from Salem. In terms of land and animals his potential wealth probably far exceeded that of any other individual settler in central Oregon. It has been estimated that he owned a million dollars' worth of horses at 1917 prices, 22,000 sheep, 40,000 acres of land, with grazing rights on 100,000 additional acres.[56]

Bill never married, and was eccentric. When his socks wore out, he dispensed with socks entirely. He continued to pay taxes to Crook County after Deschutes County was formed simply because he had acquired the habit. It took an irritatingly persistent Deschutes County assessor some

27

time to convince him otherwise.[57] He wrote checks on can labels, paper bags, shingles—in one instance a nun's handkerchief—all perfectly legal tender.[58] George Tackman, an early rancher, once told us that Bill refused shelter and food to the governor of Oregon, Os West, one evening because West had recently pardoned a horse thief Bill had helped put behind bars. "He did feed the governor's horse," Tackman chuckled.[59]

In time, Bill owned land in Crook, Lake, Deschutes and Harney counties. His headquarters were on Buck Creek, but he bought up other ranches as his empire grew. He engaged in a many-years' battle against coyotes which killed his sheep, poisoning them with strychnine which he is reputed to have personally taste-tested at purchase for purity and strength. Bill gave generously to many foundations and institutions, including Pendleton Academy and Willamette University. After World War I economic conditions forced a decline in Brown's property. After signing a blanket mortgage, he retired at Methodist Old People's Home in Salem, which he also had supported. He died, there, penniless, in 1941.[60]

Vigilantes

Why, nobody over here locked their doors. We were all honest.[61]

People liked the freedom on the east side of the mountains. Laws were not oppressive, there was room to move in any direction, and the open spaces kept down claustrophobia. Some of the boys were harmlessly boisterous, others were downright dangerous.

Among the latter was Henry "Hank" C. Vaughan, grandson of the Billy Vaughan who came through central Oregon in 1845 with the Stephen Meek train.[62] Leaving Lane County, his first recorded scrape occurred in 1867 when Frank Maddock, sheriff of Umatilla County, tried, with an early morning posse, to arrest Vaughan and a companion for horse stealing. Somebody started shooting and when it was over the companion and a deputy, Jackson Hart, were dead. The sheriff had a bullet wound through the mouth. Hank got away, but he later surrendered, stood trial, and spent some time in the Oregon State Penitentiary.[63]

In 1881, in Til Glaze's saloon at Prineville, Hank quarreled with

28

another hard case, Charley Long. They were both anesthetized with frontier whiskey. As Sheriff Jim Blakely recalled in 1939:

Sam Smith and I were in the Dick Graham saloon. Charley Long, who was in the vigilantes up to his neck, and Hank Vaughan were sitting there playing cards. Sam Smith and I rode down country and when we came back in the afternoon Long and Vaughan were in Til Glaze's saloon, drinking and talking. They got to talking pretty mad and one of them says, "we'll just settle it!" . . . . *They walked out into the middle of the floor of the saloon and commenced shooting. The first shot creased Hank's scalp, not deep, and Long's next shot got Hank in the left breast over the heart. Hank shot Long three times in the left shoulder. We took Vaughan down to Dick Graham's saloon and he says to me: "Jim, take my boots off. My dad said I'd die with my boots on, so take 'em off." But Hank got well. So did Charley Long.*[64]

The Prineville *Ochoco Review* reported May 24, 1890: "Hank Vaughan, pretty well known here, had his leg broken in two places, while riding on the Umatilla reservation last week. Hank is a stayer and intends to leave this world a small piece at a time." Vaughan was finally killed in Pendleton in 1893, as a result of his horse throwing him in the street in front of the newspaper office.[65]

When Crook County was established in the fall of 1882, county officials were appointed until the time of the general election in 1884. But before that, in the spring of that year, the only peace officer in the Prineville country was John Luckey, Wasco County deputy sheriff. Secretly organized in the winter of 1881 was a vigilance committee for protection against outlaws, especially those bent on stealing horses. These vigilantes considered themselves the principal arbiters of right and wrong, and in a number of recorded instances used the collective power of the committee to destroy individuals who openly defied their rule. One such case was Lucius Langdon, who shot Aaron Crooks and Stephen Jory in what appears to have been a property line dispute in early March, 1882. Crooks, Jory (his son-in-law) and Langdon all lived on the north slope of Grizzly Mountain near Newbill Creek, tributary to Willow Creek. Nearby was

29

Jim Blakely's ranch. When news of the killings reached Prineville, members of the vigilance committee, and others, went looking for Langdon, who surrendered finally to Blakely. At Prineville, in custody of deputy Luckey, Langdon was shot and killed by masked intruders. These dragged away W. H. Harrison, Langdon's hired hand who had come to town with him, and they hanged him from the old bridge across the Crooked River.[66]

Other men were killed, some openly murdered by individuals known to be part of the vigilance committee. Control of county and city governments by these men made justice impossible. Consequently an opposing group organized, termed itself "The Citizens Protective Union," and counted among its members responsible merchants like Isaac Ketchum, whose daughter Wilda married Dr. Horace Belknap, like David Stewart, who was credited with being one of five who organized The Citizens Protective Union (he built the first electric plant at the Cove, now covered by Route Butte Reservoir), like indignant Jim Blakely who led them to victory over the vigilantes, becoming Crook County sheriff in 1884.[67]

Blakely was first and foremost a cowman in whose private business the vigilantes interfered. He came to the Deschutes country the first time in 1866, when he and his father drove 600 head of cows across the Cascades by the South Santiam route. He grazed herds in 1869 near the basin where Madras would be established. By 1882 he had moved to Willow Creek, had about 1,500 head of stock, when the vigilante organization ordered that no one could ride range without a permit.[68]

"I was born in this Oregon country and I'll be damned if anyone is going to tell me when I can go out after my own stock," Blakely told them. He armed his riders and was not molested.[69]

But in the years between 1882 and 1883 others were, and the vigilantes had the upper hand. "I fought the gang from the first, and I had a few friends, but none of them stood by me better than Hank Vaughan. I know he's been called a lot of hard names by the history writers, but he was a good friend to me," Blakely stated in later years. "I was against killing, but I knew what had to be done."[70]

Blakely personally challenged Gus Winckler, a storekeeper, to load his gun and start using it or get on the stage out of town. Winckler,

30

one of the leaders of the vigilantes, left—promptly. Blakely served two terms as sheriff, and moved to a ranch in Wallowa County in 1888.[71] He stands out against the early time as a citizen who got involved.

Cattle & Sheep Wars

You might say we were raised in the saddle.[72]

First settlers learned to appreciate the remarkable variety of the land, its deep, carved valleys and canyons, great pine forests, meadows running with clear, sparkling streams, those streams filled with fish. They came to love the lakes in the park-like "high country," even the sage and sand and juniper. There were spring wild flowers in profusion, and overhead the blue, clear sky where sunsets quickly exhausted the supply of adjectives. The night stars shone with a diamond brightness that was almost light enough to read by.

They learned, too, that the country's weather was unpredictable, that winters could be mild or severe, and when they were severe, stockmen faced bankruptcy. So they began to put up meadow hay against those uncertainties, and when alfalfa was introduced, their ability to feed stock through the hard times was improved.

But when stockmen built houses and barns in the grass-rich bottoms of the streams, the day of transient grazing was past. For the graze had limitations. With more arrivals in the country every year, more animals eating the grass, stockmen ranged farther, reaching up under the Cascade peaks for summer range. There were cows at the site of Crane Prairie Reservoir before the dam backed water over the meadow. Sparks Meadow hosted fat, summer herds. By 1897 in Crook County the census counted 320,000 sheep and 40,000 cows. And there were an estimated 10,500 horses.[73]

So the grass went, eaten down in places to a point of no recovery. And some changes occurred. Sagebrush sprouted on former grasslands; juniper seedlings found root in the exposed soil. Hard rains and occasional cloudbursts poured tons of water into stream beds, and with the water went tons of soil no longer held fast by grass rootlets. Camp Creek and

31

Bear Creek both deepened, and Crooked River, once clear as the North Fork at Summit Prairie, turned the color of coffee with a liberal amount of cream in it.

While grazing disappeared, the competition for range sharpened and sheepmen pushed into cow country. Cowmen pushed back, and there was a period of sheep slaughter and other violences. In 1896 cattlemen east of Paulina in the Izee country organized "The Izee Sheep Shooters" to protect the range and to discourage invasion by sheepmen. Members would ride out to a band, hold up the herder and tender, and shoot sheep until they tired, sickened or ran out of cartridges. They operated until 1906, the year national forests were established in Oregon, withdrawing these lands from public domain. Their members boasted "thousands" of dead sheep. Paulina cattlemen followed suit and established deadlines beyond which no sheep were permitted. They too rode out.[74] Cartridge sales improved markedly, and hardware stores in Prineville took note.

The greatest slaughter of sheep at one time took place at Benjamin Lake in 1903 (on the High Desert between Camp Creek and Silver Lake). There a band of 2,700 wethers came under the fire of 11 Camp Creek cowmen. When the smoke cleared, 2,400 sheep lay dead.[75] In 1904, 1,000 sheep belonging to Morrow and Keenan were destroyed, and in January, 1905, 500 more sheep were slaughtered near Paulina.[76] It was a cruel method of control; there simply was not enough grass left to go around.

Sheepmen, apprehensive for herders and tenders, met at Antelope in 1904. Local members of the Oregon Wool Growers Association voted themselves an assessment of $500 to pay for information "leading to the arrest and conviction of any person or persons guilty of shooting, killing or maiming any member of the...association, or any employee...while engaged in his duties or the herds of such a member while engaged in his duties." The state association added $1,000.[77]

In 1885 Roscoe Knox came to Crook County, spent the winter three miles from Pringle Flat in a partially dug-out cabin. The next winter, cattle were fed by plowing the snow off the natural grasses. In 1887 the family moved to Newsom Creek where Knox engaged in sheep and cattle raising. But in 1904 Knox took an active part in quelling the range war. Pretending to be a sheep shooter in order to expose the sheep shooters' depredations, he wrote arrogant letters to the *Oregonian*. He signed these letters "The Sheep Shooters' Corresponding Secretary."[78] A sample:

"Sheep-Shooters" Headquarters, Crook County, Oregon, December 29, 1904—Editor Oregonian: *I am authorized by the association (The Inland Sheep Shooters) to notify the* Oregonian *to desist from publishing matter derogatory to the reputations of sheep-shooters in Eastern Oregon. We claim to have the banner county of Oregon on the progressive lines of sheep-shooting and it is my pleasure to inform you that we have a little government of our own in Crook county, and we would thank the* Oregonian *and the governor to attend strictly to their business and not meddle with the settlement of the range question in our province.*

We are the direct and effective means of controlling the range in our jurisdiction. If we want more range we simply fence it in and live up to the maxim of the golden rule that possession represents nine points of the law. If fencing is too expensive for the protection of the range, dead lines are most effective substitutes and readily manufactured. When sheepmen fail to observe these peaceable obstructions we delegate a committee to notify offenders, sometimes by putting notices on tent or cabin, and sometimes by publication in one of the leading newspapers of the county as follows: "You are hereby notified to move this camp within twenty-four hours or take the consequences. Signed: COMMITTEE.*"[79]*

Relations were still strained in 1916. In that year Cowman invited Sheepman to a peaceful meeting at the Pilot Butte Inn at Bend. As a result the Bend-Burns road became one of the boundary lines, with cattle to the north and sheep to the south.[80] In the end, market gluts, scant grazing and fenced ranges all contributed to a decline in free-ranging herds. Cattlemen turned to intensive hay growing as a substitute. Sheep, without adequate free range, were just not profitable.

Businessmen/Town Builders

Once a year my folks would take a wagon and cross the mountain by the old McKenzie Road, then up the Valley to Independence where we had relatives. We'd visit and bring back fruit and berries, squash and pumpkins.[81]

Part of the settler experience here was an annual or biennial return west across the Cascades for fruits and vegetables not ordinarily available in the harsher clime. These were sorely missed in pioneer diets, could be obtained by the pleasant late summer device of taking a wagon or two across the mountains to visit friends and relatives. Claude Vandevert recalled: "Mother would take jars, and can fruit over in the Valley, then we'd put those jars down in the wagon and cover them with oats."[82] This way, families prepared for the winter at minimal cost. Canned produce was almost unobtainable from local merchants, and prohibitively expensive.

Travel into central Oregon generally took two routes until work on the Santiam and McKenzie roads improved them considerably. New residents often came to The Dalles and then southeast to Prineville. The other road came from Eugene City or up from California. By both trails early settlement of the upper Deschutes country was possible.

The Dalles Weekly Mountaineer for April 15, 1871, recounts passage through main street of four wagons of immigrants, two families named Hodges and Allen (the former with seven children, the latter with six) from Polk County en route to Ochoco Valley. Monroe Hodges platted the town of Prineville, filing the papers at The Dalles land office in 1887. He built the first hotel and livery stable in the village.[83] Benjamin F. Allen is credited with bringing the first jersey cattle to central Oregon. A native of Illinois, he settled on McKay Creek, later (1887) helped organize the First National Bank in Prineville and served as county commissioner in 1882.[84]

Francis "Barney" Prine came across the plains from Missouri to Oregon in 1853 with his parents, at 12 years—old enough to drive one of the wagons and to stand guard. The Prines settled in the forks of the Santiam about six miles from Scio. "Before long we began feeling a little crowded," said Barney, "and I decided to go east of the mountains where I would have more room."[85]

34   He was 27 when he came to the Ochoco country in 1868, lately corporal of the First Oregon Volunteer Infantry, Company "F". With his

blacksmith shop and little store established, two years later he opened a saloon.[86] As a friend told it:

During that summer Barney Prine started Prineville by building a dwelling house, store, blacksmith shop, hotel and saloon. I think he was all of one day building them. They were constructed of willow logs, 10 × 14 in size, one story high and all under one roof. His first invoice of goods cost $80; his liquor consisted of a case of Hostetter's Bitters, and the iron for the blacksmith shop was obtained from the fragments of an old emigrant wagon left up on Crooked river. In addition to his other business ventures Barney laid out and made a race track that ran from the banks of Crooked river up along where now is the north side of First street, and many were the bottles of Hostetter's lost and won over that track by the local racers of the period. Right here I want to tell of the first poker game played in this country which was also my first venture in that direction.

A few days before the game some one from The Dalles had brought out a wagon-load of apples which Barney had purchased. On this day I happened to go to the "town" and Barney took me out and very solicitously inquired if I was versed in the mysteries of "draw," stating that if I would go in with him we could make a "raise" out of some Warm Spring Indians who were camped on the river and wanted a game. I very frankly confessed my almost criminal ignorance in that useful branch of a boy's education; that my parents had not been able to send me to college, so my education was limited to a country school grade; but I was willing to learn; as he told me that if I would sit just to his right and "cut" the cards just to his "break" we would go through those Indians like a case of the itch in a country school. I consented and we soon had the game in full blast; Barney and I and two of the Indians. Barney would run up hands and I would "cut," generally using both hands to get the "cut" correct. My work was a little "coarse" but I got there "Eli" all the same. Those Indians could speak only two English words, "I passe," and every time Barney and I would get in a good shuffle and "cut" those confounded

35

heathen would ejaculate, "I passe," with a unanimity that was paralyzing to our hope as it was astonishing, and when it came their turn to deal, the surprising hands that would be out! But the most singular part of it all was, invariably one of the condemned Indians would have the top hand, and it was not long before the Indians had all of Barney's money, and I am inclined to believe that it was all the money in the settlement at that time. After our money had all been lost we bet apples at $4 a box, and it was not long before the Indians had won the entire load of apples. Then the game stopped. We were busted. We had nothing else the Indians wanted. I stood and watched them load their ponies with the apples and when they started off I turned to my partner and whispered, "Barney, I passe."[87]

Settlement meant a main street embryonic business district, with dry goods (and wet goods), hardwares, groceries all freighted in, usually from The Dalles. It meant professional offices for lawyer, doctor, dentist; it meant newspaper, church and school. Ike Schwartz built the first sawmill on Mill Creek in the early 1870s.[88] Daniel Thomas was Prineville's first postmaster in 1873. Til Glaze came in 1879 from Dallas, and established a famous saloon which served as a church on one occasion and location for a number of gun fights. Across the street he built an opera house.[89]

Friend to Til Glaze was Benjamin Franklin Nichols, who was at 21 the first sheriff of Polk County—when that county stretched to the summit of the Rockies. Later a druggist in Prineville, he studied law when he was 54. Admitted to practice, and elected to the state legislature, he introduced the bill which created Crook County in 1882.[90]

Friend to Frank Nichols was Marshall Awbrey, fellow Missourian who came to Oregon in 1850. The *Laidlaw Chronicle* had it, in 1908, that "M.C. Awbrey was the first white man in here, and it is told that he came in ahead of the jack rabbits. After pioneer Awbrey had planted a few junipers, in came John Sisemore." Actually, Awbrey came to near Prineville in 1868. A founder of Yreka, California, and a Missouri veteran of the Mexican War, "Uncle Marsh" lived long at Pickett's Island near present Tumalo. Although he "never used liquor or tobacco," he ran a saloon in Bend for a time.[91]

36

Steve Yancey came to Prineville in 1881. He and his brother Jesse freighted, ran cows, and Steve had three bands of sheep by 1905. Together he and his brother freighted the first electric generating plant into Prineville—200,000 pounds of it—in 1898. The Yanceys contracted to haul it from Moro with two ten-horse teams for one and one-half cents a pound. It took seven round trips, each requiring eight or nine days. They also hauled wool to The Dalles (and later to Shaniko), returning with merchandise for Prineville merchants. "They didn't have automobiles in those days, but you could tie a lot of money up in a good driving team," Steve Yancey commented in later years. He recalled one, with harness and all, that represented about $500—a lot of money at that time.[92]

When friend Guy Dobson announced that he was starting a bank in Redmond, M. A. Lynch jokingly said, "If it looks good to you, let us know; 'Lord' Roberts and I will open a store." Lynch and his partner, J. R. Roberts, established Lynch & Roberts Department Store in Redmond in 1910. Evidently both felt some risk since Roberts stayed with his wholesale job in Portland, "just in case." Six months later he, too, came to Redmond. They opened a successful mail order business (1913-16), distributing a catalog to points as far away as Paulina and Izee. Once they received a 13-ton order from Sheep Mountain. Roberts laughed, remembering two trips to Paulina in an old Reo, carrying 50 crates of fresh strawberries each time.[93]

Although Frank and Josephine Redmond lived in a homestead tent in the sagebrush in 1904, by 1906 the town was platted and Ehret Brothers had a general store. First postmaster was Carl Ehret, 1905.[94]

After John Palmehn platted Madras in 1902, Joshua Hahn erected, in 1903, the first store and hotel there. Following a familiar pattern for central Oregon, he was also postmaster.[95]

Philip G. Carmical settled near the place now called O'Neil in 1872, establishing what came to be known as Carmical Crossing or Carmical Station on the road to Prineville from the west. Three of the sons of William G. O'Neil—Charles, George and Walter—operated a store at this site after 1904. To the north, on Crooked River, Francis Forest settled at the most feasible western crossing of the river, Forest Crossing, 12 miles west of Prineville. In addition to operating a small store he raised cattle, acquired 1,200 acres of land.[96]

Marshall Awbrey is authority for the statement that a Robert Carmical (Carmichael) was an early settler at Cline Buttes. Awbrey believed the buttes should properly have taken their name from that early settler who pre-dated Dr. Cass Cline. Cline, for whom Cline Buttes are named, came to Prineville in 1891. He was a dentist with a vision of more than teeth, for in 1887 he brought his family across the Cascades to the Deschutes area, taking a homestead at Cline Falls. Cline commuted by horseback to his practice in Prineville.[97]

John Sisemore and W. H. Staats were the only cattlemen permanently at the site of Bend between 1880 and 1902. Sisemore built a hotel of sorts, had a post office, and built a wagon bridge across the Deschutes. W. H. Staats also kept travelers, had a small store, and was in 1899 the postmaster. In those days the salary equaled the amount of stamps canceled; Bill Staats canceled 75 cents worth of stamps in three months.[98]

High O'Kane, portly and pleasantly Irish, was born in Antrim, Ireland, in 1854. He stowed away to enter the United States in 1867. In his time he was newsboy, tailor, packer, horseman, hotel owner, miner, athletic contest promoter and world traveler. During the Sioux campaign he packed provisions for Major Reno in 1876. He came to Bend in 1903, built the old Hotel Bend in 1905. After it burned, he built the O'Kane Building in 1915. In 1910 he joined the homestead excitement and announced that he had filed on a vinegar spring near Hillman (now Terrebonne). His idea was to plant most of the land to cabbage, water it with vinegar from the spring and corner the sauerkraut market. And pigs feeding on his sauerkraut would produce pickled pigs' feet![99]

Sisters post office was moved from Camp Polk to the homestead of John J. Smith in 1888. Later Smith opened a store in Sisters and moved the post office there. He sold to Alex Smith in 1898.[100]

Doctors, too, sought the early villages. Dr. James R. Sites took up a homestead at Lone Pine in 1875 and afterwards lived in Prineville. A veteran of the Mexican War, Dr. Sites was one of those surviving Missourians captured by Mexican forces and herded on a death march across the Jornada del Muerto—the White Sands of southern New Mexico.[101]

Horace Belknap's father moved to Prineville in 1875, educated Horace at Willamette University, Michigan University, and Bellevue Medical College in New York City. In 1886 the new doctor stopped in Prineville to visit his parents on his way to practice in Chico, California, when a typhoid epidemic broke out. He stayed to help, and stayed the rest of his life, serving Prineville and as much of the outlying area as he could.[102]

Soon after Dr. Belknap's arrival, a rider came from Sisters, bringing news of a man badly in need of medical care. The older doctor, not liking the long, hard journey (by horseback or buggy), prevailed upon young Dr. Belknap to make the trip. This was Horace's first case, and he started out not knowing until his arrival whether the patient was still living.

Returning to Prineville another similar case was reported at Paulina, and thus the young doctor's first two cases were 100 miles apart. On returning to Prineville [again] *another rider came reporting a shooting scrape south of Farewell Bend, about where Camp Abbot is today* [now Sunriver]. *Again the young doctor was prevailed upon to make the journey, and leaving Prineville in the night he arrived at Farewell Bend in the early morning. His team was exhausted and as no other horses were available to continue the journey two young unbroken mules were substituted. As was the custom in those days they tied the buggy tongue to a tree until the young mules could be "lashed in," one on each side of the tongue, and when all set they cut them loose—headed south. The doctor said the mules did not quit running until near the cinder butte* [Lava Butte] *some 10 miles south of Bend. When at last he arrived at the destination he found the patient lying under a pine tree. There being no men near at the moment two women attempted to assist as he probed for the bullet, but they soon vanished from the scene. The doctor had a can of ether which he administered to the patient with one hand while he probed for the bullet with the other. When the patient began to swear he knew it was time for more ether. In due time the doctor retraced his journey back to Prineville. The doctor related he did not learn*

39

whether the man lived or died until three months later when he met him on the street in Prineville.[103]

Among other early physicians in central Oregon, Dr. William Snook came in 1899, settling at Lamonta. He was tubercular, thought the dry air would be beneficial. Shortly, he moved his family to Madras, built an office and drugstore in the center of town. The closest hospital was at The Dalles, but Dr. Snook believed people healed better in their own family surroundings.[104]

Dr. James Thom visited central Oregon in 1904-05, looking for a "location." Bend had a new doctor, Urling C. Coe, so Dr. Thom looked further. At Silver Lake, residents guaranteed him a bonus of $1,000 to help him get started if he would stay a year. He took the offer, reminisced in later years about treating the mangled thumb of a sheepman who had been shot by a cowman. The doctor had to amputate the thumb and suture the flap, all without anesthetic. "Men, and women too, took a sort of pride in their ability to bear pain in those days, and sometimes refused anesthesia because they didn't want to appear to be sissies," he said. "I always carried chloroform in the buggy along with the complete medical, surgical, and obstetrical equipment that went everywhere with me. . .I never knew what to expect." Dr. Thom moved his family to Bend in 1924 where he practiced for a long while.[105]

Dr. Charles S. Edwards, the first doctor in Bend, moved to Prineville in 1904 where he remained in practice until 1927.[106] When his successor, Dr. Urling C. Coe, came to Bend there were two small sawmills, eight saloons and a red light district down by the river on the lower end of town.[107] Coe became *the* doctor at Farewell Bend as Belknap was in Prineville, Snook in Madras, Hosch in Redmond.

Coe dispensed medicines and treatments to homesteaders, businessmen, whores, and horse thieves, to ranchers and their families, to "timber beasts," "gandy dancers," and "sawdust savages." His book, *Frontier Doctor,* is illuminating; particularly amusing is his account of the baby who was delivered by telephone. The doctor, on his way to another case, relayed the necessary obstetrical information (over a series of telephones owned by ranchers along the route he was traveling) to the switchboard operator in Bend, whose maidenly modesty took second place to her job responsibility. She repeated to the attending midwives upriver all the necessary instructions. It was better than television; everyone on the party line was listening.[108]

When A. M. Drake, who platted the town, and his wife first came to Bend they drove their wagon right into the Staats's front yard. Prince Staats recalled it as a curious arrangement—a little house built right on the wagon bed. Prince's father sold the site of Bend to Drake for $4,000, asking twice what he privately throught it was worth.[109] Drake, from St. Paul, Minnesota, was one of the 226 people in Bend in 1903, and played an important part in bringing irrigation to the area.[110] N. P. Smith described Drake as "a small man, not tall. Some people didn't like him. Early stockmen fought him—they didn't want the country opened up to settlement."[111]

E. M. Lara, who established an early mercantile venture in Bend, also was cashier for the Deschutes State Bank of Bend, and the First National of Bend. He recalled in 1934 that bank robberies were virtually unknown during his more than 20 years' experience in central Oregon. Mr. Lara attributed this to two reasons: the difficulty in getting out of the country, and the disposition of the people here to shoot first and hold the trial later.[112]

First sheriff of Deschutes County, S. E. Roberts, came to Bend in 1910, and worked for the Deschutes Irrigation and Power Company; he was the bane of moonshiners during central Oregon's prohibition period.[113] However, his part in the Bend Commercial Club's and the Bend Emblem Club's reception for the Portland Ad Club in 1914 is less well known. Under the combined leadership of William Duncan Cheney, Harvey DeArmond and George Palmer Putnam the Bend clubs decided to host the Portlanders, bringing them to Bend by rail, and then touring the Deschutes area in cars. Part of the entertainment was a surprise eruption of Lava Butte, carefully primed for the occasion with dynamite, black powder and fireworks. Roberts, then chief of police, set off the charges as arranged, with properly horrific results as the open mouths of the visitors attested. "The entire top of Lava Butte seemed to tremble, the riven lava boulders were hurled high in the air, the aerial bombs rattled like volleys of thunder, and streams of writing fire ran through the ragged lava fields around the crater's base."

Unfortunately, some of the charges went off prematurely, burning the police chief severely about the face and hands. To preserve the hoax, he had to remain in hiding until the cars rattled away, when he could go for medical assistance.[114]

When Eugene Guerin built a telephone line into Bend in 1904, it marked a link with the outside, for the new line stretched to Prineville, to Madras, to Wasco and The Dalles. The Bend office formally opened August 17 and among the interested participants was Gerald Groesbeck, son of a New York millionaire, a true remittance man who lived for a time in Bend with his wife. Frequently intoxicated, he often availed himself of firearms with which he blazed away at the sky, not the citizenry. On this memorable occasion he wanted to call Lucknow, India, and talk to one of his friends there, a rajah's son. Since it would be 11 years before the first transoceanic telephone line, Groesbeck was finally persuaded to send a cablegram instead. It cost him $47.[115]

N. P. Smith came to Bend in April, 1902, from Bemidji, Minnesota, in company with E. A. Sather, John Steidl and Tom Tweet. He worked for Drake in 1904, laying the first board sidewalk and pulling juniper out of the right-of-way for Wall Street. In 1910 he opened a hardware store at 935 Wall. Smith brought the first gasoline into Bend in five-gallon cans. That fuel sold for about 40 cents a gallon. In 1953 he remembered a Fourth of July celebration fish fry for which he and three other anglers took 3,125 trout from the Deschutes in four days' fishing.[116]

The heir of G. P. Putnam's Sons, publishers, George Palmer Putnam, came to Bend in 1909 by stagecoach. He published the *Bulletin,* and he was largely responsible for hiring Robert Sawyer who succeeded Putnam as publisher and editor. Putnam became mayor of Bend at 24, wrote between 1909 and 1916 three books and other articles, served Governor Withycombe as aide. In his time in Oregon he assisted in Deschutes County's birth and in resolution of the long conflict between farmers and irrigation companies in central Oregon.[117]

42

Another sort of businessman, the timber buyer, came early—between

1893 and 1903. In 1902, R. E. Gilchrist bought about 60,000 acres. And in the same year S. S. Johnson of Bemidji, Minnesota, purchased a large tract of pine timber from A. J. Dwyer. Johnson later established the Deschutes Lumber Company, and he sold timber to Shevlin-Hixon interests in 1915. His son, Colonel S. O. Johnson, retained extensive timber holdings in the Sisters area and, in partnership with Bert Peterson, operated the Tite Knot Pine Mill. Colonel Johnson died in Berkeley, California, age 71.[118] S. S. Johnson's grandson, Sam Johnson, has also continued the family's interest, has served the Deschutes country well as state representative and more recently as mayor of Redmond. He and his wife, Becky, in August, 1967, donated a part of their land at the headwaters of the Metolius at Black Butte (see frontispiece) to the U. S. Forest Service as a park.[119]

Education

First, you have to get their attention.[120]

Education was not neglected on the frontier. In Ochoco, school was taught in 1869. At Farewell Bend, Electa M. O'Neil taught pioneer children in 1881. Crook County District 9, two miles north of Sisters, built a school in 1882. Sisters' first school opened in 1884; Big Meadows, 1887; Lava, 1889; La Pine, 1897; and Cloverdale, 1898.[121] Discipline sometimes called for imaginative solutions. Rae Knickerbocker Clark, who taught the Plainview School in 1918, remembered

some older big boys who misbehaved in school. I thought it over and the next day I lined them up and told them severely that since I obviously couldn't punish them, I would punish myself instead. I whacked mightily away on my left hand with a wooden ruler. It hurt like the dickens—but it worked. One of them burst into tears and swore he'd *behave himself (and looking meaningfully at the others), so would* they. *I didn't have any trouble after that.*[122]

The fact is that every frontier educator became not only inured to the vicissitudes of the life, but remarkably versatile at doing a lot of things, and some of these at the same time. As the custodian of learning (no pun intended) the teacher was also a social necessity at community gather-

43

ings in the schoolhouse, and depending on education and knowledge (and the level of knowledge in the community), an arbiter of disputes and a walking encyclopedia of useful information. A teacher was expected to know the rudiments of science, to have some knowledge of governmental designs, and to know how to get information if he didn't have it.

If the teacher was female, and reasonably young and comely, she could expect to be courted by various swains in the community—with varying degrees of seriousness—for unattached women with a teacher's acquirements were rare in frontier communities. As a "good" woman she could be assured of no lack of partners at community dances, and a great deal of well-meant advice from married ladies. She was also an object of considerable curiosity and gossip. Clara Bliss Koenig found that "there was more to teaching school than just the three 'R's' back in 1913 in rural central Oregon. There were things such as splitting wood, getting a fire started on a frigid morning and carrying the day's supply of water to school in a gallon jug. There were brisk hikes facing a stiff wind over a trail through head-high sagebrush with the possibility of an unexpected encounter with a rattlesnake."[123]

Early teachers in old Crook County needed only to present evidence of graduation from the eighth grade or pass an examination. They tended to be peripatetic. By 1888, 640 pupils were enrolled in Crook County schools while 620 school-age persons were not attending. There were 37 teachers, 27 school houses, 35 school districts.[124]

Irrigation

That the climate of the whole section was temperate and healthful; that there was abundant water, and that such parts of the grant as were included in the tract misnamed the Oregon desert in the maps of the day, would, when irrigated from the rivers issuing there from the Cascade mountains, prove to invite home making by thousands of new settlers.[125]

44   Population came to the Deschutes country in trickles which became

rivulets occasionally freshened to flood stage, when circumstances were attractive. With the natural grasses gone, except for grazing in the Cascade Range Forest Reserve and on the Warm Springs Reservation, stockmen turned to the streams of the area, making small diversions onto land for irrigating hay crops (and home gardens). The lands could be developed if enough water could be found. From these small beginning segregations (as early as 1873)[126] grew the next stage in the settlement of central Oregon.

Thousands of acres of sandy soil, sagebrush and junipers could, in the optimism of the frontier period, be transformed into green fields—productive, profitable, affording to every man willing to make the effort the sine qua non of common man yearnings: His Own Place! And here in the "last frontier" were available the "last of the public lands" waiting to be claimed. Attractive circumstances, indeed. The Deschutes Valley Land and Investment Company in 1910 claimed: "The Road to Success is short if you know which one to take—the door to fortune is open if you know which one to enter—this is *your opportunity. Embrace it NOW!*. . . 'Fortune knocks once at every man's door and if not admitted, she leaves and next day sends her daughter, Miss-Fortune.' Which will you admit?"[127]

Senator Joseph Carey, once governor of Montana, introduced a bill which Congress approved in 1894.[128] The Carey Desert Land Act provided for federal relinquishment to states of arid lands within state boundaries where such lands exceeded one million acres. Since in Crook County alone there were an estimated 3,277,000 acres, such a qualifying feature was, for Oregon, awfully apparent.[129] The state, in turn, would arrange for the construction of necessary ditches and diversion points, for the lands must be irrigated. Thus large acreage segregations were made by the state land board after 1901.[130] Those who rushed to file on waters available found that much of the Deschutes and tributary waters were already claimed.

The earliest filing on record on the Deschutes was that of the Cline Falls Power Company in January, 1892, but that filing was intended to provide hydroelectric energy rather than irrigation water.[131] "The Father of Irrigation in the West," Charles C. Hutchinson, formed the Oregon Development Company in 1898 and filed on Deschutes water that spring.[132] The Deschutes Reclamation and Irrigation Company formed by Jim Benham and George W. Swalley was also incorporated in 1898.[133]

Irrigation development companies multiplied in the Deschutes country; by 1914 water filings above Bend totaled 61,000 cubic feet per second, or about 40 times the stream flow![134] Inevitably there was competition; the most notable developed between C. C. Hutchinson and A. M. Drake. Hutchinson was on the Deschutes with engineers making surveys and water filings two years before the wealthy Minneapolis capitalist, Drake, appeared in 1900. Since Hutchinson needed capital, in 1899 he wrote to Drake at Spokane, representing to him the potential profits in irrigation development near Bend. Drake came, assessed the prospect and asked for Hutchinson's proposition. He was offered half of the company stock, with agreement that he be president and manager, conditional on his supplying needed capital. Drake agreed to the terms, and paid for surveys. About two months afterwards, Drake informed Hutchinson that he saw no reason for partnership in the venture, in effect elbowing Hutchinson aside.[135] "You have no interest here and nothing to sell," Drake told Hutchinson, who calls Drake a "disorganizer and blackmailer" in his letter of complaint to Congressman Malcolm Moody.[136]

Drake's Pilot Butte Development Company and Hutchinson's Oregon Irrigation Company then proceeded to make new water filings, in two instances side by side. Hutchinson also wrote to Oregon's Binger Hermann, then commissioner of the General Land Office, pointing out that his prior filings on Deschutes water took preference over Drake's and effectually prevented Drake from complying with Carey Act regulations.

The squabble did not really delay development of irrigation: in 1903 Secretary of the Interior Hitchcock affirmed a General Land Office dismissal of Hutchinson's protest, and recognized legitimacy of the Pilot Butte Company claim.[137] Local sentiments were strongly with Drake, probably because he had the money to make the development, and Hutchinson did not. Both companies sold in 1904 to a successor, the Deschutes Irrigation and Power Company, owned principally at that time by W. Eugene

46

Guerin, also president of the Central Oregon Banking and Investment Company.[138] Other companies followed, advertising widely the potential of the valley of the Deschutes:

In one's mind's eye the cycles of time pass rapidly, and lo! one beholds. . .a busy city. . .massive stone structures. . .the beautiful river is harnessed and giving its power to turn the countless wheels of mill and factory. . . . All about one sees great tracts of land re-claimed from the desert wilds and now groaning under the weight of fruit, vegetables, hay and grain, while in pastures green one beholds the sleek jersey cow, the noble horse, the sheep and swine.[139]

Central Oregon's lava veneer proved stubbornly resistant in those days of dynamite, black powder and hand drills. Yet with teams of horses and scrapers, with crews of pick-and-shovelers, the main ditches crept slowly north and east, their laterals extending long, wavering tendrils. In November, 1904, Deschutes Irrigation and Power Company made things considerably easier for its employees by purchasing two portable steam boilers which were shipped out from Columbus, Ohio. One boiler was of twenty horsepower, the other of six; both were to furnish power for operating rock drills. The larger boiler drove four drills; the smaller, one. Together they would bore 400 feet a day in lava rock, where ordinar-ily it would take a rock crew of three men to bore 18 or 20 feet a day. About 50 Italian laborers had been brought in during September, bringing the company's work force to 200 men and 100 teams.[140]

With so many horses in demand, wild range horses were bought, then broken and provided with harness by the company. One of the suppliers of horses was Jesse Yancey of Prineville, who sold 68 animals from the ranges at Bear Creek and Alkali Flat during September of 1904.[141]

Even in those days there were some labor disputes. In March, 1905, Deschutes Irrigation and Power Company posted notices at ditch camps that men receiving $2.25 and teams receiving $2.50 a day would get only $2.00 a day—the same rate of pay that was given in 1903 for a 10-hour day. (A man and a team received $4.50 in 1903.) Immediately men threatened to quit, with 200 men actually leaving along with 125 teams.

There was no violence—the men moved to Klamath Falls and other areas to work on reclamation jobs.[142] Eventually, the local pay was raised again and more men were hired.

The irrigation projects took their toll in lives. Men were blinded and maimed by blasts, and there were other injuries, even suicides. Babies and young children died at the project camps of pneumonia, meningitis and other diseases until companies prohibited families from living at project sites. Percy Walzer was struck by an axe head suddenly leaving its handle—the blade cut the lower leg severely and severed the ligaments and tendons.[143] Irvin Reed, December 12, 1905, was thawing out the dynamite by an open fire, preparatory to blasting a stretch of the Arnold Ditch when all 24 sticks went off.[144] Reed was within two feet of the blast, and he suffered lasting injury to his eyes, and a series of operations. Ultimately he had vision in one eye.

Walt May was a pioneer powder man who worked largely in road construction, although he blasted the holes for Bend's first street lights. He came to Bend in 1905, left powder work in 1939 when a powder charge misfired at the Redmond CCC camp. Walt remembered in 1955 that he "had charge of all the powder and rock work on the canal to Madras, and shot the first holes myself."[145] That canal extension with CCC labor brought the water closer to Jefferson County's Agency Plains, but water did not reach those thirsty acres until 1949.[146] Now, those desert lands grow grain, potatoes and mint.

Sometimes there were simply "close calls." One of those close calls happened at the office-warehouse of the Pilot Butte Company in September, 1904. The company was doing some blasting of rock at the edge of the river near their warehouse, where a wing dam was under construction. Jim Overturf, in charge of the mill yard, noticed a broken box of giant powder on the warehouse floor. Concerned that someone might stumble against the box, he set it up on a shelf in plain sight where its dangerous nature would be apparent to all. A few minutes later Overturf was sitting in the office when an unusually heavy blast was set off and a rock weighing a hundred or more pounds sailed through the air, falling squarely upon the warehouse roof. The rock crashed through the roof

48

to the floor, precisely in the spot where the giant powder had been situated only a few mintues before.[147]

Slowly the network spread, slowly the water reached sandy acres newly cleared. In time two-thirds or more of the Deschutes near Bend was detoured into irrigation ditches. Wooden flumes were built across difficult stretches of terrain, necessitating the establishment of early sawmills in the Bend area. These mills also sawed boards for new construction, including homes. By 1904 a small acreage near Bend was being watered, and about 500 people lived in the town.[148]

First watered from the Pilot Butte Canal was the homestead of Deschutes Irrigation and Power engineer Levi D. Wiest, in spring, 1904. The June 3, 1904, *Bend Bulletin* notes on page 1: "After about four years of work and the expenditure of tens of thousands of dollars the soil back from the river is slaking its thirst and pushing plant life in a surprising manner."

The spirit of irrigation entered the bosoms of almost all of central Oregon's human inhabitants. Marsh Awbrey, "Sage of the Deschutes," in 1904 exclaimed: "Talk about crops! We've got the Willamette valley skinned. I see oats, rye, alfalfa and potatoes and even fruit on this side of the range that tee-totally skunks anything they've got on the other side this year. The only trouble over here is that too few people are farming and so little of the land is now actually under cultivation."[149]

And the idea of using the lakes at the headwaters of streams tributary to the Deschutes as reservoirs for storage was born. In time that idea would be improved upon, and man-made lakes like Crane Prairie and Wickiup would add thousands of acre-feet storage.[150] But successful irrigation projects were, in those earliest days, very few. Between 1901 and 1906 seven projects were approved under the Carey Act, covering a total of 194,138 acres of segregated land. Of these projects only one—the Deschutes Reclamation and Irrigation Company project for 1,280 acres—was completed in 1913.[151]

Around Redmond, new settlers were disappointed with the new, unwatered land. A 1905 pioneer, Mrs. Joe McClay, remembered that "it was wild and desolate. . . . When we came here there wasn't much here but tents." Another wife who came to Powell Butte the same year, Mrs. S. D. Mustard, said: "It only seemed like a slow road to starvation." In 1906 Henry Schumacher said: "Boy, when we landed here, we wondered where in the world the opportunity could be." Mrs. Ezra Eby (1905) wondered: "What in the world are we going to feed the children—rocks for bread?"[152]

Sometimes the scarcity of water led to violence. In December, 1906, on the homestead of Harrison Melvin, shooting occurred. "Old Man" Melvin (he was about 60) had entered into an arrangement with S. H. Dorrance, an early resident of Bend who had worked for the Deschutes Irrigation and Power Company and accumulated enough to buy a small portable mill. With it he proposed to cut Melvin's timber and pay Melvin a share. Melvin was at first agreeable, but Dorrance came to demand more water than Melvin could spare. Melvin Creek was only a brook; the sandy soil of Dorrance's log pond drank it thirstily.

So there was trouble. Melvin went to Prineville to get an injunction; Dorrance disregarded it. The two met at the diversion headgate, and the aggressive, younger Dorrance knocked Melvin to the ground. Melvin warned Dorrance not to come at him again. On December 2, 1906, according to contemporary report, Dorrance came to the ranch house carrying a shotgun. Melvin took his rifle and went out the back door, trying to avoid Dorrance, but he was seen. Dorrance "came at him," and when within 150 yards fired the shotgun at Melvin. Some pellets struck. Melvin's return shot pierced Dorrance just above the navel; his second missed; his third struck the shotgun and Dorrance's hand. Dorrance staggered to his house at the mill, died at 10:30 that night. Melvin rode to Prineville, gave himself into custody. A preliminary hearing bound him for trial. Freed on bail, he returned to his ranch. But the grand jury refused to indict and the case was dismissed: local sentiment was strongly in the old man's favor.[153]

Under Oregon law of 1901 the state land board's duty was to enter into contract with any person or company desiring to reclaim desert lands. There were some interesting provisions to that early law. One stated that, though title to the land passed to the settler who purchased it, the title to the irrigation works—canals, laterals, dams—remained with the company and with it the right to charge a company-determined use fee for water in perpetuity.[154] This made the independent farmer not very independent at all, and caused considerable friction bewteen companies and user-purchasers. It was clear the new lands, waiting for the eager settler, were not "free." They were available to those able to pay the costs to the company—far different than the provisions of the 1860s' Homestead Law.

In 1909 Oregon passed a revised irrigation law which established a state engineer's office, thus providing a means for supervision and control of projects, but irrigation projects begun prior to that year did not generally prosper. Contractors underestimated costs of reclamation and overestimated water available; seepage in the sandy soil and evaporation lost an estimated 40 percent.[155]

Nevertheless, settlers appeared with down payments, and waited anxiously for the water to make the Dream come true. Those who came to Carey Act projects were, for the most part, not speculators. Their intent was fixed on agricultural development of the land in a pattern parallel to settlement in the Willamette Valley. As a consequence, most were men of property and prior experience. While some found the climate and the shortage of water finally too oppressive, some stayed, their presence marked today by green fields, by rock fences built from the fragmented lava which dotted the cleared fields, by tall old Lombardy poplars planted for shade and wind breaks, by grange halls of which more remain today than one-room schools. Generally, farmer settlers in the Deschutes country fared worse than early stockmen. Use of the resources of land and water required unrelenting labor to claim the land from its natural state, and it has remained for the third and fourth generations to reap the benefits.

Principal relic of those early projects, lying now in abandonment and disrepair, is the "Tumalo Project" or Columbia Southern. Begun in 1902 by the Three Sisters Irrigation Company, the original segregation application was for 27,000 acres. W. A. Laidlaw was president of the company and other principals were W. N. Moore and E. E. Lytle. In 1903 this same group formed the Columbia Southern Irrigation Company and advertised the land widely across the United States and abroad. In 1905,

51

Laidlaw appeared before the state land board with a list of 6,293.2 acres which had received water. Then in October of that year, with settlers who had moved onto lands in anticipation of water that growing season becoming increasingly and vocally unhappy, articles of incorporation were filed in Portland for a new company, the Columbia Southern Irrigating Company, with new officers. The purpose of the company was to purchase capital stock and own land in Oregon. A principal stockholder was William A. Laidlaw, a native of Oxbow, New York.

At the first company meeting the decision was made to purchase the Columbia Southern Irrig*ation* Company. Then, in a domino effect, the Three Sisters Company sold its rights to the Columbia Southern Irriga*tion* which sold to the Columbia Southern Irrig*ating* Company, which mortgaged the company to the Oregon Trust and Savings Bank for $475,000. Of this amount, $277,000 was due the Three Sisters Irrigation Company.[156]

William D. Clark was one settler who sued the Columbia Southern Irrigating Company, in December, 1906, for damages resulting from failure of the company to furnish him water during 1905 and 1906. A jury awarded him $200. Grandfather Clark tried desperately to make the homestead a success, but was finally defeated by the arid land. In reporting the verdict for Clark's suit, the *Bend Bulletin* stated: "Settlers living on the company's segregation report that there will probably be many similar cases brought against the company in the near future."[157] The desert land board filed suit against the company in 1907; in 1909 the case was decided for the company.[158]

In April, 1907, some Laidlaw citizens were surprised to find a dummy hanging from the crossarm of a telephone pole. While blame seemed at first to attach to prankish youth, ultimate community sentiment declared the "lynching" a regrettable substitution for the person of W. A. Laidlaw. Laidlaw left Deschutes country about 1916, moving to San Diego where he died in 1936.[159]

Finally in 1913 the state took over the project; $450,000 was appropriated for reconstruction and new contracts and terms were issued to the settlers. A large reservoir capable of holding 22,000 acre-feet of water was proposed by state engineers, together with dams, feed canals, diversion works. Construction went forward to completion in December, 1914.[160]

Anticipation over the long-awaited water delivery ran high as the growing season neared in 1915. Water from Tumalo Creek and Bull Springs ran steadily into the reservoir which rose as steadily, and soon almost all of Bull Flats was covered with water shining and lapping at the base of the main dam. Then disaster! Water pressure and seepage broke through to a fissure on the northeast side of the reservoir, and within hours a mad vortex raged while thousands of gallons roared into the ground. Project children on their way to the schoolhouse lingered, awestruck, by the side of the maelstrom, throwing sticks and branches into the water to watch them be sucked under. Tumbling down that fissure were their futures as well. Freda Clark McDaniel, one of the project children, recalls: "I looked around for Rollie [her brother]. He was just about to throw a big board into the water. The plank tipped on end and disappeared into the ground. What if he had fallen in!"[161]

The state in 1917 appropriated $10,000 for extensive geologic investigations, and concluded that the costs of repair were prohibitive. That portion of the reservoir to the south which could hold water was utilized and the rest abandoned; after spending almost $458,000 the project's ultimate maximum irrigable acreage was about 8,000 acres.[162]

Today Deschutes water finds its way into six irrigation systems: the Swalley District, the Central Oregon Irrigation District, the North Unit, the Lone Pine, the Arnold and the Tumalo.[163]

Until the latest flood of settlers, in this latter part of the 20th century, that irrigation development provided more impetus to settlement than any prior movement. Agricultural communities at Lone Pine, Powell Butte, Bend, Redmond and Tumalo all grew rapidly, and a part of that growth was the development of towns serving the needs of the agricultural communities.

At the height of the irrigation enthusiasm, when it seemed the desert was finally to be overcome for settlers within reasonable distance of a water supply, plans were made to form a Suttle Lake irrigation district which would utilize water in Blue and Suttle lakes by construction of a dam 58 feet high across Lake Creek. Water storage of 21,500 acre-feet could be obtained and a canal built 18 miles to bring water to the Lower Desert at Grandview and Geneva. The estimated cost was $50 an acre.[164] Grandview farmers voted $600,000 in bonds and preliminary work was begun.[165] In February, 1916 bids were opened, and the low bidder was the Henry J. Kaiser construction company of Vancouver, B.C. But by June, Kaiser's company failed to produce its earnest fee of 10 percent of the amount of the bonds. The contract was severed. Other contractors, looking at the project, looked away, and Suttle Lake water continued to pass freely down Lake Creek to the Metolius, to the Deschutes, to the Columbia, to the Pacific.[166]

Homesteaders

Two things were ever uppermost in a homesteader's mind: Water and Credit.[167]

In the 1870s it was fashionable for westside Oregonians to take their immigrant wagons up into the mountains to escape the summer heat and to recreate themselves among the timber, the streams, the lakes. But few drove on over the passes.

For a time, with ranches established, with no developing industry, population levels seemed likely to remain stable. The railroads changed all that dramatically. Men of vision and ambition had conceived the idea of an east-west rail link in the mid-1860s. Ex-Confederate "Col." T. Egenton Hogg had plans to build from Yaquina Bay to a link with transcontinental rails on the Snake River in 1871. Such a line would have opened the interior of Oregon to settler and homesteader, provided for trade with the Orient and Europe and offered an avenue whereby the products of the interior could flow to markets.[168]

It remained for another time, at the beginning of the 20th century, for developments in central Oregon to become reality. After 1911 when the line crept to Madras, to Redmond, and finally to Bend, the rails carried thousands of pounds of freight and many passengers. During that period population rose sharply, as Carey Act and Desert Act lands became available. Rails meant cheaper goods; rails meant jobs, homesteaders, professional people. Rails also meant that the great yellow pine resource could be tapped. Rails brought the population necessary for industry, and they carried to national and international markets the produce of the region. For the next step in central Oregon settlement, rails provided the means.

The desert homestead rush followed. Promoted by local developers and the railroads, companies printed prospectuses of fair lands stretching golden fields of grain under clear, blue skies, with glimpses of date palms in the distance, and with enthralling accounts of record crops. These glowing reports were foisted on an unsuspecting and land-hungry public—they were honest about the clear, blue skies. D. B. McFadyen, a Hampton Buttes homesteader of 1919

> *was visiting the Bert Meeks home one evening when a car with New York license plates stopped for gas. The man and wife asked how far it was to Imperial as they had bought there. When Mr. Meeks tried to explain there was no hotel at Imperial and the closest one was Bend 75 miles (and long ones in those days)—a 4 hour drive, the lady didn't believe him and drove on. About two hours later they were back to stay all night. They showed us some pictures of "Imperial" they had received from the promoters showing well laid out streets, buildings, fountains, and palm trees. The woman had bought several lots and had come west to check on her investment.*[169]

The February 12, 1920, weekly *Bend Bulletin* reported the arrival in Bend of a person who

> *inquired when the Imperial train would leave, and was finally persuaded to remain over night and make the 70 mile journey in a specially chartered car the following morning. On the trip out, he mystified his driver with occasional questions as to the relative merits of the Imperial banks, and how many hundred children were enrolled in the high school. Outside rooms were all that the Imperial "hotel" could boast, and he returned the same night. He will pay no more taxes. But many will, for payments still come in to the office of Sheriff S. E. Roberts, from Canada, England, Alaska, and some even from China and Australia.*

Actually, as "Doug McFadyen remembered it, there were few buildings still standing at Imperial in 1919: "There was a bank building, a school house and two or three more. But cattle and horses were using them for shelter."[170]

When, by 1908, it looked probable that a rail line was coming to the interior, attention turned to the vast acreages which constituted the High Desert—that is, the approximate area between the Deschutes River on the west and present site of Burns on the east; between the Maury Mountains on the north and the present site of Lakeview on the south. Between 1908 and 1917 a number of private companies were formed for the purpose of bringing settlement to desert lands, both High and Low.[171] In 1916, under an enlarged version of the Homestead Act, a man and wife might take 640 acres of land, if they met the loose requirements.[172]

But the High Desert country is just that. Growing season is short, frost occurs every month, and rainfall is sometimes eight inches a year.[173] These facts, however, were skillfully shunted aside, and the skeptical buyer who came in summer saw large stands of natural grasses and a generally promising landscape.

So the homesteaders came. They withdrew savings, sold businesses, borrowed money to buy equipment and railroad passage, and they came—by rails' end to Shaniko, later by rail to Bend. They even came by wagon on the old historic route across the country. By May, 1911, 300 land filings on 96,000 acres in Crook County had been made.[174]

Recently John L. Garske, a homesteader at Hampton Buttes and now a resident of Seattle, wrote of his experiences:

During 1911-12, when the first railroad was constructed up Deschutes River canyon and rails ended at Bend, a big land rush began. My father became deeply interested. In May, 1913, he arrived in Bend.

And it was booming!—landseekers, ranchers, teams and saddle horses tied to hitch racks along board sidewalks, loaded freight wagons—six to eight teams with lead bells, a jerkline skinner mounted on a wheel horse, pulling out of town in dense clouds of dust.

Charley Bangston located us on 320-acre claims in Clover Creek valley, Hampton Buttes, a corner of the old west. The Buttes were strictly cow country—homesteaders not welcome. And not healthy for sheep. Traveling 78 horse miles on winding wagon trail for two days by team and wagon, we arrived on our claims June 6, 1913. Lumber was hauled from the small Ammons sawmill on Maury Mountain about 20 miles to the north.[175]

The greatest activity occurred in 1914. In April the *Bend Bulletin* reported the homesteaders arriving in large numbers: men with families and full carloads of goods, stock and farm implements—more to come. . .bound for different points in the interior, including Rivers, Imperial, Arrow and Fremont, La Pine, Crescent and Fort Rock. "None are coming here broke."[176]

They came with high hopes, with great anticipation and enthusiasm, with confidence that the frontier was not really gone after all. Bend, Prineville, Madras and points south, all felt their impact. They bought lumber from local mills, large and small, freighted it by wagons to their claims, and built small, unpainted "yellow shacks." They picked tons of rocks from the land, often using them for fences which stand today as monuments to their industry and enthusiasm. They grubbed sage, blasted stumps, broke ground, rooted out bunchgrass, built fences of wire where there was not enough rock, established schools, small villages and post offices. They hauled water from distant sources—wells, springs, creeks—carried the precious stuff home for storage and prayed for rain.

Domestic water was never wasted. Reub Long remembered that water started out in the cooking pot, progressed to dishwashing, bathing, clothes washing, and finally was used to nourish the landscaping—a matrimony-vine next to the house. Reub said it was the only plant that could flourish with the application of soapy water, and one of the first "necessities" procured by the lady of the house.[177] If she were to keep her sanity, there had to be at least one living domestic plant in the yard.

The homesteaders held meetings to discuss development, for social reasons as much as any, to shore up their enthusiasm collectively—almost in desperation, for this thing *must* work for all of them. They talked with farmers on the irrigated lands and thought of grandiose irrigation schemes such as tapping East and Paulina lakes.

The first few years for the homesteaders saw a partial return in rye and barley, some wheat, as the virgin ground responded and a wet cycle afforded more rainfall than usual. But when the young crops were green, there came another burden: jack rabbits, by the thousands, attracted by the tasty grain, in many cases removed entire crops.

So means were employed to control rabbits. There were attempts to poison them, to shoot them and even to use dogs to catch and kill them. Finally, concerted community rabbit drives were proposed, and they became social events in the desert communities. Where the country was favorable a stretch of woven wire fence would be erected and a long line of men, women and boys armed with clubs would beat the brush, driving rabbits toward the fence corner where they would club them to death by the thousands.[178]

Old pictures exist of some of those drives, reminiscent of Paiute days, with the group of settlers standing happily by a huge mound of rabbit carcasses. Still, the rabbits seemed to thrive. In some instances, in an attempt to adjust to the situation, schemes were laid to exploit rabbit hides, furs and meat for export. Farmers in 1916-17 learned that a manufacturer in Philadelphia would buy rabbit pelts for hats. The skins would bring 35 to 40 cents per pound—and it took four to five skins to make that pound. With Crook County bounty, each rabbit was now worth about 10 or 12 cents.[179]

Despite rabbits and other hazards, the country "held" some settlers. Mr. and Mrs. Horace Brookings spent 10 years at the "Halfway House" (Hampton Station) from 1909, "the happiest of my life," Mrs. Brookings recalled in 1948. "We met so many interesting people, and two times we had 100 guests for dinner." On Halfway House registers were names from nearly every state in the Union.[180] Mary Addie Watts, who died in 1951 at 78, was found collapsed on the floor of her two-room homestead near Brothers in 1949. A North Carolinian, she had lived there alone since 1917, stoutly refusing to leave. She once told Olive Jameson, a Deschutes County Welfare worker, "It is peaceful. All one has to do here is to think the right way, and there is no one here to talk for the other side."[181]

58   On the Lower Desert, the Grandview and Geneva communities, there stand today the most impressive of homesteader relics—the stone fences

and rock piles built up with tremendous labor around once-cultivated fields. The soil there is not deep. It is a frosting of nutrient on a multi-layered cake of rocks. Homesteaders dug the rocks from the fields, did something useful with them, like constructing fences and root houses or cellars, and then plowed as deeply as they could. The next spring they found, to their dismay, a new crop of rocks working up through the thin soil. These caught the plowshares and had in turn to be removed. Ultimately the rocks and the crop prices defeated these people, but the rock piles and fences remain.

Harry Heising came to central Oregon in 1902. His family settled in the Lytle Addition at Bend until 1905 when they took a homestead on Tumalo Creek. In 1908 they moved to the Metolius: "The lack of water was a great drawback for the few springs and wells did not supply the demand. Some of the people hauled from the Deschutes river and Fly lake on the head of Fly creek. It was a common sight to see some woman going up the road driving an old poor team of ponies and an old wagon with the tires wired on with hay wire, three or four barrels and several old tin wash tubs and the same amount of children going after a load of water, a full day's trip."[182]

It was to be expected that bitterness would set in when the sad realization came that the desert could not offer or produce the prosperity that had been anticipated. No doubt there were many oral confrontations between homesteaders and real estate people, but one rather severe criticism reached John Steidl at Bend by mail. The letter, dated July 23, 1910, read as follows:

I and my brother and two other relation have come to a agreement two make you pay us back a little money that you robbed from us by lokated us up there on de hay desert and miss represented it to us and told us that it would raise and it won't a dame thing and yare node it wouldent—all you wanted was to robaf our hard erned cash. We are men with a family and sold our good homes and came here and now we are broke if you will just pay the 4 of us $600$50 six hundred and fifty dlars we will [call] it square this money must be put in a can and beried the 4th telephone pole starting from your house on the laidlaw road and in gold

*coin on the north side of the pole and beried 2 inches under the
soil and if you will give (?) or any thing or let this letter out for
12 months we will blow your head off if this moneys isn't there
rite away we will blow your house and family to hell. because
this is to much to stand. and dount you go there to look for
12 monthes either Yours truly,*

JOHN STEDC

And be sure you dont let this be known.[183]

Steidl maintained that the threatening letter was nothing more than
a joke and in an interview with the *Bulletin* he stated that the ten men
he had located on the desert were on the best of terms with him; that
the demanded reimbursement was more than the amount that would have
been collected in a sale. Steidl buried the can near the telephone pole—with
a piece of lava in it—and invited the letter writer to come get it. Nothing
further seems to have happened.

Those people who located on water fared better, but even then, other
factors conspired against them. By 1920, John Garske remembered,

*the entire Garske family had procured a large amount of land-
homesteads and [was] purchasing others. It developed into a pros-
perous ranch of 4200 acres—grazing sheep, cattle and horses.
About 1920 my father established the official "Mountain Spring
Ranch."*

*In 1929 the Big Depression arrived. Many large ranches through-
out the West, including the Mountain Spring Ranch, went
under. . . . My parents returned to their old home in Seattle. . . . In
1934 I began life again in Bend and was employed by Shevlin-
Hixon Company.*[184]

Other homesteaders, too, found employment with Shevlin or Brooks-Scanlon.

The inevitable followed, with dry years, no crops, mounting indebtedness; men and women whose lonely lives became unbearable began to
feel the pressure to abandon their land. And eventually they did, leaving
the shacks to dot the desert stretches from Crooked River to Harney
Valley, from Sisters to Grandview.

In 1920, Isabel McKinney, her husband John, and daughter Claudia, took over a cattle ranch on the High Desert on which a Bend bank had foreclosed a mortgage. Her recollections and impressions are most vivid in describing her trip to her new home:

What a strange country we drove down into. The past seemed to be unrolling before us. Silent houses, mere one room shacks, stared at us vacantly through gaps that once were windows. They stood there like monuments to an abandoned hope. This land seemed to have absorbed everything and given nothing in return. It just lies there silently waiting—waiting for water—water for irrigation which has never come.

The McKinneys stopped to give some homesteaders their mail from Millican, and observed that the

ranch had a well. The windmill was turning furiously. Water, precious stuff, was pouring into a trough. There was an enclosure made of boards and inside this was a small garden. Rhubarb and a few hardy vegetables were sticking their noses up out of the ground. Nourished by water and protected by the fence from marauding jack rabbits they had a chance for survival. A small, unpainted house was close by.

Mr. and Mrs. Percival were English. They were delighted to see us and invited us in for tea. She must have been a beautiful woman when she was younger, before the desert sun baked her skin and bleached her hair to a dry, dead, gray color. But she dressed this hair in a very high, elaborate pompadour and walked with the air of a queen. Like Queen Mary I thought. They gave me the impression of well educated, cultured people. . . . In contrast to the scanty furnishings, a piano remained aloof in one corner along with a fine collection of pipes.

Mrs. Percival placed a rough, home made chair for me to sit on with as much courtesy as would have been accorded me in a lovely dining room and she gave us tea in dainty little cups. Claudia was given a glass of cold milk. It seemed queer that they should be living in such surroundings. Tactfully, I expressed this thought and with a charming English accent she told me that her family objected to their marriage because she belonged to the nobility and Mr. Percival did not.

He left England and came over to Canada. She broke with her family and followed him. They were married in Canada. He wanted to come to the United States and finally they drifted this way to the desert and took up land. She also said she received an allowance from her family which helped them to improve their property and buy stock.

The McKinneys traveled on into the desert:

Deserted dilapidated houses still stared at us and banged their doors dismally as we drove past. We stopped at one shack out of curiosity to read a sign hung over the door, "Abandon all hope, Ye, who enter here.". . . The shack had the luxury of two rooms, but it had been ransacked. What people didn't take, the rats cut up. The walls had been papered, but only a spot here and there was left. A few rags fluttered in front of some shelves. Boxes had been broken into and were now full of debris that the rats had stored away.

I noticed an old tin trunk and walked over to it and lifted the lid. Down in the bottom were some old faded portraits and books. I picked up a book. It was a complete volume of Shakespeare's works. There were many notes written on the edges of the pages. Its owner must have been a lover of the classics. I couldn't make out the owner's name. The writing was too dim, but the date was still clear enough for me to see that it had been written May 17th, 1893.

They visited another couple:

Pete told me, between juicy expectorations of tobacco juice, that before they had their well drilled he had walked ten miles a day to get domestic water, which he carried back in two five gallon cans attached to a yoke that he made of wood to wear across his shoulders. He made shoes for the children and when the last child was born there was no doctor around; Pete took charge.

62   In 1926 the McKinneys left central Oregon for good, and Isabel reminisced in 1960: "Sometimes now, when the jets thunder over my home

in Portland and break the sound barrier with a terrible blast, my thoughts go back to the log cabin on the edge of the desert, the sage with its pungent odor, the cowboys who always managed to drop in just at meal-time, the sheriff on his galloping horse, ever searching for his man, the purple sunsets, and the lonely howl of a roving coyote."[185]

In 1930, 70 homestead shacks could be counted along the road between Bend and Burns. That year 19 were occupied.[186] In 1978 four or five were still visible from the road. (It has been popular these last years to use the weathered boards for picture frames.)

Central Oregon Leftovers

Our little Ford car used to haul lots of things to the ranch. We carried everything in it, including tiny pigs.[187]

All kinds of special vignettes of the Deschutes country remain. Such "leftovers"—often of things irretrievably past—are in good company: all central Oregonian settlers were very familiar with leftovers. (One man we knew, raised on leftovers, was never sure how he missed the meals they were left over from!) Many of these memories carry along to the present something vivid and lively. Like the times when Mrs. E. A. "Grandma" Bussett and all her neighbors hauled water from the same spring on the old Vandevert place at Powell Buttes. There was a large tank, and those seeking water could drive under the faucet and let their containers fill. In the winter the weather was cold, stormy and unpleasant. Mrs. Bussett always took a sack of chips and some wood along and built a small fire to keep warm while the tank was filling. Soon others were doing the same thing. Some of the happiest visits were around these bonfires while the water tanks and barrels were filling.[188] Or the times "when you could throw bread crumbs in the [Deschutes] water and the fish would just make the water boil."[189]

In the late 1850s Mrs. John Y. Todd was one of the first white women settlers in the region, living "on the route between the Warm Springs reservation and the Indian fishing grounds at Celilo." The Indians, she said, "would come into the house, take dishes off the shelves to look at them. . .[but] what was more unbearable [was] to have them come

63

in and turn her babies up side down to see how their clothes were made; however, after she learned to talk the Indian language she managed to get along."[190]

Mrs. Dell Allen, an 1881 pioneer, remembered that "Crooked river was as clear as a mountain stream. . . . There were lots of beaver and beaver dams. . . . And all kinds of berries grew along the banks—wild currants, wild gooseberries, service berries and choke cherries."[191] Fisher Logan, 1883 pioneer, "thought nothing of riding 25 miles on horseback to get to a dance."[192] The year before, the *Prineville News* had reported that "about one hundred thousand pounds of deer pelts" had been shipped from the town "since early last fall. It has been a wholesale slaughter merely for the hides. . . . Deer hides 20 cents a pound."[193] A little exotic flavor comes from Mrs. Elizabeth Bogue, who came from California in 1898 and homesteaded south of La Pine on the natural meadows. Later she worked at the hotel in Prineville operated by Mrs. McDowell. She cooked, while two Chinese men washed the dishes: "I learned to count to 100 in Chinese."[194] Another homesteader (Powell Butte, 1905), Mrs. S. D. Mustard, kept a .22-caliber rifle handy because the coyotes came right to her door to carry off her chickens.[195]

The pioneers also described towns: Mrs. Ethel Smith, 1903 homesteader and teacher, remembered two stores, a post office, dance hall, blacksmith shop and a school at Lamonta when she was there.[196] Describing Redmond, Mr. Jim Toney said: "It was just sagebrush and nothing for a long time, and then it grew into a farming district."[197]

Though C. W. "Bill" Jensen, on railroad survey in 1904, exclaimed: "Give the country back to the Indians,"[198] and Blanche Herschner Henderson, early teacher and 1910 homesteader in Jefferson County, recollected that "it doesn't seem like I did much of anything but chase cows all over the hills."[199] Mrs. G. E. Stadig felt that "the Lower Bridge community—that's the only place in the World!"[200]

When the rails came to Madras in 1911, Sadie Sias Huntington Cochran remembers, everyone "went down there. The train—Jim Hill's car—pulled in, and for a moment you could hear a pin drop. Then there was every kind of sound you could imagine: people crying, shouting. The thing I remember is the emotion of the crowd."[201]

And on the other side: "Klondike Kate" Van Duren, a 1914 homesteader, called the desert

my surgeon of souls—it does something if you've got a heartache or there's anything in trouble. . .go out on the desert for just an hour. You'll come back all clean and no bitterness in your heart. The whole world's lovely, everybody's good, everybody's kind. That's what I think of this part of Oregon.[202]

fig. 9

fig. 10

fig. 11

Fig. 9: Aerial view of the central Oregon Cascades, looking almost due north, Bachelor Butte (more properly, The Bachelor), the Three Sisters, Broken Top and (in the far distance) Mt. Jefferson. Fresh snow covers this scenic wonderland (©Delano photo).
Fig. 10: Todd Lake and Bachelor Butte. The surface of the lake stands at 6,100 feet and the top of Bachelor at over 9,000. A favorite location for summer activities, such as hiking, climbing and fishing, this area provides great winter sports opportunities—downhill skiing on The Bachelor, and cross-country touring on Todd and Sparks lakes, and nearby Dutchman Flat (Dept. of Trans., OHS Coll.).
Fig. 11: The shattered volcanic rim of Broken Top. This mountain lies directly east of the South Sister, and provides stark contrast to the smoother shape of that much larger mountain. Seen here from the east,

Broken Top's Crook Glacier rests in the cirque below the summit wall (Dept. of Trans., OHS Coll.).
Fig. 12: Central Oregon's loftiest peak, Mt. Jefferson stands athwart the crest of the Cascades Range. Olallie Butte (7,214 ft.). rises in the foreground, and beyond are Black Butte and the Three Sisters (©Delano photo).

fig. 12

69

fig. 13

Fig. 13: Wickiup Reservoir and Twin
lakes. Located almost due west of La
Pine, man-made Wickiup Reservoir
backs up the waters of the Deschutes
(foreground) and Davis Creek. Wickiup Butte stands to the right of the
Deschutes outflow, and the long, low
dam (left center). Gilchrist Butte is
the highest peak in this view (middle
distance) (©Delano photo).

fig. 14

Fig. 14: Lava fields at McKenzie Pass, near the western border of the Deschutes country where Lane and Deschutes counties meet. The North Sister (10,085 ft.), with Linn Glacier hanging on its near flank, and the Middle Sister (10,047 ft.), with the Collier Glacier occupying special stature as Oregon's largest, stand as silent sentinels to earlier violent eras (Dept. of Trans., OHS Coll.).

fig. 15

Fig. 15: Turning north from the previous view (fig. 14) one finds the stark aspect of the great lava flows from Belknap Crater (foreground), and the dangerous rock spire of Mt. Washington. The latter is not quite 8,000 feet high, but its volcanic plug remnant challenges the best of Oregon Cascade climbers because of the steep, loose composition (Dept. of Trans., OHS Coll.).

Fig. 16: Oregon's second crater lake is in fact two lakes. Lying within Newberry Crater (the rim of which can be seen beyond the lakes) are Paulina (left) and East lakes. This massive volcanic area provides a great outdoor classroom for geologists and volcanologists. It is also a major recreational spot. The road to the top of Paulina Peak (7,894 ft.) can be seen at the lower left, visible also is a magnificent obsidian flow—a whole field of volcanic glass (©Delano photo).

fig. 16

73

fig. 17

fig. 18

74

Fig. 17: Tiny Le Conte Crater (its crest at 6,575 ft.) lies next to the South Sister. Taken from the Rock Mesa side of the cone, this photograph delineates the petite volcano and the edge of Wickiup Plain (upper right) (OHS Coll.).

Fig. 18: Ingeniously harvesting the ice found in a lava cave near Bend, these men and their team provided a service for early settlers in the region. Formed by the cooling of molten lava, and ubiquitous throughout the landscape south of Bend, a number of these caves can be spotted on highway maps (OHS Coll.).

Fig. 19: Placing his tripod where U.S. Highway 97 now runs, Benjamin Gifford framed this shot of Lava Butte, a 5,015-foot volcano, one of many small cinder cones south of Bend (other include Klawhop, Luna and Bessie buttes). South and west beyond this peak lies today's resort, Sunriver (Gifford photo, OHS Coll.).

75

fig. 20

fig. 21

fig. 22

Fig. 20: Mt. Jefferson stands majesti-
cally in the distance in this westward
view across the uplands above both
Crooked River and the Deschutes,
taken from Smith Rock State Park
(OHS Coll.).

Fig. 21: Crooked River's multi-
layered gorge southeast of Prineville
(Dept. of Trans., OHS Coll.).
Fig. 22: Smith Rock, which stands
just northeast of Terrebonne and almost directly north of Redmond, is
one of the great climbs in Oregon and
one of central Oregon's most striking
features, where the Clarno ash and
tuff formation is cut by both aeolian
forces and riverine action of the
Crooked River at its base (OHS
Coll.).

fig. 23

78

fig. 24

Fig. 23: The northern "prow" of a formation known as The Ship guards the confluence of the Crooked and Deschutes rivers. Part of Cove Palisades State Park, this formation now floats in an arm of Lake Billy Chinook, the reservoir behind Round Butte Dam (Dept. of Trans., OHS Coll.).

Fig. 24: "The Horseshoe" of the Deschutes River's lower course marks the boundary between the counties of Sherman (far shore) and Wasco, and lies about ten miles downriver from Sherars Bridge. The track of the Oregon Trunk line (later Spokane, Portland & Seattle, and now Burlington Northern) follows the river on the Wasco County side. Rattlesnake Canyon meets the main stream at the left in this 1922 photograph (OHS Coll.).

fig. 25

fig. 26

80

fig. 27

Fig. 25: The town of Warm Springs, with the reservation's administration, school and other structures. Looking east, the scene illustrates the lovely rimrock setting where Shitike Creek (running through the trees to the right of the settlement) joins the Deschutes River flowing through the canyon beyond (Boychuck photo, OHS Coll.).

Fig. 26: Indian cemetery at Simnasho, on the Warm Springs Reservation. Flags flew over some of the graves when this photograph was taken in August, 1938. The stone monument marks the grave of Taih chief Que-pa-ma (OHS Coll.).

Fig. 27: An unknown photographer captured this long-lost scene. It is thought that the location is now part of the Warm Springs Reservation (OHS Coll.).

Fig. 28: Baby beef being driven toward Ochoco Dam (background) on the way to Prineville and the Portland market. The dirt road would eventually become U.S. Highway 26 (OHS Coll.).

81

fig. 28

82

fig. 29

fig. 30

fig. 31

Fig. 29: Range cattle beind herded along the banks of the Deschutes River, probably near Maupin (Gifford photo, OHS Coll.).

Fig. 30: Cowboys branding on the open Deschutes country range (OHS Coll.).

Fig. 31: Saddle-bronc action during the 1919 "Crooked River Roundup" at Prineville (OHS Coll.).

Fig. 32: Sheep grazing on Sparks Lake meadow, at the base of Bachelor Butte (OHS Coll.).

Fig. 33: Charles Nash, a surveyor, took a series of photographs along the Deschutes during a study for a prospective railroad, including this flock of sheep grazing on a hillside above the stream (OHS Coll.).

Fig. 34: M. R. Biggs stock ranch near Prineville (OHS Coll.).

Fig. 35: Benjamin Gifford carefully composed this bucolic scene near Madras, replete with remarkable haystacks and a graceful barn (Gifford photo, OHS Coll.).

fig. 32

fig. 33

85

fig. 34

fig. 35

86

fig. 36

fig. 37

fig. 38

Fig. 36: High Wasco County straw fields. The round stacks and the remaining stubble helped support the important cattle ranching industry of the Deschutes area (Gifford photo, OHS Coll.).

Fig. 37: Team horses being fed in the Wasco County hills, about 1907 (Gifford photo, OHS Coll.).

Fig. 38: Stopping only long enough to have their picture taken, a group of six men perch on their combine, used to cut and bag the grain in this Deschutes Valley field (OHS Coll.).

Fig. 39: Sacked wheat is towed across the fields near Madras, Jefferson County (OHS Coll.).

Fig. 40: Working horses (background, right), men and women take a dinner break in this central Oregon scene (OHS Coll.).

88

fig. 39

fig. 40

89

fig. 41

fig. 42

90

fig. 43

Fig. 41: Ashwood, Jefferson County. Named for Whitfield Wood and a nearby landmark, Ash Butte. It was August, 1898, when James Robinson halted this team and wagon-load of lumber in front of his relative John W. Robinson's store. Nine miles east of Ashwood, A. K. Chandler discovered the fossil remains of an ancient fern—*Osmundites chandleri* (OHS Coll.).

Fig. 42: Looking across Ashwood toward Ash Butte. Trout Creek flows through the town in the background. At various times Ashwood has been a mining center for silver, lead, copper, zinc and cinnabar (Gifford photo, OHS Coll.).

Fig. 43: Wasco County community of Dufur. While settlers built dwellings in the area as early as 1852, the town did not have a post office until 1878. Mt. Hood lies 25 miles to the west (Gifford photo, OHS Coll.).

fig. 44

Fig. 44: W. A. Laidlaw was one of the principals behind the ill-fated Tumalo irrigation project (1902-15). This blacksmith's shop (with a dappled Percheron looking alert) was located in the town named for Laidlaw. Problems with the Tumalo project eventually led to the hanging-in-effigy of Mr. Laidlaw. About the time the waters of the Tumalo irrigation project were seeping their way to failure, the town's name was changed to Tumalo. It is located on the highway between Sisters and Bend (OHS Coll.).

Fig. 45: Looking the part of a movie set, La Pine's main thoroughfare housed (from left) the garage, abandoned post office, J. M. Bogue's Pioneer Store ("Terms strictly cash"), a building (behind the trees) that was occupied by the new post office and the La Pine Supply Co., and (at right) the *La Pine Inter-Mountain* ("The Newspaper That's Different") (OHS Coll.).

Fig. 46: The coming of the railroad to central Oregon brought a new prosperity, and allowed the previously remote area to develop its agricultural, lumber and livestock resources. The Metolius Warehouse Co. building stood at the Spokane, Portland & Seattle siding on Agency Plains (OHS Coll.).

fig. 45

fig. 46

fig. 47

fig. 48

94

fig. 49

Fig. 47: Hotel in Madras (either in the Green or Josh Hahn establishment), probably before 1910. Wagons are parked behind the building; the six persons (one holding the triangle used to ring persons for dinner) and two dogs may have had some association with the business in room 10— "real estate." (OHS Coll.).

Fig. 48: The western section of Maupin (named for Howard Maupin, who operated a ferry across the Deschutes at this spot) sits above the canyon in central Wasco County. Only one automobile appears in this 1921 picture (OHS Coll.).

Fig. 49: Wagon pauses at the entrance of long-gone Sherars Hotel at Sherars Bridge (OHS Coll.).

fig. 50

fig. 51

Fig. 50: Missouri-born Francis "Barney" Prine (for whom Prineville was named in 1872) was one of many Oregon pioneers who came west to the Willamette Valley, only to move later over the Cascades to the Deschutes country. Prine established himself as the community's first businessman in 1868 (OHS Coll.).

Fig. 51: Prineville's "hanging bridge" across the Crooked River. W. H. Harrison was hanged on this structure by Prineville's vigilance committee in 1882 (Bowman Museum, Prineville).

fig. 52

N°5. MAIN ST. PRINEVILLE, ORE.

Fig. 52: Main Street, Prineville, looking north. A plank-covered fire well is situated in the middle of the intersection. The round-roofed Lyric Theatre (left) was owned at one time by Til Glaze (Bowman Museum, Prineville).
Fig. 53: Looking east across Crooked River, Prineville spreads toward the gap through which flows Ochoco Creek; that stream's last few yards before reaching its confluence with Crooked River can be seen at middle left (Andrews photo, OHS Coll.).

Fig. 54: Aerial view of Prineville from the southwest. Crooked River is at the bottom right, and the Ochoco works its narrow way through the city. U.S.. Highway 26 leads east from this ranching and lumbering center (©Delano photo).

fig. 53

No.7. BIRDSEYE VIEW, PRINEVILLE, ORE.

fig. 54

99

fig. 55

fig. 56

fig. 57

MAIN ST. REDMOND. CENTRAL ORE

Fig. 55: First known photograph (taken on 1 July 1905) of the Deschutes County town of Redmond— the settlement was then part of Crook County (OHS Coll.).

Fig. 56: Redmond's Main Street. Jim Toney once described it as "just sagebrush and nothing for a long time." (OHS Coll.).

Fig. 57: Redmond in the 1920s. Running along the opposite side of Main Street are the Hotel Redmond, Gregory's Variety Store, the bank, Redmond Grill, drugstore, the baths, and at the end of the street, Ehret Brothers general merchandise (OHS Coll.).

fig. 58

Fig. 58: Aerial view of Redmond, taken in 1961 (©Delano photo).
Fig. 59: Sisters, looking southwest toward the community's volcanic namesakes, the Three Sisters. Currently a popular year-round resort and vacation center, Sisters was platted in 1901 (OHS Coll.).

Fig. 60: C. J. Van Duyn's store in Tygh Valley. Among the many elegant items offered in this establishment were hats manufactured with names such as "Harvest," "Treasure," and "Maurice." Van Duyn stands at the center (OHS Coll.).

fig. 59

fig. 60

103

fig. 61

fig. 62

104

fig. 63

Fig. 61: Wapinitia in central Wasco County is situated about ten miles west of Maupin. The combination store and post office was run by H. T. Curum. The group here posed in front of it in 1889 (OHS Coll.).

Fig. 62: Identified as first in Crook County, this schoolhouse on the Ochoco was built in 1868. Men are probably Jehu and Ewen Johnson (OHS Coll.).

Fig. 63: Only a year before all their families' dreams were dashed, these children stood outside school at Camp 6 of the Tumalo project. In 1915 all hopes for the success of this much ballyhooed irrigation development were thwarted when the rising waters of the system broke from their man-made containment walls (OHS Coll.).

fig. 64

Fig. 64: Pilot Butte Canal and Central Oregon Irrigation Ditch at the diversion point on the east bank of the Deschutes, two miles south of Bend, about 1905. The irony of this photograph is that there should be such a poor garden plot associated with a project to bring water for agriculture in the Deschutes area (Gifford photo, OHS Coll.).

Fig. 65: Completed in 1910, the Bend Water, Light & Power dam supplied the wattage for the town's first electric lights on 9 November of that year. The dam and power plant (out of the picture and downriver) cost $40,000 to construct. The two-story building at the left is the second Pilot Butte Inn (OHS Coll.).

Fig. 66: Trestle built to support the galvanized-iron flume used in the Tumalo irrigation project (OHS Coll.).

fig. 65

fig. 66

fig. 67

fig. 68

108

fig. 69

Fig. 67: Part of siphon for the Tumalo project (OHS Coll.).

Fig. 68: One of the audacious schemes that made up the Tumalo irrigation plan was this siphon, constructed to carry water up and over the rolling landscape near the Deschutes (OHS Coll.).

Fig. 69: A substantial looking section of an irrigation canal near La Pine. This earth-walled construction was one of many water-carrying plans developed in the Deschutes country after the turn of the century (OHS Coll.).

fig. 70

Fig. 70: The Ochoco Dam nearing
completion. Built across a gap in
Ochoco Creek canyon east of
Prineville, the project was designed
for irrigation (OHS Coll.).
Fig. 71: Crooked River and North
Unit Main Canal north of Redmond.
The canal tunnels through a flank of
Smith Rock at the upper right
(©Delano photo).

fig. 71

111

fig. 72

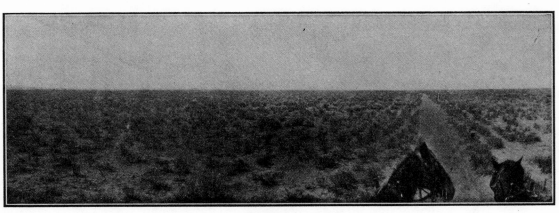

SAGE-BRUSH LAND.

fig. 73
fig. 74
fig. 75

IN THE RICHEST GRAIN, FRUIT AND STOCK SECTION IN THE WORLD

FREE LANDS IN OREGON

Thousands *of* Acres *in* Crook County *at* Actual Cost *of* Irrigation — Deed Direct *from* THE STATE *of* OREGON

BE AMONG THE FIRST *to* MAKE A SELECTION

This Book Gives Particulars

WRITE TODAY

DESCHUTES IRRIGATION & POWER Co.
610 - 11 - 12 McKAY BUILDING
PORTLAND, OREGON

— OR —

The Deschutes Improvement Company
BEND, CROOK COUNTY, OREGON

Union Printing Co., Portland, Oregon.

A Land Flowing With Milk and Honey

IRRIGATION is as old as the eternal hills. The foundation of a civilization ages old in the Nile regions of Africa, was the control and artificial use of water in sterile regions. From that day to this agriculture by irrigation has never ceased to be the surest and safest and always, far and away, the most profitable.

The centuries old wisdom of the Orient is now being applied to the fast developing Occident. Oregon's sage and juniper covered plains are already being rapidly transformed into blooming gardens and fragrant meadows of alfalfa, timothy and clover. Orchards of winter apples, peaches, pears and apricots; vineyards of American and semi-tropical grapes and broad pastures for cattle and all kinds of live stock will replace the arid waste, until lately inhabitated only by jack rabbits.

Free Irrigable Lands

Irrigation and free land in the State of Oregon form the magic combination that is now peopling Crook County and transforming it into a veritable bower of pleasant fields and thriving, happy homes for people who come here from less favored regions. That day and generation in which the humble wage-worker or the farmer of moderate circumstances could obtain cheap homes in the West is now rapidly waning. Little land remains to be taken in the West under the homestead laws that can easily or cheaply be reduced to cultivation. Practically all the choice irrigable land in the North Pacific Coast states has been withdrawn from entry under the Desert Land Act by the United States Government. Within a few years that which yet remains to be taken under the provisions of the Carey Act and watered by contracting irrigation companies will be gone.

1

SPECIAL NOTICE

We desire to call special attention to the fact that any citizen of the United States (male twenty-one years of age or female eighteen years of age), may apply for and secure from 40 to 160 acres of these lands.

The right to take land under the Carey Act, by virtue of which The Deschutes Irrigation and Power Company is irrigating these lands and has secured a lien thereon, does not interfere with your other Government rights, such as the Homestead, Desert, Timber or Stone right.

Both husband and wife may take these lands. Consequently it is possible for a family to secure a large tract of land and pay less for it than they would for a small and inferior farm in a thickly settled community. There is no reason why this land should not show a very large increase in value during the next few years, as lands of a similar character but in less favored parts of the Pacific Northwest are now selling for $100 per acre and more.

Keep in mind the fact that this is not a rough wilderness, but an exceedingly fertile tract of land capable of high cultivation. The profits from it are limited only by the purchaser's energy.

The following is an extract from a letter written by R. W. Thatcher, Chemist of the Washington Agricultural College at Pullman, Washington:

REPORT ON RESULTS OF ANALYSIS: Shows the soil to be richer in potash, lime and humus than the Yakima Valley soil. The fertility extends to a good depth, the sub-soil at three feet being almost as rich as the surface soil. This soil is similar to but better than Yakima Valley soil.

Inasmuch as the Yakima Valley has long been considered the richest valley in the Pacific Northwest, we consider this letter of great importance, and coming as it does from a rival state, it is of more than usual significance.

The land is deeded to the applicant by the State Land Board at the cost of reclamation, which amounts to from $2.50 to $14.75 per acre.

For further particulars address:

The Deschutes Irrigation & Power Co.
610-12 McKay Bldg., Portland, Or., or
The Deschutes Improvement Co.
Bend, Crook County, Oregon.

Fig. 72-78: After construction of railroads in the Deschutes region, and with the promise of irrigation development, many persons were lured to central Oregon by literature prepared for that purpose. "Promoted by local developers and the railroads, companies printed prospectuses of fair lands stretching golden fields of grain under clear, blue skies, with glimpses of date palms in the distance, and with enthralling accounts of record crops." The four photographs and three printed pages shown here are from several of these promotional pieces (OHS Coll.).

fig. 76

INTENSIVE FARMING.

fig. 77

ALFALFA-FED HOGS.

fig. 78

113

CROOK COUNTY, OREGON, IS PRIMARILY A STOCK COUNTRY.

fig. 79

Fig. 79: On the flat lands east of the Deschutes near Culver, Jefferson County, this farmer checks his dry land potatoes. Such endeavors were vulnerable to slight changes in the weather, and most failed when conditions did not meet the hyperbole of the land promoters (OHS Coll.).

Fig. 80: Four men affectedly sample somewhat undernourished watermelons on the W. D. Moore ranch on Agency Plains, near Madras. Both this photograph and the one opposite were taken by the local railroad company, in an effort to gather evidence about the hoped-for railroad-induced prosperity of the Deschutes country (OHS Coll.).

Fig. 81: The late 1940s' Deschutes Irrigation Project was promoted to "make a garden spot out of . . . 50,000 acres, many of which were all but abandoned before irrigation was brought into the picture" (OHS Coll.).

fig. 80

fig. 81

115

fig. 82

Fig. 82: An early group of buildings in the rimrock country near Prineville (Gifford photo, OHS Coll.).

Fig. 83: Well-turned-out woman draws water from a central Oregon well, about 1910. The implication is more that this is a vacation home than a working homestead (OHS Coll.).

fig. 83

117

fig. 84

118

Fig. 84: The four major regions of the High & Mighty country of the Deschutes watershed, as delineated in the following chapter. CS: the Cascade Slope; DP: the Deschutes Plateau; BM: Blue Mountains; HLP: High Lava Plains (OHS Coll.).

3

DESCHUTES COUNTRY GEOGRAPHY

From snow-covered South Sister a small stream courses down the slope on its long, tortuous, and rapid journey to the Columbia River. This little stream, together with a hundred similar streams on the east side of the Cascade Range and on the slopes of the Ochoco Range, are the sources of the Deschutes (Falls) River of central Oregon, named, strangely, not for its own numerous and spectacular falls, but for Celilo Falls of the Columbia River near the mouth of the Deschutes.[1] (Celilo Falls is now covered by the waters of Celilo Reservoir, backed up by The Dalles Dam.) In many ways the Deschutes is a unique river;[2] it is the only Oregon river with its source in lofty, snowy mountains which flows, for most of its length, through semiarid country. The main stem, unlike most rivers, has few floodplains and almost no floods.[3] The Deschutes is even-flowing in spite of the long dry season, thanks to the heavy slow-melting snow pack in the Cascades and to the porosity of the rocks in its watershed. Water from melting snow and rain soaks readily into the porous rock which includes volcanic ash, pumice, cinders, various flow lavas, and sediments. If the river rises a bit, water soaks *from* the river into the porous banks; if the river falls a trifle, water seeps from the banks *into* the river. If a cubic foot of water could be traced from the melting snows to the Columbia, much of its journey would be found

Samuel N. Dicken

underground, sometimes sinking, sometimes reappearing in springs. Springs are numerous throughout the watershed; in fact the Deschutes might just as well be called the "River of Springs." Or, on the basis of its even flow and few floods, it could be called the "Dependable River."

The watershed of the Deschutes River (see map on p. 118), otherwise known as the Deschutes country, covers an area of 10,300 square miles. Of Oregon's interior rivers only the Willamette has a slightly larger watershed. Included are the major parts of five Oregon counties: Wasco, Sherman, Jefferson, Crook, and Deschutes; also lesser parts of six other counties: Hood River, Klamath, Lake, Harney, Grant, and Wheeler. Four of Oregon's nine geographic regions are represented.[4] The east slope of the Cascade Mountains covers the western parts of Wasco, Jefferson, and Deschutes counties. The northwestern part of the High Lava Plains covers parts of Deschutes and Crook counties. The Blue Mountain region, represented by the Ochoco and Maury ranges, covers most of Crook County. And the Deschutes-Umatilla Plateau, sometimes called the Columbia Plateau, includes central Jefferson County, the eastern part of Wasco County, and all of Sherman County. Each of these regions has distinctive landforms, surface rock, vegetation, and drainage patterns; also a variety of land use, productive activity, population distribution, and land ownership. But in all of the regions, igneous activity has played a major role. In some areas the surface is much like it was when the lavas cooled; in others, streams have carved canyons, some shallow, some deep, in the surface.

The Cascade East Slope extends from the Columbia River to northwestern Klamath County and drains mostly to the Deschutes River; a small part, in the north, drains directly to the Columbia. The western parts of Wasco, Jefferson, and Deschutes counties are included. The outstanding features are the crestline peaks, the drainage from which the Deschutes shares with the Willamette River. From north to south, Mt. Hood, Olallie Butte, Mt. Jefferson, Three-Fingered Jack, Mt. Washington, the Three Sisters, and many lesser crestline peaks and buttes contribute water from rains and melting snows to the Deschutes. Additional peaks, such as Black Butte at the headwaters of the Metolius River, are located on the slope below the crest. Some of the peaks are young and little dissected, forming almost perfect cones, such as South Sister and Black Butte; others, like Mt. Hood and Mt. Jefferson, have been glaciated and carved by stream erosion and are, therefore, more rugged.

The general slope from the crest of the Cascades to the High Lava Plains and the Deschutes Plateau is moderate from Mt. Hood, elevation 11,237 (only a small part of Mt. Hood drains to the Deschutes), to about 4,000 feet in a distance of about 20 miles. This is the maximum slope. The average slope is from the crestline at about 5,000 feet to 4,000 feet in a distance of 20 miles. Here also the amount of dissection varies: on the recent lava flows, very little; on the older ones the slope is cut by narrow canyons; some of the ridges between are flat-topped, others narrow and sharp. Most of the Cascade slope is forested, although the vegetation has been greatly modified by logging and forest fires.

The High Lava Plains Region in eastern Deschutes, western Crook, and northern Klamath counties contrasts sharply with the Cascade Slope. It is part of a large region which extends eastward to the Harney Lake area. The surface is made up of young lava flows, covered in places by pumice, ash, and alluvium. It is little dissected, except in the northwestern part where the Deschutes and Crooked rivers have cut canyons. The Deschutes and the Little Deschutes are the only major streams and for the most part they meander through the region at low grade. Much of the region has no exterior drainage. Water from the light rains and melting snows sinks into the porous surface or drains to shallow closed basins, where it evaporates. Although much of the surface is nearly level, some areas have numerous cinder cones and there is one large shield volcano, Paulina Peak, in southern Deschutes County, elevation 7,985 feet, rising nearly 3,000 feet above the plain. The crest of the mountain is a large caldera containing two lakes, East and Paulina. Paulina Peak covers a circular area about 25 miles in diameter, all of which is forested.

Crook County drains to the Deschutes River via the Crooked River. Most of the county is in the western part of the Blue Mountains, a large region which extends from the Deschutes country eastward to the Snake River Canyon. The chief divisions in Crook County are the Ochoco Mountains and the Maury Mountains. Unlike the two areas described above, this region is much older and has been uplifted, folded, faulted, and

121

eroded. In many places sedimentary rocks are interbedded with lava flows. The result is a rugged landscape of ridges, flat-topped uplands, and narrow valleys. Elevations range from about 2,900 feet near Prineville to 6,793 feet on Round Mountain in the eastern part of Crook County. Most of the area above 4,000 feet is forested, some of it cut and burned over. Some of the flat summit areas are treeless and are called prairies. The Crooked River and its tributaries form a tree-like pattern; the main stem drains the southern and eastern part of the county; Mill, McKay, and Ochoco creeks drain most of the northern portion of Crook County.

The Deschutes Plateau is part of a large region which extends from the Cascades to and slightly beyond the Umatilla River. The larger region is called the Deschutes-Umatilla Plateau. It is also sometimes called the Columbia Basin because of its proximity to the Columbia River. In the Deschutes drainage is the eastern part of Wasco County, the western part of Sherman County, and the central part of Jefferson County. This is a classic case of a plateau with nearly horizontal lava flows dissected by the lower Deschutes River and its tributaries which have cut deep, steep-walled canyons in the uplands to a depth of up to 2,000 feet. Some of the uplands between the canyons, called variously "flats," "benches," or "plains," are nearly level; others have been slightly dissected to form a low hilly or rolling surface, but most of the uplands are not too steep to be cultivated. Agency Plains, for example, in the vicinity of Madras is nearly level; Metolius Bench in Jefferson County and Juniper Flat in Wasco County have been slightly dissected to form a somewhat hilly surface. In some places gentle folding of the lava beds has produced ridges such as Tygh Ridge and Summit Ridge in Wasco County and a few isolated buttes rise above the general level.

From the Air

The brief regional descriptions above give a general idea of the variety and contrasts in the Deschutes country. Flying over the area and the study of airphotos provide more specific descriptions and help to place the various elements, both physical and cultural, in a proper perspective. Familiarity with the country on the ground and the study of maps contribute to the understanding of many features, as seen from the air. Our flight takes off from the Willamette Valley and leads over the rugged western Cascades and we are soon over the south slope of South Sister in the Deschutes National Forest where the Deschutes River begins. It is early summer and the snow which usually covers everything in winter has melted up to the 7,000-foot level, above which the snow remains in patches and streaks.

The plane circles at 12,000 feet and provides a 360-degree panorama of striking variety. To the west is the plateau-like surface of the High Cascades, with scattered conical peaks and buttes rising above the general level. To the north are the Three Sisters, each with its own individuality. South Sister is the smoothest with the fewest wrinkles and grooves; the other two are somewhat older, showing some of the wear and tear of time and glaciation. Beyond are Mt. Washington and Mt. Jefferson and, in the distance, more than 100 miles away, the small white dot is Mt. Hood. Turning to the east the wooded Cascade Slope is below us, sloping eastward to the High Lava Plains. The city of Bend is 25 miles away and 50 miles to the northeast is Prineville, nestling at the edge of the Blue Mountains which appear at this distance as hills rather than mountains. To the south are the High Lava Plains, broken by the darkly wooded shield volcano, Paulina Peak, but reaching on to blend with the Basin-Range Region of southern Klamath County. On the crest of the Cascades to the south are Diamond Peak, Mt. Thielsen, and Mt. McLoughlin. Mt. Scott is visible, as is the rim of Crater Lake, but we are not high enough to see the lake.

We now descend to 2,000 feet above the ground, fly southward over Moraine Lake on the slope of the South Sister and note that very few streams are visible, in spite of the melting snows above. Most of the drainage is underground and although this area *must* drain into the Deschutes River, no continuous stream is visible until we reach Little Lava Lake. Several small lakes have been dammed by lava flows and, in most cases, the dark brown and black unweathered lava is visible. We are now over Century Drive highway and the slender ribbon of the river flows southward in its narrow strip of prairie. At Crane Prairie Reservoir the stream gathers strength from several tributaries: Cultus River springs full blown

123

from the base of Bench Mark Butte (which is really a mesa); Cultus Creek drain Cultus Lake; several other creeks enter the reservoir from the Cascade crest to the west. With these additions, the Deschutes leaves Crane Prairie Reservoir and flows into Wickiup Reservoir as a full-fledged river. Wickiup receives the drainage from Odell and Davis lakes, adding to the volume. The low dam on the east side of Wickiup is more than a mile long and from the spillway the Deschutes takes off in a northeasterly direction to be joined by the Little Deschutes River. Part of its course leads through small prairies, other parts follow narrow openings in the forest.

We leave the main stem of the Deschutes River, temporarily, and fly south to the source of the Little Deschutes River on the Cascade Slope in Klamath County. On the way are several buttes, some of them, like Odell Butte, almost perfect volcanic cones. Some have rugged lava flows in the vicinity obviously younger than the cones. The Little Deschutes rises on the crest of the Cascades between Cappy and Miller mountains. Its first course is to the east but in a few miles the direction becomes northerly. It crosses State Highway 58 and after some wandering parallels U.S. Highway 97. It picks up Crescent Creek from Crescent Lake and enters the High Lava Plains where the gradient is low, producing many meanders. A few ranches are located near the river. We fly over the small towns of Crescent and Gilchrist, located on small prairies. Near the junction of State Highway 31 with U.S. Highway 97, the town of La Pine lies at the center of a larger prairie. Below this point the river meanders through the narrow prairie like a miniature Mississippi; some loops are cut off forming nearly circular ponds or "oxbows." The light green grass of the prairie contrasts with the dark green of the pine forest. A detour to the east gives us a good view of Paulina Peak and Newberry Crater. Paulina Creek, with its own little band of prairie, drains to the Little Deschutes.

So far our flight has revealed comparatively few evidences of man's activities, excepting a few roads, railroads, dams, and scattered ranches. North of La Pine the works of man, the cultural landscape, are very apparent. Between La Pine and Bend there are at least 50 subdivisions; hundreds of lots are laid out in rectangular patterns with streets gouged out in the woodland. Only a few are occupied by houses.

A little farther to the north the two Deschutes rivers are joined, forming a broad, nearly level plain. This level area is probably the result of damming of the Deschutes River by a lava flow, forming a lake into which sediments were deposited. Later, as the river eroded its bed, the lake was drained, leaving this broad plain. Below the confluence of the two rivers is the extensive recreation community of Sunriver with an area of 5,500 acres, which includes a golf course, swimming pool, lodge, tennis courts, marina, artificial lakes, clusters of condominiums, and individual houses. Sunriver has about 500 permanent residents and many thousands of visitors, summer and winter.

Below Sunriver the Deschutes changes its character and begins its steep drop to Bend—nearly 600 feet in 10 miles—in a series of falls of which Benham, Dillon, and Lava Island are the most spectacular. All the falls are apparently the result of lava flows. We fly over the falls and circle over Bend, the largest city in the Deschutes country, in both population and area. The city is located where the High Lava Plains meets the Cascade Slope. Here for a short distance the Deschutes again has a low gradient and small dams create quiet pools. The river is easily bridged and the city, originally located on the east bank, has expanded to the west side and even onto the foothills. The business district and the older residences are laid out along the river which, for a short distance, flows to the northeast. The newer parts of the city are laid out in the usual east-west, north-south grid. The city evidently grew first to the east toward Pilot Butte, a cinder cone rising 500 feet above the city. Recently suburbs have grown both to the north and south including clusters of movable homes and trailer courts. The main industrial area is on the south; a large lumber mill is in operation on the right bank of the Deschutes; one formerly on the left bank has been dismantled, as some of the timber in the hinterland has become exhausted. Obviously Bend is a commercial and recreational center rather than an industrial town.

Heavily traveled U.S. Highway 97 runs through the eastern part of the city and is joined by U.S. Highway 20. The Burlington-Northern Railroad follows a parallel route. A number of secondary paved roads radiate from the city to the east, one of which goes to the airport. Four irrigation canals take water from the Deschutes River in the vicinity. The Arnold and Central canals tap the river above the city and lead to the east toward Powell Buttes. The North Unit Irrigation Canal removes water at a small diversion dam on the north edge of the city and leads for more than 40 airline miles to the Agency Plains north of Madras.

Leaving the Deschutes we fly northeastward over the High Lava Plains toward the towns of Powell Butte and Prineville. Most of the plain here is too rough and rocky for irrigation and cultivation. The irrigation ditches run many miles to reach the smooth gentle slopes of the alluvial fans at the foot of Powell Buttes. Hay fields and irrigated pastures cover most of the slopes. Farther north is Prineville on the irrigated floodplain of the Crooked River. The main stem has a reservoir and so does one of the tributaries, Ochoco Creek. From Prineville the canyon of Crooked River runs west and then north to join the Deschutes. The floor of the canyon is about one mile wide and is irrigated. A secondary road and the City of Prineville Railroad follow the floor of the canyon before climbing to the upland north of Redmond.

We return to the Deschutes below Bend, where, robbed of most of its water by the large irrigation ditches, it is now but a trickle as it flows in a shallow canyon. At Cline Falls a modern bridge with easy approaches marks the site of the Willamette Valley and Cascade Mountain Road crossing in pioneer days. It is now used by State Highway 126. The second city of Deschutes County, Redmond, is six miles to the east on an open plain. It appears to have little direct relation to the river, although its location is undoubtedly related to the river crossing. A large irrigation ditch, derived from the Deschutes near Bend, serves the area. From this point the Deschutes Canyon becomes deeper and deeper, making it impractical to divert or pump water to the adjacent uplands. Only one incorporated town, Maupin, is located on the Deschutes below Bend.

We now fly into Jefferson County and almost at the same time reach the Deschutes Plateau, leaving the High Lava Plain behind. The outstanding difference is in the canyons of the Deschutes and its tributaries. We approach Billy Chinook Reservoir, with its three arms, one in the lower

Crooked River, one in the Deschutes, and one in the lower Metolius. All three rivers are deeply intrenched with steep cliffs of basalt rising from the water's edge. Here and there are narrow rock benches at intermediate elevations. One of these on the Crooked River has a guest ranch. The bottoms of the canyons have an elevation of 1,600 feet (from an old map), the lake level averages 1,965 feet, and the upland level in the vicinity is about 2,500 feet. Between the Deschutes and the Crooked rivers is a narrow isolated part of the plateau, called the "peninsula." On both sides of the reservoir are flats or benches which are parts of the Deschutes Plateau. On the west, south of the Metolius, is a flat called the "Lower Desert," although it has some scattered trees. To the north of the Metolius River is Metolius Bench, a slightly dissected part of the plateau. To the east of the reservoir is Culver Bench and farther north the largest and flattest "flat" of them all, the Agency Plains, which includes the town of Madras.

The Culver area and the Agency Plains are irrigated with water from the North Unit Irrigation Canal, brought all the way from Bend. Dark green fields of peppermint and alfalfa alternate with the straw-colored winter wheat, ready for the harvest. The map shows a gentle, uniform slope, ideal for gravity irrigation. Madras is at the upper end of Willow Creek Canyon on the edge of the Agency Plains. It is at the junction of U.S. highways 26 and 97 and also on the railroad. A huge grain elevator testifies to the importance of wheat in this area, just as the extent of the peppermint fields testifies to great changes in the agriculture since the North Unit canal reached the Agency Plains.

A few miles north of Billy Chinook Reservoir, Pelton Dam backs up Lake Simtustus. Here the sides of the canyon are not so steep and rock benches at intermediate elevations are used for roads. Tributary canyons include Campbell Canyon which is followed by U.S. Highway 26 on its way to the crossing of the Deschutes and Dry Canyon. On the west is the canyon of Shitike Creek, with the town of Warm Springs on the Indian reservation, where the most conspicuous feature is a large lumber mill with its piles of lumber and its "cold deck." The lower elevations of the reservation near the Deschutes have only a few scattered trees, but the upper slopes near the Cascade crest are forested.

127

The Deschutes now turns to the northeast and flows through a steep-walled canyon. On our right is the north end of the Agency Plains with wheat farms marked out in mile-square sections. The green spring wheat and the tan winter wheat contrast with the bare fallow fields. Seven miles north of the town of Warm Springs, Trout Creek flows into the Deschutes from the east. The lower course is used by the Burlington-Northern Railroad as it descends from the Agency Plains at 2,300 feet, to the banks of the Deschutes at 1,300 feet. The railroad continues at the bottom of the canyon all the way to the Columbia River, first on the east side, then on the west. The Deschutes River now turns north and enters Wasco County in a broader canyon, about two miles from rim to rim. Webster Flat is on the west at 2,300 feet and its unnamed counterpart on the east side is at the same elevation. Two miles north of Warm Springs Creek is Warm Springs River coming from the west and seven miles upstream to the west is Kah-Nee-Ta, the resort at the hot springs. Now the canyon opens up more and it is difficult to identify the rims. High on the west are the wooded Mutton Mountains, rising to over 4,000 feet, about 3,000 feet above the Deschutes River. In this vicinity the railroad crosses to the west side of the river. The river now flows through rugged canyon country about 10 miles to Maupin. A few miles to the east on the upland is the nearly abandoned town of Shaniko, once the terminus of a branch-line railroad, now only a museum.

At Maupin U.S. Highway 197, which branches from U.S. Highway 97 on the north end of the Agency Plains, crosses the Deschutes, with switchbacks on both sides of the river. Maupin is on a narrow bench about 200 feet above the river on the west side and a lumber mill is perched on a higher bench. The railroad is below the town. On the east side a narrow road leads down the canyon for many miles on the grade of an abandoned railroad. A few ranches are located along this access road. The upland here, represented by Juniper Flat, is about 1,600 feet above sea level. We fly north to Tygh Valley which, together with the lower part of White River, provides an easy approach to the Deschutes Canyon. One of the earliest crossings was by Peter Skene Ogden with a party of fur traders in 1826. Later it was on a supply route—a toll road—leading to the mines in eastern Oregon. A bridge and a hotel were built at the crossing, Sherars Bridge. The route is now followed by State Highway 216. The floor of the canyon here includes a rock bench about 20 feet above the the river. This restricts the channel to about 40 feet; the modern bridge is only 85 feet long, much shorter than bridges farther upriver. House trailers of sports fishermen are located along the old railroad grade; Indians are dipnetting for salmon. To the north of the bridge the canyon walls close in with steep cliffs of black lava.

On the uplands north of Tygh Valley, Tygh Ridge rises above the general level, probably the result of warping of the underlying lava beds. The northern continuation is Summit Ridge. From the west rim of the Deschutes Canyon, the drainage is to the west *away* from the canyon, in a series of "hollows" or shallow canyons; the east side of the canyon here is in Sherman County.

Farther north the canyon has steep sides but not quite so high. On the upland there are no large flats comparable to the Agency Plains. The surface is slightly dissected and varies from gently rolling to hilly. Much of the land is used for wheat farming, but the irregular shape of the wheat fields in contrast with the usual squares and rectangles, indicates that some slopes are too steep for cultivation. Both spring and winter wheat are growing, interspersed with grazing land. The upland surface in Sherman County appears to be somewhat smoother than that of Wasco County. This is reflected in the greater production of wheat in Sherman County, although Wasco County is much larger in area. A few small towns are scattered on the upland. Grass Valley and Moro in Sherman County and Dufur in Wasco County are still functioning and growing slowly. A few places have been abandoned, DeMoss Springs in Sherman County and Ortley in Wasco County. As the Columbia River is approached, the upland elevation declines to about 1,000 feet above the Deschutes River.

Where the Deschutes flows into the Columbia River, The Dalles Dam backs up Celilo Lake, a part of which reaches into the lower Deschutes Canyon. To the left, the Deschutes branch of the Burlington-Northern Railroad is beginning its winding course up the canyon. Almost at once a tunnel is necessary to pass through a steep cliff. Celilo Lake covers some of the small floodplains along the Columbia and there is little room for railroads, highways, or towns. Nevertheless, the Union Pacific Railroad and U.S. Highway I-84 follow the south bank of the Columbia, their routes notched into the cliffs.

The Dalles, county seat of Wasco County, is not in the drainage area of the Deschutes River, but, because it serves all of Wasco and Sherman counties, it needs to be considered in any discussion of the Deschutes country. The city occupies a low crescent-shaped band on the Columbia River with a circle of cliffs behind it. This is one of the few low-lying areas of nearly level land along the Columbia on the Oregon side for many miles. Across the river on the Washington side is also some low, fairly level land which is used, among other things, for The Dalles airport. The Dalles, the first town to be established in the Deschutes country, became an important break-in-bulk point in pioneer days. Here many of the immigrants abandoned their wagons and finished their journey by river, for many a hazardous choice. Today, thanks to The Dalles Dam, with cheap power and the growth of barge traffic on the Columbia, The Dalles has developed several industries. The dam is the most conspicuous feature, and strung out along the river to the west are a wood preservation plant, a cherry processing plant, a flour mill and elevator, a fruit packing plant, and an aluminum plant. The business district and the industrial area occupy the lowest bench near the river; a residential area is on a higher rock bench; and, still higher, are orchards of cherries, apples, peaches, pears, apricots, and prunes.

Other Geographic Features

The foregoing description of Deschutes country geography, as seen from the air and supplemented by study of airphotos and maps, has revealed the variety of geographic features in the region, but some aspects cannot be fully evaluated from the air. Studies on the ground and from the written record are necessary. Additional geographic topics include climate, natural vegetation, population, land ownership, and the nature of the productive economy.

Climate

The Deschutes country is in the rain shadow of the Cascade Range, which shields it partially from the rain-bearing winds from the Pacific Ocean. The distance from the ocean makes for greater extremes in temperature; the summers tend to be warmer and the winters colder. The most important variable factor within the region is altitude; for each 1,000 feet of elevation, on the average temperature declines three degrees Fahrenheit. Since the average elevation of the region is nearly 4,000 feet, temperatures tend to be lower both in summer and winter than in the Willamette Valley.

The temperature ranges from summer to winter are moderate but noticeably greater than in western Oregon. Almost all areas, except those along the Columbia River, average below freezing in January and the average for July, the warmest month, is generally below 70°F., again excepting the area near the Columbia. The absolute range, the difference between the very highest and the very lowest, is large. Prineville, for example, has experienced −35°F. and 119°F. Such occurrences are rare, however.

The daily range, for the region, is often high. It is not very unusual to have the highest temperature reach 100°F. at The Dalles in the afternoon and to fall to 25°F. at Redmond the following night. The daily temperature range varies with the season and with the altitude. At Bend, a representative station, the average daily range in January is from 18° to 39°F.; in April from 31° to 60°F.; in July from 46° to 85°F.; and in October from 36° to 62°F. As a result of the high temperatures in summer and limited cloud cover, the evaporation rate is high. As measured from an open water surface, evaporation exceeds precipitation for most of the region.[5] But this does not mean that the region is a desert. Most of it is semiarid; only a few small areas in the canyons and in other sheltered places are properly designated as deserts by climatologists. The low winter temperatures compensate, in part, for the low precipitation. The following table shows the elevation in feet, the January average temperature, the July average temperature, annual precipitation, summer precipitation (total for

June, July, and August), and the average snowfall.[6] Crater Lake and Chemult are slightly beyond the limits of the Deschutes country but together with the other stations listed give a good idea of the range of climatic elements in the region. Data for Portland are given for comparison.

Station	Elevation (ft.)	Jan. Av. (°F.)	July Av. (°F.)	Ann. R. F. (in.)	Summer R. F. (in.)	Av. Snow (in.)
The Dalles	102	34	73	14	1.0	23
Bend	3,539	30	63	12	2.2	34
Prineville	2,868	31	65	9	1.6	14
Chemult	4,752	24	59	26	2.5	16
Crater Lake	6,475	24	56	68	4.0	540
Portland	30	40	68	42	2.8	6

Natural Vegetation

The vegetation of the Deschutes country reflects both the variations in climate and the porosity of the surface materials, as well as the changes made by man.[7] The higher elevations, generally above 7,000 feet, are treeless. Here various shrubs, grasses, and flowers grow in the short season. The absence of trees is related more to the lack of sufficient warmth in summer than to the cold of winter. The tree zone extends from 7,000 feet down to about 4,000 feet; it is wide in the south in southern Deschutes and northwestern Klamath counties and narrow in the north, in Wasco County. The dominant tree is ponderosa pine which grows in open stands with an understory of grasses and shrubs under natural conditions. This is also the characteristic tree on the upper slopes of the Ochoco Mountains in Crook County. In the more porous areas, including pumice, lodgepole pine grows in nearly pure stands, usually stunted by the dryness of the situation, as well as by the shortness of the growing season. Near the upper limit of trees is a belt of grand fir. At the lower, *dry* timberline, western juniper appears, usually widely spaced, with sagebrush and grasses in between. Juniper "forests" are well developed in eastern Deschutes and western Crook counties. In the driest regions juniper does not grow, only sagebrush and various grasses occur.

Many changes have been made in the natural vegetation since the coming of man. The Indians burned the forest and grassy areas as a part of their hunting and food gathering practices, as noted by the fur traders and early travelers. But with white settlement changes were accelerated. Logging and forest fires set by man have removed much of the forest. Cultivation has wiped out the native grasses in many areas and new varieties of plants have been unwittingly introduced. Overgrazing in the original bunchgrass areas allowed sagebrush to spread.

Population

In the Deschutes country 3.8 percent of Oregon's people, approximately 91,600 (1977), live on 11 percent of the land. In 1977 the population density was 7.6 persons per square mile, compared to 24 per square mile for the state.[8] The distribution is uneven: most of the people live in the middle portions of Deschutes and Jefferson counties and in western Crook County. The population is clustered in and near Bend, Redmond, Prineville, Madras, and The Dalles.

The population is quite homogeneous: the only sizable ethnic minority is represented by the Indians on the Warm Springs Reservation in Jefferson and Wasco counties. Blacks, Chinese, Japanese, and Mexicans are present in very small numbers. There are slight but significant differences in the age composition of the population from county to county. In the state of Oregon as a whole, in 1970, 17.5 percent of the population was in the age group 15-24 years, the childbearing age for females. In the Deschutes country the average was 14.7 percent with Jefferson County having the highest, 15.3 percent, and Sherman County the lowest, 13.6 percent. The disparity in this group between the Deschutes country and the state is probably to be explained by the migration out from these counties in the period before 1970. The percentage of people over the age of 65 was slightly below that of the state as a whole, 9.9 percent as compared to 10.8 percent.

The political orientation of the Deschutes country population tends to be slightly conservative, although less so than eastern Oregon as a whole. In recent years voter registration has favored the Democrats, which is true for all counties of the state.[9] But the Deschutes country Republicans often cast more votes. In the presidential election of 1976, two counties, Jefferson and Sherman, voted for Ford and three counties, Wasco, Crook, and Deschutes, voted for Carter. At the same election, in a vote to repeal the Land Conservation Development Commission legislation, the Deschutes country voted "no," that is, to keep the legislation, while eight other counties east of the Cascades voted "yes."

The growth of population in the Deschutes country is uneven, changeable, and probably unpredictable. It was formerly accepted that western Oregon was growing rapidly and that eastern Oregon was static with some counties losing population by out-migration. In general this was true until recently—until 1970 in fact. In the period 1960 to 1970 eastern Oregon gained only 2.7 percent which, assuming that the natural increase was about a single percent per year, indicated a substantial out-migration. In the same period, the state as a whole gained 18.2 percent and western Oregon gained 21.0 percent. Times have changed; in the period 1970 to 1977, western Oregon gained 14.3 percent and eastern Oregon gained 16.3 percent. A key factor in this flipflop of population growth is the greatly increased migration to Oregon from California and Washington, and, in smaller numbers, from all the other 47 states. One-third of Oregon's growth is from natural increase and two-thirds from migration.

In the Deschutes country the imbalance between natural increase and migration is most marked. In Deschutes County, in the period 1970 to 1977, 10.9 percent of the growth was from natural increase, and 89.1 percent from migration. Deschutes County had the highest percentage gain in the state, also the highest migration rate. Jefferson County's growth was 48.2 percent from natural increase and 51.8 percent from migration. In Crook County the figures were 20.3 percent and 79.7 percent; in Sherman, 73.9 percent and 36.1 percent. In Wasco County the natural increase in numbers was 571 and the net migration was minus 304. The increase for this eight-year period was 267 persons.

Most of the growth of population in the Deschutes country in the period 1970 to 1977 has occurred in or near the towns and cities; outside the city limits much of this population is listed as rural non-farm. Suburban area growth is apparent as one flies over the region. During this period in Deschutes County, Bend grew 20 percent, Redmond, 68 percent, and Sisters, 50 percent. (Sisters had lost population in the 1960s.) In Jefferson County, Madras grew 24 percent, Culver, 12 percent, and Metolius, 67 percent. In Crook County, Prineville grew 42 percent and, in Wasco County, The Dalles grew 7.0 percent, Dufur, 18 percent, Maupin, 44 percent, and Mosier, 24 percent. It is apparent that in the slow-growth counties, Wasco and Sherman, most of the growth is in the towns and that the rural areas are probably still losing population. In the counties with more rapid growth, Deschutes, Crook, and Jefferson, most of the growth is in and near the cities and, although a part of it is technically rural, it is, in fact, urban in character. At any rate, it is distinctly non-farm.

Land Ownership

In the Deschutes country, as a whole, less than half of the land is privately owned, but the percentage varies widely from county to county, from 21 percent in Deschutes County to 91 percent in Sherman County. The U.S. Forest Service (USFS) controls very large areas in the Mt. Hood, Deschutes, and Ochoco national forests. The Bureau of Land Management (BLM) holds large areas in eastern Deschutes County and in western and southern Crook County. The Bureau of Indian Affairs (BIA) owns the Warm Springs Indian Reservation in Jefferson and Wasco counties, although the management is in the hands of the tribal council. The state of Oregon owns small areas on the Crooked River and the lower Deschutes River (Fish and Wildlife Service) and there are a few county-owned parks. Privately owned land is largely in the areas of denser population, in and near the towns and cities on the one hand, and in agricultural regions on the other. The following table gives the area of each county in square miles and the percentages of ownership. State ownership figures are supplied for comparison.

135

County	Area (sq.mi.)	USFS (%)	BLM (%)	BIA (%)	State (%)	County (%)	Private (%)
Crook	2,982	22.7	26.8	—	1.5	0.2	48.8
Deschutes	3,060	49.9	26.5	—	1.4	1.1	21.1
Jefferson	1,795	14.4	2.3	22.3	0.4	—	60.6
Sherman	1,807	—	8.1	—	0.1	0.7	91.1
Wasco	2,392	10.9	2.3	25.3	1.7	—	59.8
State	98,981	24.1	25.3	1.2	2.5	0.9	45.2

The Economy

The economy of the Deschutes country includes a variety of activities: forestry, logging, irrigation farming, dry farming, ranching, recreation and retirement, and manufacturing, as well as many kinds of service enterprises.[11] In the upper reaches of the Deschutes River and its tributaries, logging, camping, skiing, and sports fishing are most important. In the middle area, near Bend, Redmond, Prineville, and Madras, irrigation farming, recreation, and manufacturing are the leading activities. The agricultural emphasis is on livestock (mainly beef cattle), hay, wheat, peppermint, and pototoes. In the north, on the benches, flats and plains, dry farming is most extensive and wheat is the important crop. The decreased timber harvest in western Oregon has placed pressure on the forests east of the Cascades, especially on privately owned land, thus reducing the timber reserve. In recent years irrigation agriculture and recreation have increased. Dry farming varies with seasonal rainfall and the market. The price of wheat has been generally high, leading to an expansion of wheat acreage, some of it on rougher land than is ordinarily cultivated. Camping, sightseeing, fishing, hunting, skiing, and boating have increased very rapidly, along with the construction of camps, motels, condominiums, supermarkets, and ski lifts. Recreation is big business now, especially in Deschutes County, and the influx of out-of-state people has led to a great inflation of property values. Manufacturing is mainly in lumber, plywood, metal fabrication (mobile homes), and food processing such as flour milling and fruit packing. The chief centers are Bend, Redmond, Prineville, Madras, Warm Springs, and The Dalles.

136

The Counties

Most of the Deschutes country is included in five counties: Wasco, Sherman, Jefferson, Deschutes, and Crook. The watershed of the Deschutes River, however, includes small parts of Hood River, Klamath, Lake, Grant, Wheeler, and Harney counties. Of the major counties, Deschutes is the largest, 3,060 square miles, and the most populous, 46,800 (1977). Jefferson is the smallest, with 1,795 square miles, while Sherman has the least population, 2,200 in 1977. Wasco is the oldest county, dating from 1854 when it included all of Oregon east of the Cascades. Crook County was formed from Wasco in 1882, Sherman from Wasco in 1889, Jefferson from Crook in 1914, and Deschutes from Crook in 1917. It is obvious that effective settlement of the Deschutes country began along the Columbia River and moved southward; a decade or two after these beginnings, some moved eastward from the Willamette Valley.

Boundaries of the counties are based mostly on drainage divides, but in detail most of the lines follow township, range, and section lines, giving a zigzag effect to many of the borders. The crest of the Cascade Range forms the west boundaries of Jefferson, Deschutes, and part of Wasco counties. Streams form boundaries in some cases: the Deschutes River together with a tributary, Buck Creek, marks part of the boundary between Wasco and Sherman counties, while the John Day River marks the eastern border of Sherman County, the southeastern edge of Wasco County, and the northeastern corner of Jefferson County. The entire boundary of Crook County follows range, township, and section lines; selected, however, to mark out approximately the watershed of Crooked River.

Deschutes County

When Isaiah Bowman, president of the American Geographical Society, studied the Bend country half a century ago, he found that the area had already experienced four stages of occupation. The first stage was pre-railroad in which ranching, along with some wheat farming, was the chief activity. The region was isolated but cattle could be driven long distances to the nearest railroad, since the price of beef and wheat were

137

relatively high. The second stage was dry farming before and after the railroad came to Bend in 1911. Dry farming failed, except in a few most-favored locations, and cattle ranching again became the chief activity; this was the third stage. The fourth stage was introduced when the big lumber companies arrived and began large-scale production in 1916. The lumber industry stimulated agriculture and the expansion of irrigation took up the slack from the failure of the homesteaders. Bowman also noted that the porous soils of Deschutes County were not suited for dry farming and that the line of wheat cultivation should be drawn two miles north of the Deschutes-Jefferson county line. Bowman observed the unusual phenomenon that trees will grow on the porous soil, too dry for wheat. Usually the reverse is true.

Deschutes County is divided physically into two regions, the Cascade Slope and the High Lava Plains. In both areas igneous activity has played a major role; basalt and andesite are the common rock types along with deposits of ash and pumice. Sediments have accumulated in shallow lake beds, most of which are now dry. Deschutes County shares with Linn and Lane counties a number of prominent crestline peaks, Mt. Washington (7,794 feet), the Three Sisters (all over 10,000 feet), Elk Mountain (5,936 feet), and Maiden Peak (7,818 feet). East of the crestline are Broken Top (9,175 feet), Bachelor Butte (9,065 feet), an important ski resort area, Black Crater (7,251 feet), Tumalo Mountain (7,775 feet), and many others. Away from the peaks and buttes the surface is usually rough, especially on recent lava flows, as in the McKenzie Pass area. Although these flows are at least several hundred years old, vegetation is just beginning to be established. At this elevation the long, cold winters and comparatively dry summers are not favorable for the formation of soil and the germination of seeds. Small streams such as Squaw Creek, Trout Creek, and Tumalo Creek have carved shallow canyons in many parts of the Cascade Slope but some parts do not have well-established drainage lines. Lakes are common, most of igneous origin; a few are related to glaciation.

The Cascade Range presents a barrier between Deschutes County and the Willamette Valley, especially in winter when snow tends to block the passes. State Highway 242, leading over McKenzie Pass (5,324 feet), is closed in winter usually from November to June. Two other passes

138

are kept open year round, except for temporary closing during severe storms. U.S. Highway 20 crosses Santiam Pass (4,817 feet) and State Highway 58 and the Southern Pacific Railroad cross Willamette Pass (5,128 feet). The approach to these passes is easy on the east but steep and winding on the west.

The High Lava Plains extend from the foot of the Cascade Slope in the vicinity of Bend eastward to the Blue Mountains and, farther south, all the way to Burns and beyond. The surface is made up of recent lava flows, together with deposits of ash, pumice, and sediments. The maximum relief in this section of Deschutes County is from about 3,500 feet near Bend to 7,985 feet at Paulina Peak. The general level is over 4,000 feet. A number of buttes and peaks rise above the general level in some localities. Surface streams are generally rare; only the Deschutes and Crooked rivers have cut deep canyons in the surface. Dry River, which flows through the eastern part of the county, was formed in more humid times. U.S. Highway 20 follows this channel in the vicinity of Millican, 35 miles to the southeast of Bend. Most of the High Lava Plains, except at higher elevations such as Paulina Peak, are covered with sagebrush and a sprinkling of junipers.

Only a small part of Deschutes County is in farms, about 121,000 acres out of a total of 1,940,000.[12] In 1974 there were 438 farms, averaging 276 acres each, the smallest average farm size in Oregon east of the Cascades, where large farms and ranches are the rule. The fact that most of the farms are irrigated and that large, dry land farms are rare accounts for the small average size. Harvested cropland amounts to 19,000 acres of which 15,700 acres are irrigated. Cropland pasture, about 40 percent of it irrigated, covers 15,000 acres and farm woodland, 13,500 acres. Most farmers emphasize livestock rather than cash crops based on extensive hay production, irrigated pasture, and rangeland. Hay, wheat, potatoes, and grass seeds are the most important crops. Livestock includes 7,500 beef cattle, 3,100 sheep, 1,100 horses and 900 hogs. The average value of an acre of farmland increased from $269 in 1969 to $409 in 1974. Recently 10-acre investment or recreational tracts have been offered at $5,000 an acre. Most of the water for irrigation is diverted from the Deschutes River and from the creeks on the Cascade Slope. Groundwater is available at depths of from 300 to 800 feet, but drilling in basalt is expensive and few wells are used for irrigation. Plans are being made to reduce the excessive loss of water by seepage in the irrigation system by lining the ditches and by other improvements.

Crook County

Crook County was named for George Crook, a major-general in the U.S. Army, but Crooked River was named by the early fur traders for the winding nature of its course. The county lies on the western margin of the Blue Mountain Region, which, in its entirety, extends from the middle Deschutes River to the Snake River Canyon. Two of the subdivisions of the Blue Mountains, the Ochoco Mountains and Maury Mountains, are in Crook County. The total relief of the county is about 4,000 feet, ranging from 2,800 feet near Prineville to 6,800 feet at Mt. Lookout in the eastern part of the county. Landforms include many irregular peaks and ridges, separated by narrow valleys. The general trend of the ridges is east-west and some of them have fairly level summit areas, called prairies.

Crooked River has a nearly uniform gradient of eight feet per mile while its main tributaries, North Fork, Beaver Creek, and Ochoco Creek, have steeper grades. Most of the streams have narrow floodplains which are subject to fairly frequent floods, unlike the Deschutes and its tributaries. All streams have a very low stage in late summer. Two reservoirs, one on Ochoco Creek and one on the main stem, provide storage for irrigation water and are also used for recreation. Numerous campsites are provided in various parts of the county by the U.S. Forest Service, the Bureau of Land Management, and the state of Oregon for sightseers, fishermen, and hunters.

Crook County is unique in that nearly half of the 12,100 people live in the only incorporated town, Prineville. Small unincorporated towns include Powell Butte on the west, Post near the center, and Paulina in the east. The average density of population is four per sqare mile; only Sherman County, in the Deschutes country, has a lower density.

Most of the 290 farms in Crook County are better described as ranches with very small areas of cultivation and large areas of grazing land, supplemented by rangeland in the public domain, administered by the BLM and the USFS. The average ranch size is 3,500 acres or five and one-half square miles, the largest in the Deschutes country. Of the million acres of land in ranches, only 46,000 are usually harvested, 64,000 acres are irrigated of which 25,000 are in pasture. The chief crops are hay, 36,000 acres, wheat, 4,000 acres, and potatoes, 2,400 acres. Other crops such as fruits and vegetables are of minor importance. Emphasis is on livestock which is valued at more than seven million dollars, with 31,000 beef cattle, 1,300 sheep, and lesser numbers of horses, dairy cows, and hogs. The value of ranch land, per acre, is the lowest in the Deschutes country, increasing, however, from $54 per acre in 1969 to $78 per acre in 1974, a gain of 44 percent.

Jefferson County

Jefferson County was named for Jefferson Peak which was named by Lewis and Clark for President Thomas Jefferson. The county is divided into three regions, from west to east: the Cascade Slope, the Deschutes Plateau, and the Blue Mountains. Most of the county's 9,900 people live on the plateau on the east side of the Deschutes River.

The Cascade Slope is dominated by Mt. Jefferson, the second highest peak in Oregon at 10,497 feet. Another conspicuous peak is Three-Fingered Jack, 7,841 feet. On the whole the slope appears to be more rugged and dissected than in Deschutes County. It drops steeply to the upper Metolius River which collects many small tributaries and flows northward before turning east to the Deschutes River. The Metolius flows from a large spring at the foot of Black Butte. To the east of the upper Metolius is Green Ridge, a fault block trending north-south with a steep 2,000-foot scarp facing west. Farther north Seekseequa and Shitike creeks, each with several tributaries, flow directly to the Deschutes. There are very few lakes, limited mostly to the southwest corner of the county, such as Suttle and Blue and, to the northwest, Olallie and Monon.

141

The Deschutes Plateau in Jefferson County consists of many large upland areas separated by the Deschutes, Crooked, and tributary canyons. Individual plateau areas include Metolius Bench, Tenino Bench, and the Agency Plains. These somewhat isolated fragments of the plateau are similar in that they are based on horizontal lava flows which have been weathered to produce fairly thick soils. One of these plateau fragments south of the Metolius is called the Lower Desert, although it grows scattered trees.

The smooth plateau surfaces with good soils, less porous than those farther south, make it possible to grow wheat and other grains without irrigation and for many years wheat farming represented the chief use of the land. But with the introduction of irrigation, by way of the North Unit Canal, land use became more intensive and the crop system was changed. Large, dry land farms were divided into smaller fields with peppermint taking the place of some of the wheat. Irrigation also increased the yield of wheat.

The eastern part of the county is along the western edge of the Blue Mountains at generally lower elevations than the Ochoco Mountains in Crook County. Much of the surface is rough hill land with many buttes and old volcanic cones. Ranches are widely scattered and grazing is generally poor. Most of the country is covered with sagebrush and juniper, with very little grass.

In 1974 Jefferson County had 341 farms with a total acreage of 458,000. The average farm size was 1,344 acres but 33 farms were over 2,000 acres each. The 32 farms with annual sales of less than $2,500 were probably parttime operations. Harvested land totaled 67,000 acres, about six percent of the area of the county, while farm woodland occupied 8,700 acres. Fifty-three thousand acres were irrigated, about six percent of which were irrigated pasture. Wheat was the most important crop with 31,000 acres, of which about one-half was irrigated. In recent years peppermint has become the second crop in acreage, the first in value; in 1977 the acreage reached 21,450. Hay crops, mostly alfalfa and clover, occupied 10,200 acres and potatoes, 2,300 acres; Kentucky bluegrass seed, 6,300 acres. Beef cattle numbered 10,300 and sheep, 6,500, with smaller numbers of horses, hogs, and dairy cows. The average price of farmland advanced from $102 to $235 per acre from 1969 to 1974, an increase of 138 percent, the highest percentage increase in the Deschutes country.

The Warm Springs Reservation was set aside in 1855 for the Tenino, Wasco, Paiute, and Klickitat tribes. It lies on the Cascade Slope in Jefferson and Wasco counties and extends approximately from the Cascade crest to the Deschutes River. It is curious that this "barren area" produces large quantities of timber, has a very successful hot springs resort, and supports a substantial livestock industry. The 2,200 residents, mostly Indians, but including a few whites, live in the towns of Warm Springs and Simnasho and near the hot springs. Agriculture is limited by the climate and terrain. A few of the flats produce hay which, together with the range areas, support the cattle industry.

Wasco & Sherman Counties

Wasco and Sherman counties make up the north part of the Deschutes country. It seems logical to include all of Wasco County in the region, although the northwestern part drains directly into the Columbia River; also all of Sherman County, although the eastern part drains to the John Day River. The Dalles is the urban center for both counties, in fact it is the only city.

Two physical regions are involved, the Cascade Slope in the western half of Wasco County and the Deschutes Plateau which includes the eastern part of Wasco County and all of Sherman County. The lower canyon of the Deschutes River and the gorge of the Columbia River are the dominant features of the region. The region is underlain by nearly horizontal layers of basalt; the Columbia River basalts occur mostly in the stream valleys while younger lavas cover the higher areas. In places the layers are warped slightly and faulted, which accounts for some of the ridges and other irregularities. Most of the surface features, however, are the result of erosion by the Deschutes and Columbia rivers and their tributaries.

On the Cascade Slope, the highest point is on Olallie Butte in southwestern Wasco County, at approximately 7,000 feet (the summit of the butte is shared by Marion and Jefferson counties). The lowest point is

143

on the Columbia River, 72 feet above sea level, which is the normal level of the reservoir backed up by Bonneville Dam. This part of the Cascade Slope appears older than the same region farther south. Recent lava flows are rare. Streams have cut parallel shallow canyons in the surface, giving a washboard effect. Some of the valleys are irrigated. A few streams are named according to the distance from The Dalles along the old Indian and fur trader trail south—Three Mile Creek, Five Mile Creek, Eight Mile Creek, and so on. This route is approximately the same as U.S. Highway 197. Further south, White River and Warm Springs River and their tributaries have carved a dendritic pattern in the Cascade Slope. Here and there are nearly level surfaces such as Government Flat and Hood River Flat.

The Deschutes Plateau in Wasco and Sherman counties is in effect a continuation of the Cascade Slope but the beds are nearly level and so are the plateau surfaces, except for shallow dissection by small streams. The general slope is northward from 2,500 feet in southern Wasco County to less than 1,000 feet near the Columbia River. In Wasco County the plateau surface is carved into shallow canyons or hollows, such as Shot, Hog, and Long hollows. This term, common in the Appalachian Plateau of the eastern United States, is seldom used in Oregon where the term "canyon" or "draw" is preferred. Its use is probably related to the settlement of some parts of the Deschutes Plateau by people from Appalachia. In Sherman County the relief on the plateau between the Deschutes and John Day rivers is much less. Most of the surface can be described as low, rolling hill land.

The Deschutes Canyon on the Wasco County border is 85 miles long by the river, approximately 55 miles as the crow flies. The canyon varies in width; in some areas it is quite narrow with steep cliffs. Wheat fields on the plateau are less than a mile from the river. In other parts, the nearest cultivation may be as much as five miles from the river. The gradient of the river in the lower reaches is comparatively low, about 13 feet to the mile.

Wasco and Sherman counties are in a wheat growing area, producing both spring and winter wheat. Farms are large, averaging over 2,400 acres (3.75 square miles per farm). Wasco County had 485 farms in 1974 and

Sherman County, 196. Most of the land is in farms, 89 percent in Sherman County, 78 percent in Wasco County, but since much of the land is idle in any one year, the harvested land is less than half the total farmland; rough land on the sides of canyons is not cultivated. Sherman County has only 7,000 acres of cropland pasture, and Wasco only 19,000, part of which is irrigated. It is not an unusual sight in early summer to see a number of fields of winter wheat ready for harvest and next to them a green field of spring wheat to be harvested in September, and on the rougher, adjacent slopes dry pasture land. Irrigation is not generally used except in the Wapinitia district of Wasco County since the Deschutes River is too far below the plateau level where most of the farmland is located. Wheat dominates the crop system, almost all of it grown by dry farming methods. In 1974 Wasco County had 81,000 acres in wheat and Sherman County, with larger areas of smooth land, had 135,000 acres. Other crops are minor except for hay in the Wapinitia district which had 13,000 acres in 1974. Livestock ranching is generally secondary to wheat farming but in 1974 Wasco County had 20,000 beef cattle and Sherman, 6,000. In recent years (1969-74) the price of farmland in the two counties has increased rapidly, from $96 per acre to $147 in Sherman County and from $77 to $123 per acre in Wasco County.

Prospect

To Isaiah Bowman's four phases of development in the Deschutes country a fifth has been added in recent years—recreation and retirement. Although the region began attracting fishermen, hunters, and even a few sightseers many years ago, growth began to accelerate in the last 25 years. Skiing did not become popular until about 1960 and since that time camping, fishing, hunting, and backpacking have doubled and redoubled. Many visitors came for a vacation and decided to stay or, at least, make the Deschutes country their second home. The rapid increase in tourism and retirement has had a strong impact on construction of houses, motels, resorts, camps, condominiums, and also on the price of land.[13]

Growth has been uneven. Obviously the Bend area is favored because it is located on an even-flowing, alive but not too rapid river, which can readily be bridged. Plenty of level land is available for building and development. But apart from the attractiveness of the Bend area is the fact that the whole Deschutes country is available for recreation and other uses.

Ranching and irrigation farming appear to face a slow but steady growth. Most of the readily available water is in use but more efficient methods, such as lining the irrigation ditches to reduce the very large losses by seepage, should make it possible to irrigate more land. Dry farming, so important in Wasco and Sherman counties, will continue to wax and wane with the price of wheat, government support, and the foreign market. But the potential is there; this is perhaps the most stable dry farming region in the United States, with its capacity to grow both spring and winter wheat. Lumbering is a big question mark; inroads in the three national forests in recent years have been heavy. The demand for lumber and plywood is excellent and prices are high. The question is, will U.S. Forest Service policy be relaxed to allow an increase in the annual cut? Otherwise the cut must decline. The Deschutes country is a unique region with a variety of resources. The outlook appears to be favorable but it is only fair to point out that future growth will depend, in part, on continued import of investment funds from outside the state of Oregon.

4

IMAGES OF THE DESCHUTES COUNTRY

In Oregon the Deschutes country, with its great and penetrating contrasts, has a special fascination and reality. Lovers of the region think of the fragrances of pine and juniper and sage, of the rushing green water in the river and the dry lands through which it flows, of deep canyons and high mountains, of rimrock and lava fields, of panoramic views and bluebirds, of meadows unexpectedly full of tiny flowers and mosaic-marked butterflies. They remember the light from the sun, hot days and frosty nights, blue sky and towering thunderheads, or sometimes the wind and the dust, the quiet, lichen on a pile of stones, fading traces of the land—an axe-marked juniper limb or a bleached board. The imagery can strike deep.

It is lighter, higher and harder country than the Oregon west of the Cascades. And it came later to general public knowledge as a part of the Oregon Country.

The first transferable written records and maps of central Oregon, the Deschutes watershed, were supplied by parties who passed through during the first quarter of the 19th century. Though the native-born inhabited and moved through the region for centuries, adjusting to some spectacular changes in the landscape, Indian "maps" were trails on the earth.

Priscilla Knuth

In time these came to be utilized by European and American record makers, along with native advice and guides.

European visions of the Pacific Northwest preceded any personal experience, but gradually the real geography of the "high and mighty" landscape of the Deschutes drainage—from the east flank of the Cascades down through the high plateau country through lower Crooked River drainage, and north to the Columbia—began to be recorded by land explorers and fur traders. Lewis and Clark, on the Columbia, only passed the mouth of the Deschutes, but fur traders reached upstream parts a few years later, perhaps as early as 1813,[1] and Crooked River in the mid-1820s. Finan McDonald, Peter Skene Ogden and Tom McKay were on the Riviere des Chutes[2] by that time, and Nathaniel Wyeth followed in the 1830s.

Still, their knowledge was hardly circulated. Even the few details of the Deschutes country printed on a U.S. map (see fig. 85) in 1838 were a tremendous advance in public material. The courses of the Deschutes ("Chutes or Falls R.") and Crooked (so named) rivers are portrayed on the "Map of the United States Territory of Oregon West of the Rocky Mountains, Exhibiting the various Trading Depots or Forts occupied by the British Hudson Bay Company connected with the Western and northwestern Fur Trade," a map "Compiled in the Bureau of Topographical Engineers from the latest authorities under the direction of Col. J. J. Abert, by Wash[ington] Hood, M. H. Stansbury, del[ineator]." Most of the new geographic knowledge of the Pacific Northwest on the Hood map had come from the British fur trade through a map published by the Arrowsmith firm of London in 1834 and described as a "monument" with "a whole new geography."[3]

It seems ironically appropriate that the Hood map, including the first real concept of central Oregon published in the United States, appeared with Senator Lewis F. Linn's report asking for occupation of Oregon, dated June 6, 1838.[4]

A few years later in the mid-1840s, Frémont explored south from the Columbia River to California, following the Klamath Indian trail and adding much more to the delineated map of the Deschutes. South of the Dalles of the Columbia, he marked Fall River (Deschutes) and "Taigh"

148

fig. 85

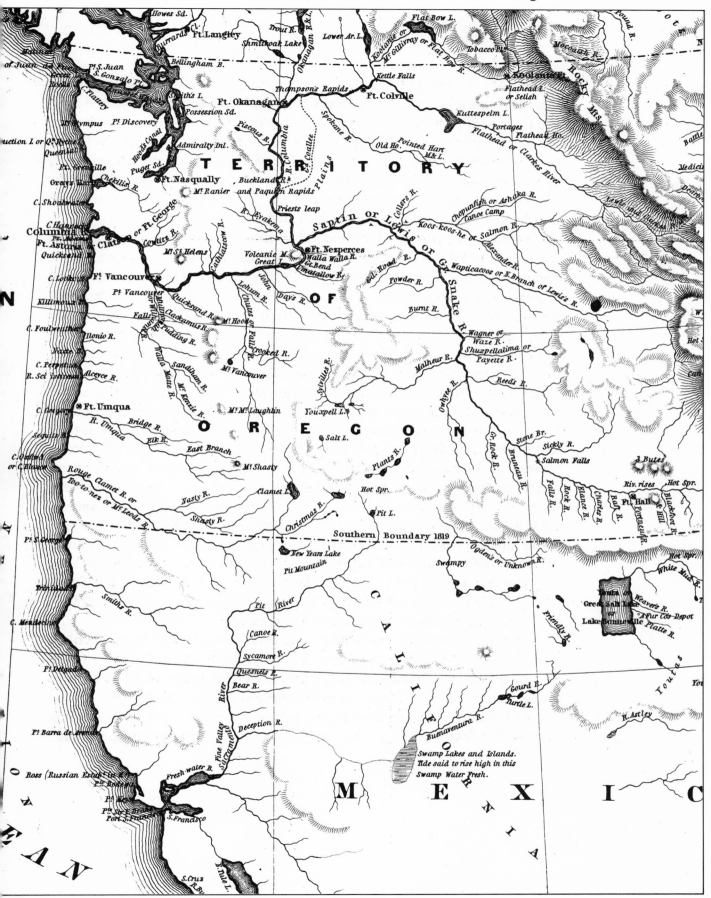

Prairie, Mt. Hood and Mt. Jefferson, moving along to the west of the Deschutes until he reached its upper branches. The section presented here (see fig. 86) is part of the "Map of an Exploring Expedition to the Rocky Mountains in the Year 1842, Oregon & North California in the Years 1843-44 by Bvt. Capt. J. C. Frémont of the Corps of Topographical Engs. under the orders of Col. J. J. Abert, Chief of the Topographical Bureau, lith. by E. Weber & Co., Baltimore, Md." At the time not much of the Willamette Valley had had such skilled attention.

Printed material in governmental circles and Congress often did not circulate very far into general public knowledge. As more and more people began using the Oregon Trail in the 1840s, heading for the fertile—and expected free—land in the Willamette Valley, the need for information spread. The travelers, now including families with wagons, cattle and sheep, gathered whatever guidance they could. On the usual Oregon Trail route, they touched the Deschutes country only on the north, heading for the Barlow Road south of Mt. Hood. Distance and traveling conditions naturally led them to try shortcuts from near Fort Boise on the Snake River more directly west across Oregon to the Valley. Sometimes they had advice from those with fur trade experience, comments from relatives and friends already in Oregon, or warnings of the hazards on other known routes; for the most part they gathered information the hard way. Frémont (if his experience was known to them) was no help between the Malheur River and the Deschutes, or across the Cascades. To these newcomers, central Oregon and the Deschutes drainage were simply a place to cross as rapidly as possible before winter snows trapped them in the mountains (to avoid the Donner party nightmare), though the river itself was reached with thanksgiving after the hazards of the drier country to the east. Those who gambled on the Meek Cutoff (1845) or the Elliott Cutoff (1853) had experiences told in families for generations.[5]

Non-governmental knowledge was usually oral and not transcribed to paper until it reached those who had to provide official records. Good examples are the Joel Palmer-George H. Belden maps of 1855, where the primary purpose was Oregon Superintendent of Indian Affairs Palmer's report of Indian land cessions. One Palmer map of 1855 roughly outlines the Warm Springs ("Wasco") Reservation, adding "wagon roads"

fig. 86

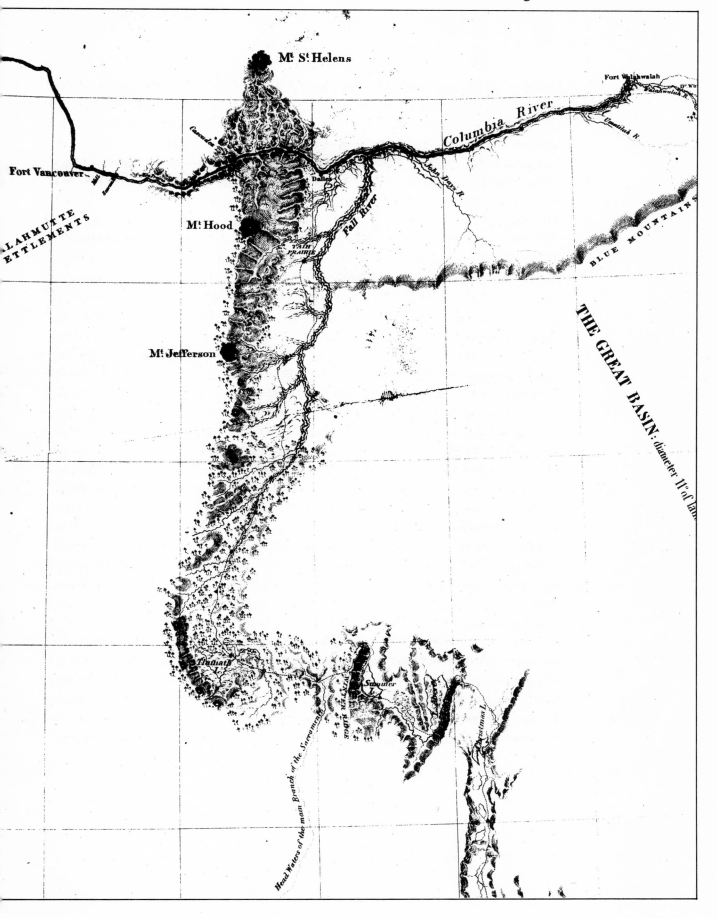

of 1843, 1847 (a shortcut Oregon Trail route to the Dalles), and a very approximate line north across central Oregon for "Meeks Cut-off."[6] South of the the "Tigh" River tributaries entering the Deschutes from the west are not named, and none is shown on the east side of the river.

A better manuscript map sent to Indian Affairs headquarters in Washington, D.C., was the Palmer map (see fig. 87) titled "Sketch Map of Oregon Territory, Exhibiting the Locations of the various Indian Tribes, the districts of Country ceded by them, with the dates of Purchases and Treaties, and the Reserves of the Umpqua and Rogue River Indians, Projected by Geo. H. Belden."[7] There are tributaries entering the Deschutes from both east and west including Crooked River, and more vaguely but deriving from recent settlers' experience, "Emigrant trail," "Old Road of 1844" (1845?—probably a different section of the Meek route), and "New Road of 1854." The crude north-south line of "Meeks Cut-off" on the "Wasco" Reservation map does not appear, perhaps omitted because its purpose was better served by the "New Road of 1854," a revision of the 1853 Elliott route. Palmer was interested in roads, not only for the pertinence of white travel to relations with the Indians.[8]

Another advance in the published representation of central Oregon was a consequence of the Pacific Railroad surveys, exploration federally provided and again involving the Army Corps of Topographical Engineers. The same year Palmer recorded Indian land cessions in the Deschutes country, 1855, Lts. R. S. Williamson and H. L. Abbot with a small Army escort moved north from California and along the east side of the Cascades, looking for a suitable railroad route and mountain passes. They explored further into the mountains than Frémont, and they also had benefit of some knowledge gained by settlers' explorations from the Valley up the Middle Fork of the Willamette, to provide a connecting road for immigrants taking a shortcut from the Oregon Trail west via the Malheur River, Harney Valley, Crooked River and the Deschutes. The engineers' work was published in the *Pacific Railroad Reports,* vol. 6 (Sen. Ex. Doc. 78, 33rd Cong., 2nd sess., Serial 768), printed in 1857, and the section here (see fig. 88) is part of the Map No. 2, "From the Northern Boundary of California to the Columbia River from exploration and surveys made

fig. 87

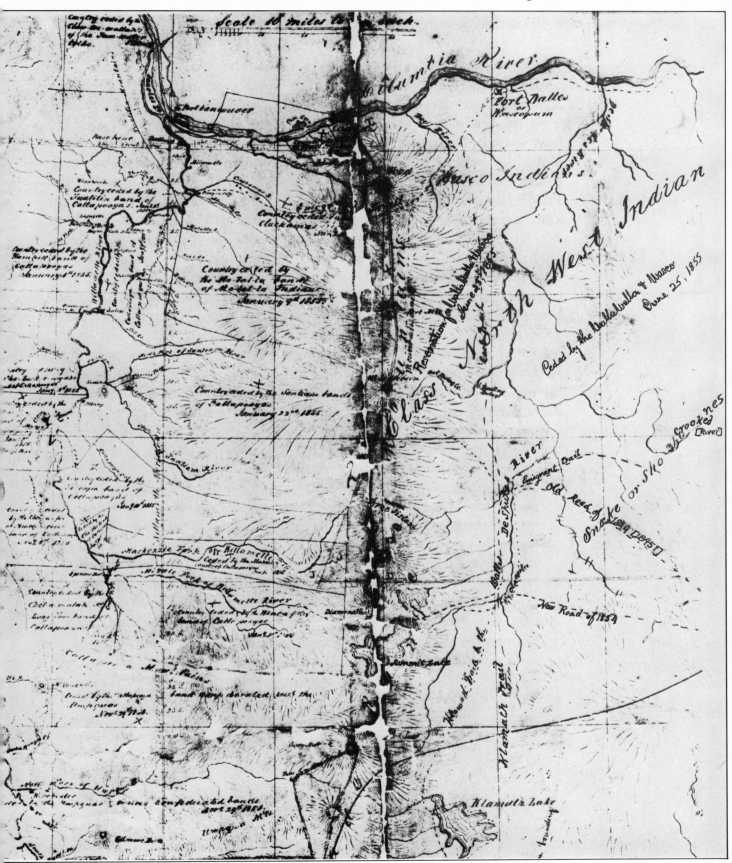

under the direction of Hon. Jefferson Davis, Sec. of War by Lieut. R. S. Williamson. . .and Lieut. H. L. Abbot, U.S. Topl. Engrs."

After examining the Three Sisters area, Williamson worked over the pass south of Diamond Peak and down the Middle Fork of the Willamette along the locally "constructed" Free Emigrant Road, while Abbot continued farther north in the Deschutes country. The "Map drawn in the Field" (see fig. 89) is from Abbot's working notebook (OHS Ms 94B), and summarizes his exploration from south of Mt. Jefferson north to Mt. Hood. Though spelling varies from the published map, western tributaries of the Deschutes have recognizable names.

The *Pacific Railroad Reports* also included beautiful pictorial representations (see figs. 102, 103) and probably the first published text appropriate to the grandeur of the Deschutes region. Early in September, 1855 the Williamson-Abbot party reached the Deschutes at a point where, as Abbot described it, "About fifty feet below us, the river was leaping, with a low murmuring sound, from crag to crag, and apparently descending one hundred and fifty feet in less than three hundred yards. The dark pines around us, and the remains of a deserted Indian rancheria, harmonized well with the scene." The next day, September 4, they were in the Sisters area. Abbot commented that

> *after riding a few miles, we emerged from the forest, and traversed an elevated plateau, dotted with cedars and sage bushes, and marked by a few low ridges and ravines. . . . The air was uncommonly clear and pure. The white summits of several snowy peaks began to appear in the distance, and we pressed rapidly forward. After travelling 17.5 miles from camp, we reached Why-chus creek. . . . It was a fine stream, about 30 feet in width, flowing rapidly over rounded rocks. Its waters were slightly turbid. There was an inexhaustible supply of fine grass in the vicinity, but Lieut. Williamson decided to travel on, and encamp near the "Forks of the Indian trail." We passed through an open forest for the whole distance, and encamped on a little brook which, a few miles below us, sank among the rocks. From a slight eminence above camp, the snowy peaks of the Three Sisters appeared quite near. A large*

fig. 88

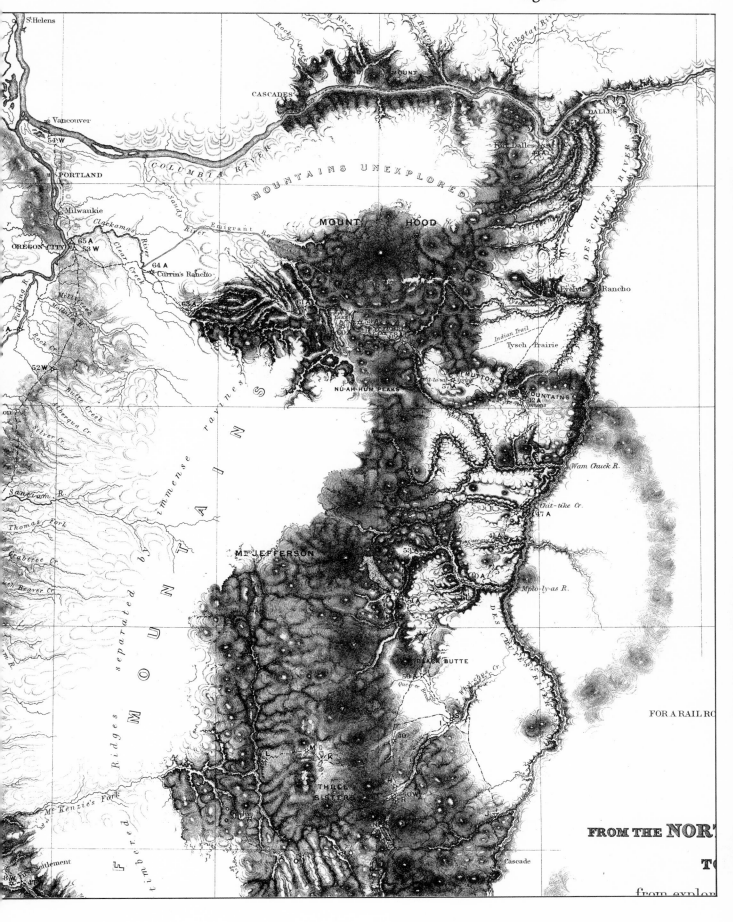

St Helens

Vancouver

54 W

PORTLAND

COLUMBIA RIVER

Milwaukie

Clarkamas River

Emigrant Rd

OREGON CITY

65 A
53 W

64 A

Currin's Rancho

Clear Creek

63 A

MOUNTAINS UNEXPLORED

CASCADES

MOUNT

DALLES

Ft Dalles

DES CHUTES RIVER

MOUNT HOOD

Frelyns Rancho

Indian Trail

Tysch Prairie

CHUTTON

51 A

NU-AH-HUM PEAKS

MOUNTAINS
Springs

Pudding R

Molalla R

Rock Cr

52 W

Butte Creek

Silver Cr

Umberqua Cr

Santiam R

Thomas Fork

Crabtree Cr

Beaver Cr

Ridges separated by immense ravines

M O U N T A I N S

Timbered

F

Mt JEFFERSON

53 A

Wam Chuck R.

Chit-tike Cr.
47 A

D A

Mpto-ly-as R.

BLACK BUTTE

50 A

Quee-ee-Br

Whychus Cr

DES CHUTES RIVER

10

FOR A RAIL RO

McKenzie's Fork

THREE
SISTERS

HOW

FROM THE NOR

Cascade

TO

Settlement

from explor

meadow, which Lieut. Williamson had previously seen, and upon which he depended for grass, proved to be a cranberry swamp and utterly impassable. A sufficiency of excellent bunch grass, however, was found among the trees. Whortleberries [huckleberries], elder berries and service berries abounded in the vicinity.[9]

Leaving Williamson and turning north toward The Dalles to get supplies, Abbot wrote on September 7:

We continued our course, and, after crossing the bed of a torrent of the rainy season, came to a very small stream called Psuc-see-que by the Indians. It was sunk in a canon about 500 feet deep, cut through successive strata of basalt, infusorian marl, tufas, and conglomerate sandstone like that found in the Mpto-ly-as canon. There was a little grass in the narrow bottom and on the sides, and some small cedars, willows, and bushes. . . . Here we encamped, after a laborious day's march, which had brought us but very little nearer the end of our journey. The view from our camp was wild and beautiful. Looking up the canon, we could see the snowy summit of Mount Jefferson closing the narrow vista; while the steep banks, with their strongly contrasting colors of black, white, blue, pink, and red, gradually approached each other below our camp, until they formed a narrow gateway, through which we had a glimpse of a little opening in the ravine beyond.[10]

The next day, on what became the Warm Springs Reservation, they reached "a fine stream called Chit-tike. . .sunk in an enormous canon, 900 feet deep." Proceeding through gorges and over hills, they reached the canyon of the "Wam Chuck" with "steep sides of basaltic rock and red earth." There they were surprised to find 20 or 30 so far unsuccessful prospectors. The gold hunters were amused when one of the railroad party tried to drink from a clear spring bubbling from under a rock near the trail, only to find it was hot water (140°F.).

Prospectors, especially consequent to the view of the West created by the California discoveries and the 1849 gold rush, now had added their voices and activities to earlier fur hunters, explorers and immigrants. "Blue Bucket" nuggets found along the Meek Cutoff were recalled, and

156

fig. 89

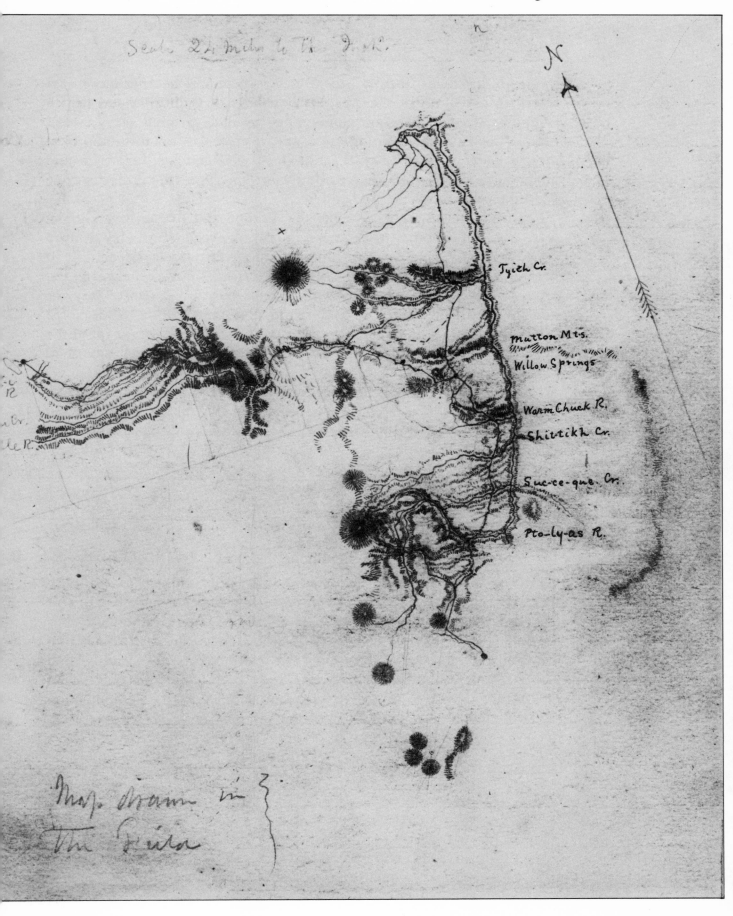

Scale 24 miles to the ½ ½.

N

Tyich Cr.

Mutton Mts.

Willow Springs

Warm Chuck R.

Shittikh Cr.

Suc-ce-que Cr.

Pto-ly-as R.

Map drawn in
the field

the quest for roads "across" the Deschutes country became more of a search in and through the area. As bonanzas in California and British Columbia played out, some immigrants brought to mind memories of central Oregon's fine grazing areas and relative ease of traveling, even though water might be scarce. Still, there were hungry Indians in and about that country, and they made their wants known to travelers one way or another.

The skirmishes and battles of the Yakima and Rogue River Indian wars, the hostile parties encountered in central Oregon, probably delayed entry to the Deschutes country more than Army orders attempting to halt settlement or gold seeking east of the Cascades during the war years. Volunteer expeditions and Army campaigns did not penetrate very far into the Deschutes region, but the size of the Army efforts to the north in 1856 and 1858 provided expanding markets for local beef east of the mountains; Fort Dalles and the city of The Dalles burgeoned almost at the Deschutes' doorway.[11]

The Army campaigns brought relative quiet by the fall of 1858, and the 1855 treaty made by Superintendent Palmer with the tribes around the Dalles began to be implemented. The Warm Springs Reservation had been set up with an agency "about 70 miles south" of Fort Dalles, at Warm Springs on the "Chit-tike" near its confluence with the Deschutes.[12] There the still treatyless and hostile Snakes or Paiutes raided for horses and cattle. On occasion the Warm Springs tribes raided in return. Various temporary and unsuccessful expedients were tried, including a small Army detachment posted at reservation headquarters for a while.

Larger Army moves into and across the Deschutes country followed. General William S. Harney, who had only arrived to take charge of military affairs in the Pacific Northwest at the end of a northern Indian war that took some sting out of two Army defeats, found other tasks for the soldiers. It was time to explore for a better wagon road route from The Dalles southeast toward the old fur post of Fort Boise, and beyond it toward the "Great Salt Lake valley" and the U.S. force stationed there, and to provide safe escort for Oregon Trail travelers. With a combination of such popular and military purposes, Harney in 1859 sent out Col.

H. D. Wallen with a large expedition directed to explore "for a military road from the Dalles of the Columbia River to Great Salt Lake."[13]

Of more interest to the Deschutes country than the official expedition maps done by Lt. Joseph Dixon of the Engineer Corps were advance scouting and mapping done by chief guide Louis Scholl.[14]

Leaving Fort Dalles June 4th, Wallen moved south on the west side of the Deschutes, on June 12 camping at the mouth of the Warm Springs River, where he had a report from Scholl that he had found "an excellent country as far as Crooked river."[15] Then the expedition crossed the Deschutes to follow that course to a "Camp on the South fork of Crooked River," where the commander heartily agreed about the country. He reported to Harney's adjutant on July 1 that once across the Deschutes, the expedition followed "the best natural road" he "had ever passed over."

Water, wood and grass is in abundance along the route; the grass full of seed and almost as nutritious as the forage used in the barrack stable.

I enclose you a small sketch of the route passed over, with the distances, water courses, springs, &c. laid down. My object in coming out by the Warm Spring river, & from thence around to this point, was to form a depot here & work the road in both directions, and, also, to map the country in the Department, such portions of it as had, heretofore, been unknown. I have had accurate surveys & maps made of the country over which we have travelled, and am fully convinced that the information will be useful to the Government. . . . The ox train and the balance of the mule teams will work their way in slowly to Fort Dalles under the command of Lieut. Bonnycastle with seventy enlisted men.

Perhaps it was a tribute to central Oregon air that Captain Wallen at the same time "respectfully" suggested "that the Des Chutes River be examined from its mouth to the Warm Springs River, or even a few miles higher up, to see if there is any impediment to steam navigation. If not," he thought the Deschutes was "the natural outlet to all the valleys through which I have passed. Having heard from Mr. Scholl, I move on today."

Scholl's advance reconnaissance sketch maps (see fig. 90) helped to direct the early part of the expedition's course through the Deschutes

fig. 90

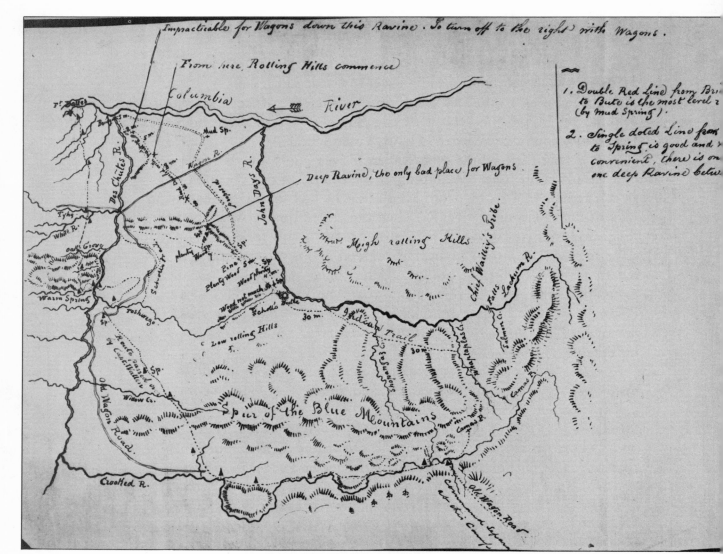

Fig. 90: Louis Scholl's map, enclosed with Col. H. D. Wallen's 1 July 1859 report. On an earlier map (with Wallen, 5 June 1859) he had marked in the "Joe Mix Trail" along the Crooked River to the Deschutes and going north along the latter stream as far as "Tyich" River. Here the label is "Old Wagon Road" (OHS Coll.).

160

fig. 91

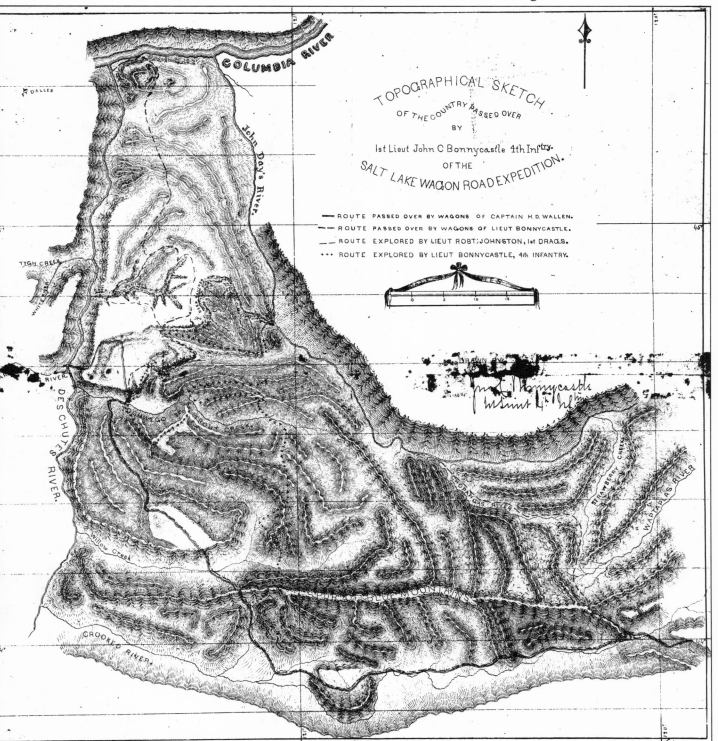

Fig. 91: Lt. John C. Bonnycastle's
1859 manuscript map. (From Record
Group 77, W56-2, Cartographic
Branch of the National Archives.)
(OHS Coll.)

country, and his and Lt. John C. Bonnycastle's work (see fig. 91) that summer made it plain from that time on that the better wagon road route south from the Columbia lay on the east bank of the Deschutes. Bonnycastle, according to Harney, stated that "the road by which I came from the camp, at which the division of Captain Wallen's command was made, I regard as a very good one for wagons, being generally over a level country, and with water and grass in sufficient quantities for large trains. . . . I brought the entire train. . .(17 ox wagons and 6 six-mule wagons) in 12 travelling days."[17]

Generally, the Wallen expedition results were encouraging, so much so that when General Harney sent all the reports to the adjutant general in January, 1860 he commented: "To enable the emigrants moving into Oregon to do so more expeditiously, I shall cause a route to be opened from the lake, named as Harney lake upon the map, to the juncture of the road from Eugene city, up the middle fork [of the Willamette], to where it crosses Frémont's road of 1843, south of Diamond peak."[18]

To carry out this plan Col. Enoch Steen and Capt. A. J. Smith went out late in the spring of 1860—and that year the Army expeditions crossed to the east bank of the Deschutes near its mouth, turning south before reaching Mud Spring. Otherwise, they followed the Wallen route—"the best natural road"—south and east along Crooked River to a joint camp at the northern end of Harney Valley, where Steen and his party turned west to explore toward Eugene and Smith (Scholl was with his party) turned east toward the Owyhee. Steen (and Dixon, again the topographical officer) found that a route directly west from Harney Lake to the pass south of Diamond Peak failed to provide enough water for immigrant trains or troops. Instead, from (Captain) Smith's Spring (Indian Springs, now Currey Springs) they surveyed by Indian Creek (Silver Creek) to Buck Creek.[19]

Dixon noted that "about two miles below our camp on Buck creek our road diverges from the road to Fort Dalles and follows nearly a due west direction for about ten miles over a level sage plain, in which the south branch of Crooked river rises. . . . From the. . .plain to Lost spring (as indicated on the map) a distance of about forty miles, the road passes over an undulating country, crossing several small streams which flow

162

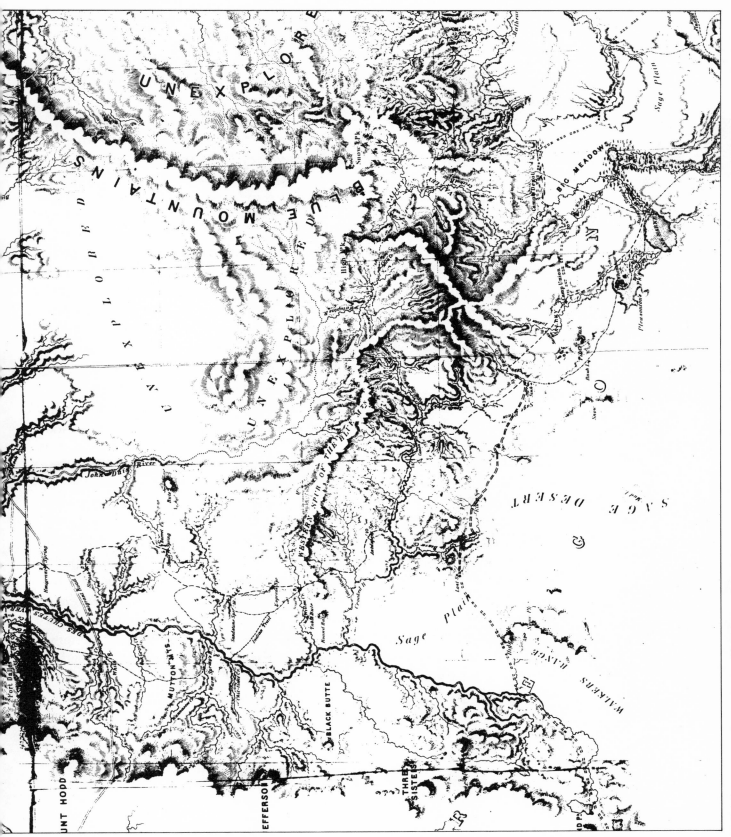

Fig. 92: Lt. Joseph Dixon's map includes 1860 campaign routes against the Snake Indians, as well as road exploration routes. Dixon's report is in U.S., Congress, Senate Executive Document No. 1, 37th Cong., 2nd sess., 1861-62 (Serial 1118); the map appears in Serial 1120 (OHS Coll.).

north into Crooked river."[20] North of the road there was luxuriant bunch grass and they saw fine groves of "cedars" and pines on the hillsides. From their camp at Lost Spring (see fig. 92),

looking west, the view of the dark, fir-coverd Cascade range presents an appearance wild and grand beyond description. Several of the principal mountain peaks stood out clear to the sky, with a pure mantle of snow. Good bearings were also taken on the principal peaks—Hood, Jefferson, Three Sisters, and Diamond Peak.

From Lost spring due west to Des Chutes river, a distance of twenty-five miles, the country is extremely level, and may be properly called the northwest portion of the great sage desert that extends from the western boundary of the valley of the lakes [Harney] to Des Chutes river, including all this region in one vast sterile sage desert, with the exception of a chain of mountains called Walker's range, bordering the east banks of Des Chutes river.[21]

Here at Lost Spring, on June 29, they received news that Captain Smith had been attacked by Indians before reaching the Owyhee, that he was waiting for reinforcements to continue. That was the end of 1860 Army road exploration in the area that year: Steen turned back and joined Smith, and other troops sent from Fort Dalles joined in the Indian campaign in southeastern Oregon that followed.

As for Steen's branch of the road from Harney Valley, Dixon concluded "that the country from Buck creek to the Des Chutes offers no serious obstacle to the construction of a very good wagon road with but little labor; and for an emigrant road, or for troops on scouting expeditions, it possesses superior advantages, such as plenty of grass, good pure water, and abundance of wood." Though Steen had not quite reached the Deschutes, or been able to follow Harney's plan to continue from the river across the Cascades to Eugene, their work, Dixon felt, had demonstrated that "the great sage desert, that has been so much dreaded by all previous travelers," could be avoided.[22]

The "sage desert" reputation of the country east of the Deschutes did not keep prospectors out. In June, three days after he left Smith, Colonel Steen was informed that a party of 62 armed men had been attacked by Indians on Captain Wallen's road, 40 miles northeast of Harney Lake.[23]

The Civil War intervened in official Army exploration, though it, too, failed to discourage gold hunters. Shortly, the trickle of adventurous miners washing back into the interior country from the Willamette Valley or north from California found paydirt in northeastern Oregon. So there was more travel, and there were more markets for meat and transport animals. Since the Regulars were busy elsewhere, Oregon Volunteers were recruited to patrol travel routes to eastern Oregon, to the Canyon City and Idaho mines. It was an enlightening experience of central Oregon, a country the Volunteers remembered for more than a few skirmishes and fruitless pursuit of disappearing Indians. The journals or recollections of Capt. John M. Drake and others are good testimony (like the movement from the Valley to east of the Cascades) that many were impressed with the cornucopias of trout in the streams, the air, the trees, the bunchgrass, the special blessing of cold clear water in the Deschutes and its tributaries. Even before problems with the Snake Indians were cleared away, enterprising men trailed in cattle to fatten for Idaho mining markets.

Guidance into the nearly trackless desert portrayed in printed information was provided by the Volunteers' personal experiences, along with those of drovers and packers, and there was some indirect help from previous Army exploration. Though all the military department records had been sent to Pacific Coast headquarters in San Francisco,[24] at least some of Louis Scholl's knowledge was transmitted on paper, and there were others like Cayuse George and Indian George who had worked with Army expeditions of 1859-60 who also worked with the Volunteers in the mid-1860s.[25] Such knowledge was reflected in the maps of John Bowen.[26]

By 1863 ex-miner Bowen was a second lieutenant in the First Oregon (Volunteer) Cavalry, and became Capt. George Currey's adjutant for the latter's 1864 "pacifying" expedition into southeastern Oregon.[27] Two known maps of his survive: from the information recorded on them, one from late 1864 and the second from 1865. He must have incorporated some data Louis Scholl sent along on a map to Gen. Benjamin Alvord, then in command of the Oregon military district, for there are names

165

that could only derive from the 1859 and 1860 Army expeditions into southeastern Oregon.[28] The 1865 Bowen map adds battle sites and dates for Indian-Volunteer skirmishes (some in central Oregon), traces of military movements of 1864 and 1865, military camps of those years, and some John Day and Idaho mining sites. A section of the Bowen 1865 map appears here (see fig. 93), part of the version in the Oregon State Archives (Sec. of State Records, Np-lp no. 23). Captain Drake, with his branch of the Oregon Volunteers' 1864 expeditions, used Scholl's names and map then and found the latter "very valuable and generally correct."[29]

The Bowen maps add only a little to the delineated knowledge of central Oregon.[30] By the mid and later 1860s that region was much more widely if not very specifically "known." Travel to mining areas in various parts of Idaho and then Nevada, added to Volunteer experiences, had spread the word that the Deschutes drainage was better watered than the "desert" east of it. Yet, despite searches, it was not a mining area, a matter reflected in the gaps in commercial maps, even those produced in the West or regionally. Alonzo Leland's 1863 "New Map of the Mining Region of Oregon and Washington Territory" (still including Idaho) presents exactly the area of its title. For the Deschutes drainage it simply has routes to the mines east from The Dalles: the Oregon Trail route across northern Oregon, a route southeast to the North Fork of the John Day, and one crossing southeast from the west side of the Deschutes to the Middle Fork of the John Day. There is nothing along Crooked River or south along the east side of the Deschutes.

Other "official" agency maps also lagged in presenting what was known of central Oregon, at least known by *some* people and recorded in *some* printed maps. A primary branch of officialdom, the general land office and its state branches, the surveyors general, had vast unknown western reaches to cope with, complicated by lack of sufficient money, skilled help, and conflicting problems of many kinds regarding policy and Indians. Recording public surveyors generally came after settlers or speculators, but by the 1860s some work began to be done in central Oregon, represented on the map of Oregon surveys up to that time only by a few townships around The Dalles.[31]

166

fig. 93

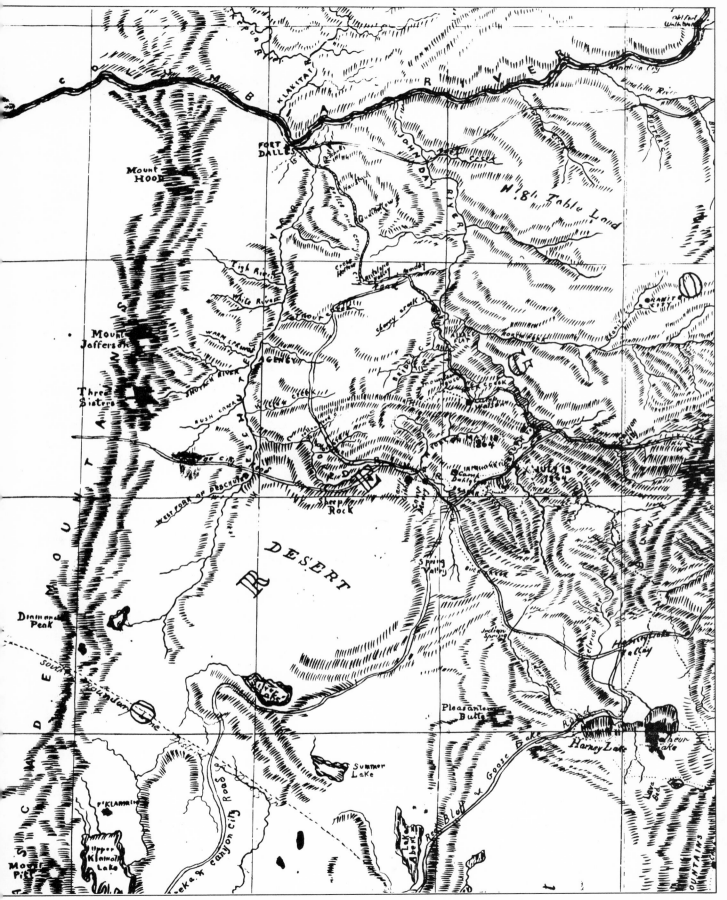

Fig. 93: A section of John Bowen's
1865 map (OHS Coll.).

Early in 1860 then Oregon Surveyor General W. W. Chapman, keeping in touch with Army exploration, was aware (as were other interested parties) of General Harney's plans to "establish a line of forts and open a road" toward Utah.[32] He wrote Harney on January 13, reporting that many in the Willamette Valley favored the establishment of a military post near the Deschutes intersection of the east-west Fort Boise-Middle Fork route to the Valley with the north-south Dalles-California route. "Last year," he said, "quite a settlement would have been made in the vicinity of the intersection of the roads referred to, and upon the head waters of the Des Chutes, had it been considered safe to do so."[33] Nor was it "safe" in 1860; the Indian attack on the civilian party Steen heard of, and that on Captain Smith with the subsequent Army campaign have been mentioned.

Tenaciously, the next year Surveyor General Bynon J. Pengra reported that "some valuable lands" were "known to exist in the Des Chutes valley and on the eastern slope of the Cascade range." Whether Indian hostility would allow official surveying or not, he added, "Many settlers from the Willamette valley are now absent in that section exploring, and from them, on their return, much valuable information is expected."[34]

Perhaps that hope and situation was the reason for a new version of the annual "Diagram of Public Surveys in Oregon" supplied by the state surveyor general's office in 1862, and published in the regular congressional documents.[35] It (see fig. 94) provides a good example of the qualifications and/or limitations of maps of the times from that office. Compared to its 1861 counterpart, Wheat comments, the 1862 Diagram was "entirely redrawn" and made "a very considerable geographical advance in the Deschutes Valley," naming western tributaries of the river "for the first time."[36] Yet what was an advance for the Oregon surveyor general had appeared in public print as early as the *Pacific Railroad Reports* (the Williamson-Abbot party, vol. 6, published in 1857) and again later in the maps of the 1859 and 1860 Army expeditions. Availability of the Railroad Report volume must have been limited, one of the continuing roadblocks to the circulation of official knowledge.

Most of the immigrant and other trails like Meek's, Applegate's, and Frémont's appear on the 1862 Diagram. But it does not include the trail

fig. 94

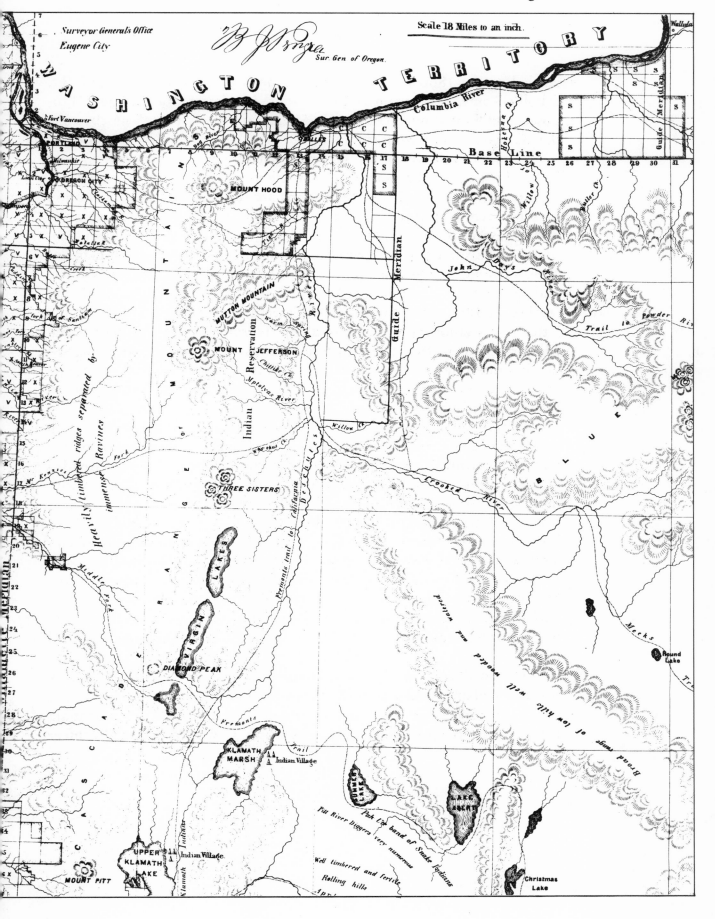

WASHINGTON   TERRITORY

Columbia River

Base Line

Fort Vancouver

PORTLAND

Milwaukie

OREGON CITY

Molalla

MOUNT HOOD

MUTTON MOUNTAIN

MOUNT JEFFERSON

Warm Spring

Indian Reservation

Chitike Ck.

Mptolyas River

THREE SISTERS

Heavily timbered ridges separated by immense Ravines

Fremonts trail to California

Des Chutes

John Days River

Guide Meridian

Willow Ck.

Wallula

Trail to Powder River

Crooked River

BLUE

Well timbered and fertile Rolling hills

Meeks Trail

Round Lake

LAKES

VIRGIN

DIAMOND PEAK

Fremonts Trail

KLAMATH MARSH

Indian Village

SUMMER LAKE

SILVER LAKE AGENCY

Pak Ute band of Snake Indians very numerous

Pitt River Diggers very numerous

Christmas Lake

UPPER KLAMATH LAKE

Indians

Indian Village

MOUNT PITT

CASCADE RANGE OF MOUNTAINS

labeled on the 1860 verison "Genl Harney's proposed Route" and "Lt. Scholl's Route," and again in 1863 (where it is less a straight line), "Proposed Emigrant Route." In the 1865 Diagram, that "route" has become the "Oregon Central Military Road."[37]

Another variation of the surveyor general's maps from year to year in the 1860s is in the number of townships surveyed or "proposed" to be surveyed. Both 1862 and 1865 maps are realistic in their presentation of a few central Oregon townships (near the Deschutes and Columbia) and an extension of the "guide meridian" south, then surveyed or proposed to be surveyed, compared to the wildly visionary survey plans of 1860—from the Columbia all the way south through the Deschutes valley and on to the California border. Even the additional planned surveys marked in 1863 along the John Day have disappeared by 1865, and the latter year's visionary surveys are along the route of the Oregon Central Military Road to the state's eastern boundary. In these years hope evidently quite often far exceeded the possible. The annual written reports from state surveyors general to the general land office had to convey the realities of what was actually surveyed.

In the mid-1860s roads, as always, were important, but now with an additional dimension. About this time Congress (in addition to the land-grants which "encouraged" the transcontinental railroads) provided grants, through the state, for so-called "military wagon roads." And with more knowledge, eastern Oregon land had become worth more speculation. The Oregon Central Military Road, even though it ran up the Middle Fork of the Willamette, when finally laid out was nowhere near Steen's 1860 exploration westward toward the Deschutes, instead turning south to the Klamath country. But one such "military" wagon road ran across the heart of the Deschutes country, from west to east, and on to Idaho; and another proceeded from The Dalles south along the lower Deschutes before turning east toward the John Day and Canyon City country and Idaho.

The road creating the most commotion for the Deschutes country was the Willamette Valley and Cascade Mountain Military Wagon Road, which proceeded east from Albany and Lebanon in the Valley via Santiam Pass, passing Black Butte on the south side, Camp Polk (the Volunteer

170

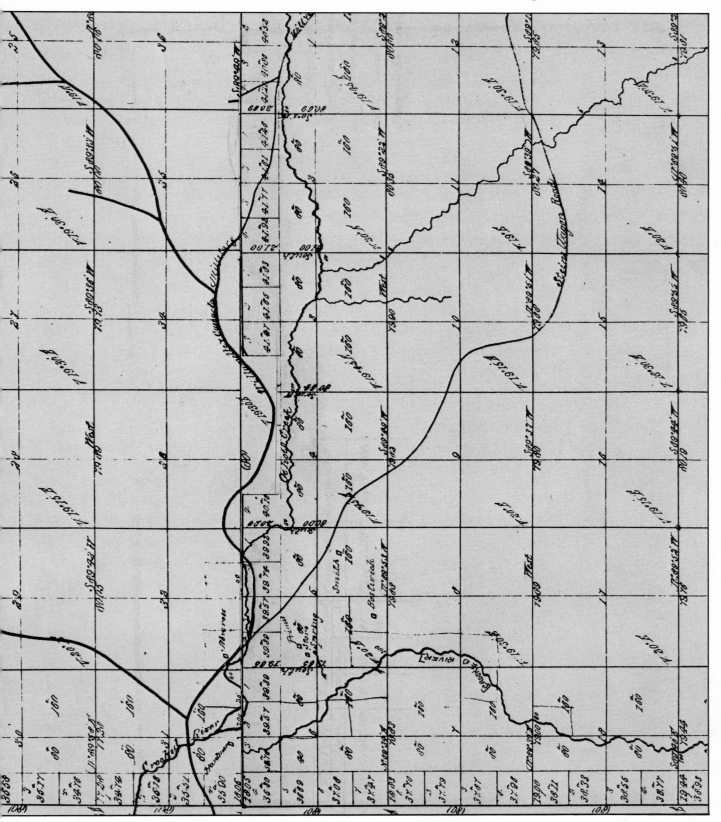

fig. 95

Fig. 95: This map shows part of the Willamette Valley and Cascade Mountain Military Wagon Road, including the Prineville area (note settlers' names on the left). (From T 14 and 15 S, R 16 E, surveyed July and August 1869 by McClurg and Meldrum, in Surveyor General's Office records.) (OHS Coll.)

military post of 1865-66 about three miles from later Sisters), then across the Deschutes and on east to "Carmichels," running between Gray Butte and Grizzly Butte on to Prineville, continuing along the Crooked River and eastward to Idaho (see fig. 95). The land granted to the wagon road company—alternate odd-numbered sections, three per mile, to be selected within six miles of the road (from Albany to the eastern boundary of the state)—and the land withdrawn from public entry so the company might select, led to congressional and state involvement and extensive court proceedings which continued for years. But the printed testimony gathered in the investigation of the road company's actual accomplishment documents much early settlement and "progress" of a part of central Oregon. Many early settlers in that region came from the Valley, from Linn, Lane, Polk and Marion counties. And many began as stock ranchers.

For example, in 1887 Prineville settler Elisha Barnes, long a prime mover to "investigate" the road company, testified that he had lived in Prineville for 20 years, that he was a farmer and stock raiser, and that he was familiar with the controversial road from Albany to Crooked River since 1866. The "bulk of supplies for settlers," he agreed, came in by way of the WV&CM road.[38] But Barnes, described by pro-road company sources as "one of those squatters on the company's land," complained that not only had there been little or no 'construction,' but "all of the odd sections of the public land lying within six miles of the entire line of the road, on either side," had been withdrawn from sale years before and still remained in that condition. Investigation would "confer a great favor on a grateful community, besides saving the government from being swindled out of a large amount of land that should be thrown open for settlement by actual settlers."[39] His son, George W. Barnes, who lived near Lebanon from 1861 to 1868 and came over the road in 1868, stated that the wagon road company had done no work from

> *the summit of Buck Mountain to Harney Valley,* [following] *an old Government road known as the "Stein* [Steen] *road"....*
> *From Camp Polk there was a faint trace of an old wagon-road, and it* [WV&CM] *followed this road down to Red Canon, and intersected this old road again this side the Des Chutes, and followed it to the lower end of Crooked River Valley, the old road*

fig. 96

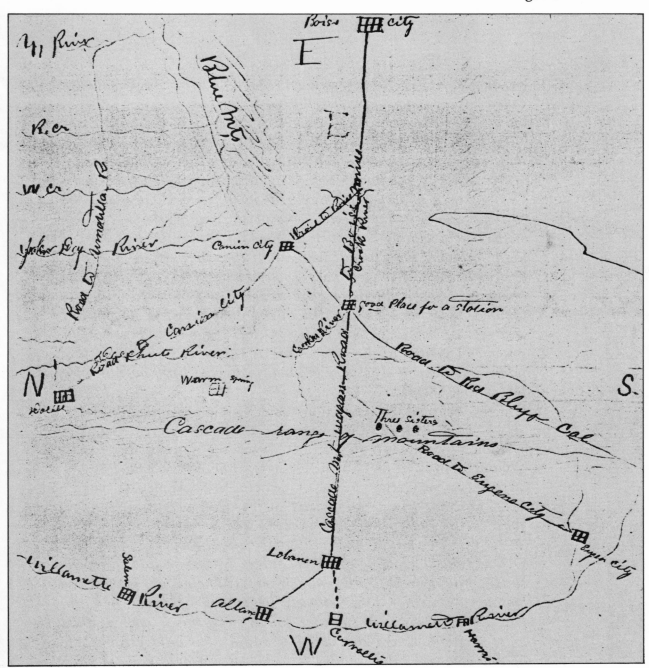

Fig. 96: A Volunteer military post was actually established on the Willamette Valley and Cascade Mountain Road about three miles from present Sisters. The post petitioned for in 1860 (see note 32) was requested again in 1865, by much the same people (road backers). Governor Gibbs forwarded the letter from L. G. Elkins (dated Lebanon, 27 July, to Colonel Currey, as mentioned in note 42), and Currey responded on 3 August (Gibbs Coll., OHS Mss 685), asking for a specific location "to designate the point where the Proposed Road is intended to cross the De Chutes River" so he could send troops. When he received this map with a letter from the "petitioners," dated 14 August (RG 393, NA, Army Commands, Dept. of Columbia, Letters Received, Box 5), he issued Special Order no. 10 (22 August 1865) from Fort Vancouver, ordering 40 men and Capt. Charles Lafollette to march for the "mouth of Crooked River by the DesChutes, crossing the Cascade Range. . .near the Three Sisters, on the new road" (Gibbs Coll.). Lafollette was to take "the necessary tools for erecting. . .huts for his Command to Winter in, at some suitable place." They built Camp Polk (OHS Coll.).

crossing Crooked River there and going north. . . . We always
called this old road a branch of the old Stein road.[40]
Roads in central Oregon could leave visible traces for a long time.

> Testifying for the company, Jason Wheeler of Linn County stated
> *that before this road was built [i.e., before 1865-67], there was*
> *not a settler in the whole section of the country between Cache*
> *Creek, which is about one hundred miles from Albany, and the*
> *eastern boundary of the State. . .except at Camp Harney. . . . The*
> *settlers were waiting with their wagons for the removal of the last*
> *log in crossing the Cascade Mountains that they might pour into*
> *the open country beyond, and in less than two years from the*
> *opening of the road, there were at least two hundred and fifty*
> *families had settled on the east of the mountains, along the line*
> *of the road entering the country by this wagon road. . . . This*
> *settlement related to the land as far as Upper Ochoco; from that*
> *point a settlement was very gradually effected little by little, for*
> *fear of the Indians.*[41]

Of course, the road "construction" and "completion" dates, 1865-68,
pretty well coincided with the years when the Snakes were being pacified,
with Paulina's death in 1867, and followed the military movements of
the Volunteers in 1864-66 and the Regulars, 1866-68[42] (see fig. 96).

Comments of Oregon Surveyor General E. S. Applegate dated September 15, 1868, reflect the interest of the time in central Oregon. He
reported "many settlements" that were "of recent exploration" in valleys
> *along the Deschutes, and in the Crooked River Country, the*
> *Ochoco and a number of other valleys in this section. . .here is*
> *certainly a fine field for the emmigrant [sic], he may in fact choose*
> *his own occupation to be either a herdsman or farmer, or both,*
> *it is almost needless to say that country like this is well adapted*
> *to raising sheep, and that wool is destined to be a great staple*
> *of this country. . .the country is well watered and in most parts*
> *is sufficiently supplied with timber, the climate here is preferred*
> *by a great many people to that of the Willamette, there is much*
> *more clear weather in the winter months, while in the summer*

fig. 97

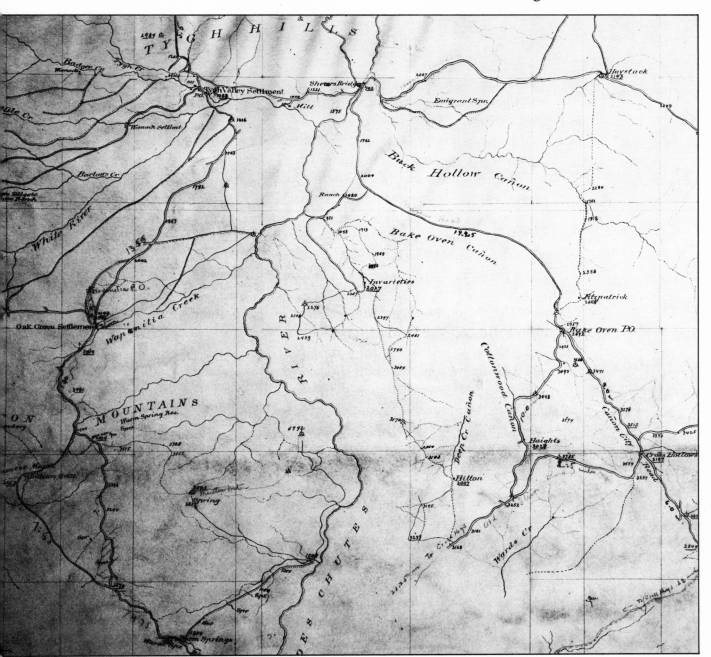

Fig. 97: Map section from RG 77 (1877-78), NA, U.S. 542/9, Pt. 2, Wheeler atlas sheet 20a. Officers in charge Lieuts. Geo. M. Wheeler, Thos. M. Symons, U.S.E., topographers Chas. P. Kahler and Anton Karl. (From U.S. Geological Surveys West of the 100th Meridian, under Lt. Geo. M. Wheeler) (OHS Coll.).

175

it is claimed there are more showers. . . . This is also a fine fruit country. Game is abundant. Elk, Deer, bear and Antelope abound, and Fowl, and Fish. To the man that is master of the fine art of trout Fishing that is certainly a paradise. All the streams abound in finest varieties of Trout. . .and in the lakes they are even more plentiful. about the head waters of Deschutes River there are some fine lakes. . .the water of which is as clear as crystal.[43]

Another advance in mapping a portion of central Oregon came a few years later with the Wheeler Survey, officially part of the "U.S. Geographical Surveys West of the 100th Meridian," one of the large Western survey projects,[44] and once more, a project of Army engineers. Lt. George M. Wheeler's vision covered the entire West, and work continued through the 1870s.[45] In the Deschutes country, some surveying was done in the summer of 1878. Though maps are available only for the section from Warm Springs north to the Columbia (see fig. 97), the survey parties moved along the full length of the river, traveling north from Fort Klamath toward The Dalles with horses and pack mules. Observations were difficult, as Lt. Thomas W. Symons reported, because of the "dense haze"— from fires often "built by the Indians for the purpose of driving game into places convenient for their slaughter," as well as from the "impalpable dust which rises from the desert."[46]

When Symons's party reached Diamond Peak September 14, he commented that the Deschutes drained "all the eastern watershed of the Cascades from the latitude 43° 10' to the Columbia, and by means of the Crooked River a large portion of the great interior basin of Central Oregon." Odell Lake, "the cradle of the West Fork of the Deschutes," he described as a "very wild, romantically-beautiful sheet of water," but there was no grass on its borders, and the fallen timber, dense thickets of brush and miry bogs made progress very slow. Finally they came to another lake, with "many acres of rich grass meadows" but no visible outlet. That night, camping beside lava bluffs with water marks 20 feet above them, they "heard strange rumblings in the vast pile."[47]

On September 22 they reached the ford at Farewell Bend where the river was "about 400 feet wide, running very swiftly over a rocky bottom,

fig. 98

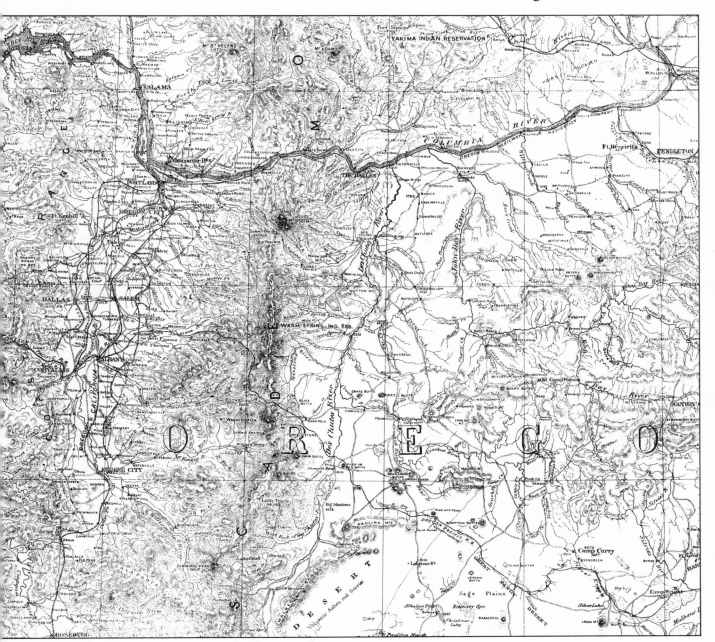

Fig. 98: "Map of the Department of the Columbia. . .compiled at the Engineer Office Dept. of the Columbia by Lieut. Thomas W. Symons, Corps of Engineers, assisted by Alfred Downing and C. C. Manning. . .3rd Edition revised to Dec. 1887. . .Compiled from. . .Map of the U.S. West of the Mississippi River. . .1879; U.S. Land Office Map of Oregon Washington and Idaho, ed. 1879; Land Office Surveys in Oregon and Washington for 1879 and 1880; Lieut. Robert H. Fletcher's Map of the Dept. of the Columbia, 1877; Surveys in the Field in 1878-79-80 by Lieut T. W. Symons; Surveys West of the 100th Meridian under Capt. Geo. M. Wheeler, 1878; The official records and maps in the Eng. Ofc. Dept. of the Columbia and from information furnished by the Railroad Companies of the Department and Officers of the Army" (OHS Coll.).

177

with a nearly uniform depth of about 2 feet." They moved on 27 miles to Crooked River "by the old emigrant road," across a rocky sagebrush desert scattered with junipers.

It was a great relief to emerge from the woods in which we had been traveling almost continuously for over a month, where our vision had been so contracted, out into the open country where the broad plains were spread out before us as far as the eye could reach. This plain. . .presents the most unmistakable evidence of having been covered with a flow of molten lava from the mountains to the west of us. It is easy to distinguish the wave fronts where the fiery mass was arrested in its course by the hardening of its elements, and which enables us to imagine these hundreds of square miles as once a seething, struggling, turbid lake of fire.

Impressively, as they were on their way to Warm Springs, a storm in the mountains

covered all the peaks with snow and cleared the atmosphere. . . . The great heights of Jefferson, the Three Sisters, Diamond Peak, and all the lesser mountains of the range, loomed up in their new and fresh robes of snow, pure white against the clear, blue sky, and their skirts of woodland showing folds and creases where sunny hill-slopes and shady canons branched from the parent mass. The exquisite beauty of this day's march will, I hope, never be obliterated from my memory.[48]

From the late 1870s Symons, with others, continued to play a part in the military maps of the Pacific Northwest, among the most useful of those times for general knowledge, and published in revised versions at least into the late 1890s. A section of the 1887 edition is reproduced here (see fig. 98), compiled not only from many military sources but from land office and railroad information. The rather grandiose plans for the "Oregon Pacific Railroad (constructing)" apparent on the map were not carried to actual construction beyond the Cascades. Railroads connecting the Deschutes region with other parts, except at the mouth of the river, arrived only at the turn of the century, and the earliest was on the east bank, south into Sherman County.[49]

For a decade or more assorted railroad plans and maneuvers were rumored. Then in 1910, less than a year after the Hill and Harriman lines had begun the actual battle of building up the Deschutes canyon into the interior, history presented another of its whimsical conjunctions. Louis Hill, president of the Great Northern Railway Company and son of Oregon Trunk owner James J. Hill, viewed the Deschutes country (and other parts of Oregon) for railroad prospects from the seat of a Studebaker "40,"[50] making one of the earliest automobile tours. Halley's Comet and Louis Hill arrived there together—and he was the bigger sensation.[51] No wonder—considering the Deschutes canyon battle and the "great plans."[52]

Louis Hill's trip with other railroad officials and publicity agents had a suitable guide (one was needed when there were no road signs) in southeastern Oregon rancher William Hanley, who took the party along the "old wagon roads." Even if this were on parts of "the best natural road" to the 19th century, it took some doing in the new horseless carriages. Newspaper reports in May, 1910 not only announced grandiose schemes for immigration to the region, but also for additional rail lines extending to the southeast, and to the south, east and west of the Cascades.[53] A special dispatch to the *Oregon Journal* dated Madras, May 11, reported that Hanley was "losing no opportunity for showing the noted travelers the country's great resources with its magnificent prospects of being a populous and fruitful empire."[54]

On that day, May 11, it was also announced that a St. Paul, Minnesota, corporation had "closed the largest land deal ever made in America, obtaining title to 800,000 acres in Central Oregon," including 660,000 acres of rich agricultural land "much of which will be improved under irrigation," and 140,000 acres containing "4,500,000,000 feet of standing pine, fir and cedar." The land was expected to "be peopled and settled at once. . . . President Louis W. Hill of the Great Northern railway, which proposes railway construction in the tract obtained by the St. Paul company, is now in Central Oregon on an inspection trip."[55]

The huge acreage, in a belt extending about 400 miles from Albany on the west to the Idaho line at Ontario (see fig. 99), was the extent of the Willamette Valley and Cascade Mountain Military Wagon Road

179

grant, which the report described as having "for 40 years. . .lain in idle uselessness, the owners refusing to sell any portion of it, except here and there a quarter section. . .and the fact that it has remained undeveloped has done much to retard development and keep out thousands of settlers who soon will be able to buy it for farming purposes."[56]

These large visions provided fertile ground for the new variety of maps which came after 1900: Forest Service maps, Bureau of Land Management maps, water resources maps, Geological Survey topographic maps and others. Among the most important to a growing number of individuals, and appearing about a decade later than the railroads in central Oregon, were the "road" maps which ultimately became maps of paved highways. Gradually a new personal freedom came with automobiles, and roads that changed from mud and dust to gravel and cinder and pavement allowed many more than visiting Army engineers to refresh their eyes and spirits.

That spring of 1910 there were other automobile "tourists" more directly involved with their travel method than Louis Hill exploring the Deschutes country. The "Oregon State Automobile Association" had appointed committees of five in each county that were "faithfully. . .putting up road signs all over the state on the principal thoroughfares" so that auto tourists within a year might be able to find their way anywhere in Oregon.[57] Though James J. Hill publicly criticized "automobiling as a pastime," G. F. Beck made an automobile touring map of Oregon "east of the Cascades" for the Portland Automobile Club.[58] Such help must have been welcome, for the Oregon State Highway Commission was not created by the legislature until 1913, and the first separate "State Highway Department's official Automobile Road Map" was not published until 1919 (see fig. 100).

The Deschutes country may not have had any paved roads, but a *Journal* report on May 31, 1910, mentioned agreements among "a number of homestead locating firms" in Bend for "building and clearing 30 miles of highway," which would "within a few weeks. . .make Bend the radial point of a 275-mile automobile road. . .the equal of which is not to be found any place in the state." As for the tourists trailing Hill south from The Dalles by auto, Simon Benson's party at Bend "hooked out three

fig. 99

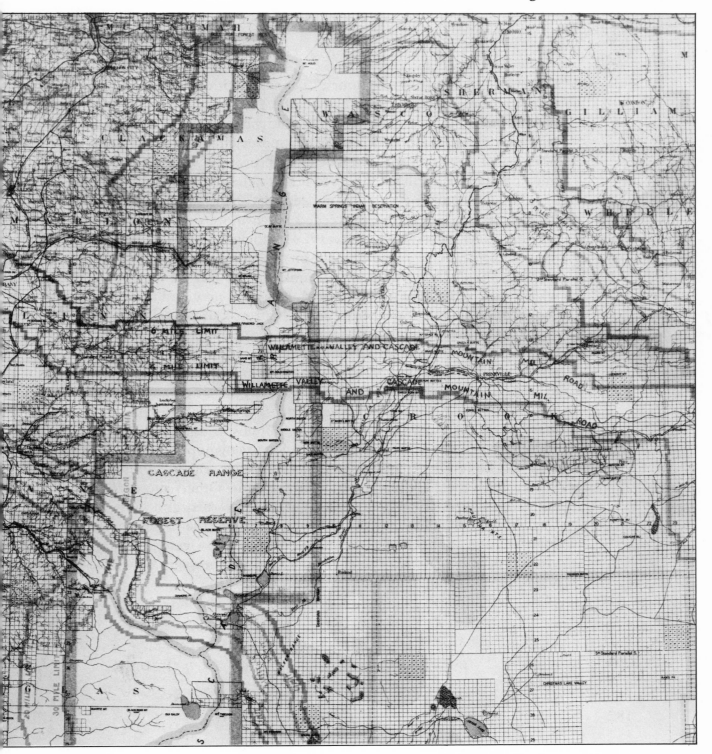

Fig. 99: This section of "Map of the State of Oregon, published in the Title Guarantee & Trust Co., compiled by Huber and Maxwell, civil engineers, 1904 (Bushong & Co. Map engravers, Portland)," shows six-mile limits of the WV&CM Military Road, running east through central Oregon, as well as part of the limits of The Dalles Military Road (top right) and the Oregon Central Military Road (lower left), all of which include some portion of the Deschutes country (OHS Coll.).

basketfuls [of trout] in two hours," probably with as much or more thrill than the Oregon Volunteers had in the 1860s. The Benson party, lost several times because there were no road signs, found the town "on the crest of a wonderful boom" and was "impressed with the marvelous possibilities of development. . . . The power project at Bend, the adjacent timber belts which will take years to market, the great irrigation project."[59]

Though coming events had indeed cast their shadows before, actual development in the region proceeded much more deliberately, or by fits and starts. As represented in the 1924 "official" roadmap, still no paved roads in central Oregon (pavement on the Columbia River Highway had reached The Dalles); the Oregon Trunk was no farther south than Bend, where it arrived in 1911, even though Prineville now had its own railroad connection; and the Southern Pacific Natron Cutoff over the Cascades was still uncompleted.

The 20th century had arrived in the Deschutes country—and the near poetry of traveling Army engineers had given way to the exuberance and panic of boom—and bust—development. Large-scale views were tempting, but there were also hopeful homesteaders and small developers among those who came to live and to strive with opposing aims, lagging irrigation and unaccustomed seasonal variations. Some saw hopes vanish under burdens too large to surmount—lack of knowledge, financial resources and the technical means to accomplish their dreams. Others succeeded; adapting to Deschutes country life, they survived, learned and grew in spirit. Over historic times the people of, in and through the "high and mighty" country have supplied the historic record in many guises. The material presented here is aimed to reflect parts of its message in words, maps and photographs.

182

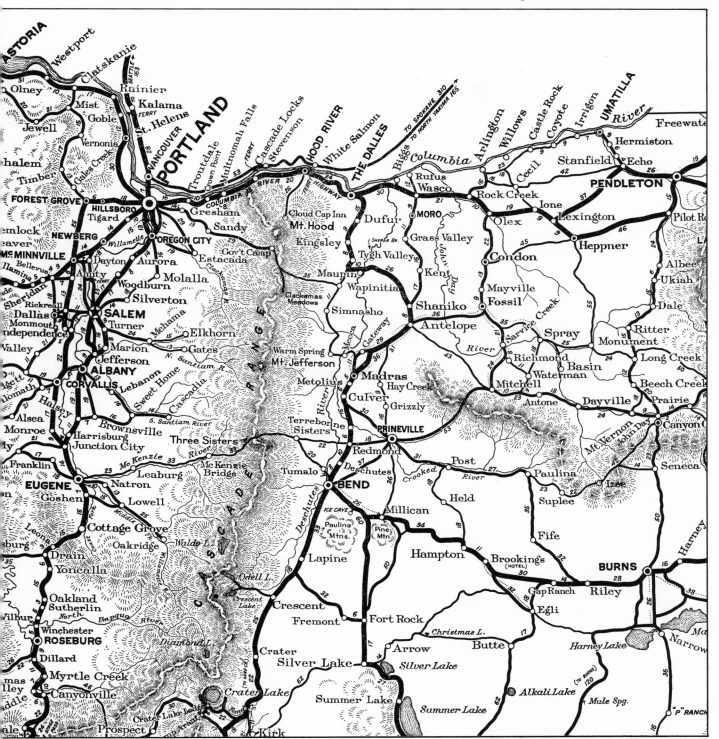

fig. 100

Fig. 100: By 1919, when this map was published, central Oregon's roads "proposed" and actual had undergone change in emphasis from the first "system of state roads" indicated in a small plate (no. 44) with the *1st Annual Report of the State Highway Engineer* (Salem, 1914). Amendments appear in the small map with the *Third Biennial Report of the State Highway Commission, 1917-1918*. The *Fourth Biennial Report, 1919-1920*, shows the first rock or gravel surfacing of the Deschutes country, on the road from Madras to some miles south of Bend, and from Redmond to Prineville (OHS Coll.).

fig. 101

Fig. 101: At the northern end of the High & Mighty country, in what Samuel Dicken refers to as the Deschutes Plateau, the great grain ranches of the area can be found. The rolling countryside maintains an even horizon, with stream eroded declivites breaking the surface. Dust devils work their way across the middle distance (Gifford photo, OHS Coll.).
Fig. 102: "Western slope of main ridge of Cascade Mountains from near Camp M," reads the caption for this illustration from *Reports of Explorations and Surveys to Ascertain the Most Practicable and Economical Route for a Railroad from the Mississippi River to the Pacific Ocean* (referred to as *Pacific Railroad Reports)* of 1854-56. (Figs. 103-106, and the frontispiece are from this *Report.)* This lithograph shows (from right) Mt. Washington, Three-Fingered Jack, Jefferson, and, over the latter's western shoulder, Mt. Hood (OHS Coll.).

Fig. 103: The rimrock land of the High & Mighty Deschutes country is captured here by one of the railroad survey artists. The legend reads: "Canon of Psuc-see-que Creek near Camp 41A." This is probably near the Deschutes canyon, for the explorers next moved across Shitake (they called it Chit-take) Creek which runs through present Warm Springs (OHS Coll.).

fig. 102

fig. 103

fig. 104
fig. 105

Fig. 104: A *Juniperus occidentalis* (western juniper) as drawn by railroad survey artist J. Young, and printed as a lithograph in the *Pacific Railroad Reports*. John S. Newberry, the expedition's botanist, states in the "Report upon the Botony of the Route": "We found it abundant on rocky and barren surfaces east of the Sierra Nevada and Cascade mountains from Pit river to the Columbia" (p. 59) (OHS Coll.).

Fig. 105: An *Abies williamsonii* (Williamson's spruce). Newberry wrote:

"This beautiful fir, one of the finest of the genus, was discovered by us on the summits of the Cascade mountains, latitude 44° north. It is the most alpine in its habit of all the firs; extending from the height of 6,000 feet to the line of perpetual snow. . . . I have given this beautiful tree the name of the commanding officer of the expedition" (p. 54) (OHS Coll.).

186

fig. 106

Fig. 106: Countless drawings appeared in the subsections of the *Pacific Railroad Reports*, those for geology, botany and zoology. Some were lithographs (see figs. 102-104 and the frontispiece), and many were line drawings. Dr. Newberry caught this white fish in the Deschutes, and he, or Dr. Charles Girard, named it for Lieutenant Williamson *(Coregonus williamsonii)* (p. 33) (OHS Coll.).

Fig. 107: The confluence of the Deschutes (foreground left) and Metolius rivers (upper right). Preliminary survey and road grading for the eventual construction of Round Butte Dam had taken place by the time of this photograph; some equipment floats in the straight section of the Deschutes (foreground). Today, the two wings of this canyon are filled with the waters of Lake Billy Chinook. Canadian Bench sits atop the canyon (background), and Metolius Bench overlooks the scene at the right (OHS Coll.).

Fig. 108: A part of Lake Billy Chinook, Jefferson County. The Deschutes River is on the left, Crooked River on the right. The isolated part of the Deschutes Plateau in the middle distance is called The Ship (see also fig. 23). Cove Palisades State Park is in the foreground (OHS Coll.).

187

fig. 107

188

fig. 108

189

fig. 109

fig. 110

190

fig. 111

Fig. 109: Early morning mists dissipate over the surface of Olallie Lake, revealing the reflection of Mt. Jefferson. The ridges in the background separate this lovely spot from equally picturesque Jefferson Park, which sits at the base of the mountain (Ray Atkeson photo).

Fig. 110: Just to the east of Lake Billy Chinook lies this flat plain. The checkered agricultural landscape has been provided by the irrigation projects of this area near Culver and Metolius. Part of Crooked River canyon shows to the left, and a section of rail line courses across the land (bottom right) (©Delano photo).

Fig. 111: Benjamin Gifford photograph of the junction of the Deschutes and Warm Springs rivers. The eastern boundary of the Warm Springs Reservation at this point runs down the middle of the Deschutes. Today, this section of that river provides quiet relief for summer rafting parties before the challenging rapids downriver on the way to Maupin (Gifford photo, OHS Coll.).

Fig. 112: One can almost hear the sound of the rapids below Benham Falls, and smell the pine woods on this 1909 summer day. In the distance are the Paulina Mountains (Gifford photo, OHS Coll.).

191

fig. 112

192

fig. 113

193

fig. 114

Shaniko Stages in Cow Canyon Oregon

fig. 115

194

A Typical Stage of Central Oregon

Summer 1911

fig. 116

Fig. 113: The grandeur of mature Ponderosa pine forest (and the absence of undergrowth) provides cathedral vistas, probably near present Sisters, about 1910. A black and white photograph cannot convey the complexities of color in the bark of these trees (Gifford photo, OHS Coll.).

Fig. 114: Rock-strewn Cow Canyon, now occupied by U.S. Highway 97, was a less attractive part of the Shaniko-Madras stage route (Bakowski photo, OHS Coll.).

Fig. 115: Before the railroads, freight wagons traveled south from the Columbia River east of the Deschutes through Sherman County to Grass Valley and Shaniko Flats, to Antelope, Madras or Hay Creek and Prineville. Part of the cargo here seems to be wagon wheels (OHS Coll.).

Fig. 116: "A Typical Stage of Central Oregon" reads this postcard, 1911. This six-horse stage carries eight persons (including the driver) and a goodly amount of baggage (Bakowski photo, OHS Coll.).

195

fig. 117

Shaniko Stages at
Madras, Ore

fig. 118

196

fig. 119

Fig. 117: B. B. Bakowski took many photographs around central Oregon, but he seemed especially enamored with horse-drawn vehicles. Here he records the Shaniko stage at a Madras hotel, 1910 (OHS Coll.).

Fig. 118: Backeoven station, Wasco County, was on The Dalles-Canyon City road. It appears that the smithy has stopped his work (bending tire irons for wagon wheels) so that he and his assistants might pose for this photograph (Silvertooth, OHS Coll.).

Fig. 119: Both battles and building took place in the canyon of the Deschutes (1910-11) as part of the railroad construction competition between the Oregon Trunk Railway (owned by James Hill) and the Des-chutes Railroad (backed by E. H. Harriman of the Union Pacific). The Oregon Trunk was built on the west bank, and the Deschutes worked up the east side of the river. These horsemen were bringing mail and emergency supplies to one of the engineering parties in 1909 (OHS Coll.).

Fig. 120: Prior to the actual construction of the railroads along the banks of the Deschutes, engineering parties had to survey the route to anticipate all problems and adjustments. This encampment served that purpose (OHS Coll.).

Fig. 121: Cuts on both banks of the river are visible at "Mile 51" of the 142 miles between the mouth of the Deschutes and the ultimate goal, Bend. Hundreds of workers were required to construct the roadbed; it was all horse and hand work. The party in the foreground may have been newly hired, for they carry clean bedrolls (OHS Coll.).

197

fig. 120

fig. 121

198

fig. 122

199

fig. 123

Fig. 122: The Oregon Trunk construction camp visible here (1911) was in the Deschutes canyon, probably just below Madras. About the time the tracks reached that town, the two railroads compromised, and agreed to use one line through the river canyon. The Oregon Trunk was the first into Bend—in late 1911, and trackage was completed as far south as Chemult in 1916, where the railhead remained until 1928, when the California connection was finished through the newly completed Southern Pacific Natron Cutoff over the Cascades.

Fig. 123: Construction gang works during the morning shift on the Oregon Trunk line's track on the west bank of the Deschutes (OHS Coll.). Fig. 124: Inexorably moving across the deep gorge of the Crooked River was this Oregon Trunk line bridge. Anchored in the rimrock, the two sides were closing in on each other, to overcome one of the major barriers between the Columbia and Bend (Kiser photo, OHS Coll.).

fig. 124

201

fig. 125

202

fig. 126

Fig. 125: This popular postcard photograph, one that indicated the Deschutes country's great pride in the completion of the Oregon Trunk's remarkable structure in September, 1911, records the "first train to cross Crooked River Bridge." The bridge spans the gorge at a point where it is only 340 ft. wide, but the railroad bed stands 320 ft. above the waters of the river (Hedlund photo, OHS Coll.).

Fig. 126: The competitive construction between Louis Hill's Oregon Trunk line and the railroad constructed by Harriman manifested itself in many ways, one of which was this crossing of the two railroads. Looking down a valley northeast of Madras, one can see the Harriman trackage crossing the canyon on this rather simply constructed trestle, while the Oregon Trunk line runs under it up the canyon. U.S. Highway 97 now runs through the valley (OHS Coll.).

fig. 127

Fig. 127: Two boxcars stand on a siding of the Oregon Trunk Railroad in the Deschutes canyon. The man on the right cliff surveys this mid-day scene, probably noting the cut for the Harriman rail line on the opposite bank (Kiser photo, OHS Coll.).

Fig. 128: Engine 702 of the Oregon Trunk line stands behind the dignitaries at the occasion of the railroad reaching Madras, "The Gateway to Central Oregon," 15 February 1911. The track layers, most of whom were now out of the picture, had moments before completed the track through the welcoming arch (Hedlund photo, OHS Coll.).

Fig. 129: Not all celebrations awaited the completion of the railroad. Bend filled its main street with celebrants when the 1909 announcement was made that a railroad would be constructed south from the Columbia, to this, the main city of the Deschutes country (OHS Coll.).

Fig. 130: James J. Hill, himself, booms railroad benefits in his speech at Bend during the golden spike ceremony there on 5 October 1911, when his Oregon Trunk reached that growing town (OHS Coll.).

Fig. 131: This may be part of the famous 1910 auto tour of the Deschutes country led by Louis Hill, the son of James J. Hill, when the group was scouting a route for the spur of the Great Northern Railway to work its way into the high central Oregon countryside. They pose in front of the Pilot Butte Inn (OHS Coll.).

fig. 128

fig. 129

205

fig. 130

fig. 131

206

fig. 132

207

fig. 133
fig. 134

Fig. 132: Emphasizing central Oregon attractions in this May, 1910 photo is Louis Hill (left), president of the Northern Pacific, then touring the region and describing "great plans" for developing the country. Well-known cattle rancher William Hanley (center) led the auto tour. The man at the right is probably Col. E. C. Leedy, N.P. immigration agent. The overhead banner celebrates James J. Hill (the region's "best friend") then pushing for the building of the Oregon Trunk Railroad up the Deschutes (Callvert album, OHS Coll.).

Fig. 133: Photographs like this one, with James J. Hill and Louis W. Hill, were part of their railroad's promotion. This 1915 shot was designed to be used by newspapers (OHS Coll.).

Fig. 134: Gloved Louis W. Hill snapping a picture in a lush, irrigated field near Bend. In 1910, when this photograph was taken, the railroad was talking of a campaign to attract thousands of settlers to the Deschutes region (OHS Coll.).

Fig. 135: An early road in the Deschutes country. The driver and his companion have stopped their auto to record this moment before paved roads made it easy for persons in the Willamette Valley to spend their weekends at the resorts of central Oregon (OHS Coll.).

Fig. 136: The *Bend Bulletin* of 5 May 1910 noted that the Madras Oil and Gas Co. was drilling for oil on the slope of Crook County's Grizzly Mountain. By May the well was 300 feet deep, expected to go to 3,000; it did not pan out (OHS Coll.).

fig. 135

fig. 136

fig. 137

fig. 138

fig. 139

Fig. 137: A slip-tongue "Big Wheel" (often referred to as a Michigan wheel, Wisconsin wheel or high wheel) carries a bundle or "turn" of logs under its axle. Generally these horse-drawn rigs were used to carry the logs to the temporary rails that connected with the main logging lines, which eventually carried the logs to the mills (OHS Coll.).

Fig. 138: A McGiffert Loader, perched over the rails, takes the logs from the big wheels and places them on the railroad flatcars, so that they might be moved to the mills at Bend. This is one of the many central Oregon pine logging operations of the Brooks-Scanlon Co. (OHS Coll.).

Fig. 139: Bend Co. sawmill. Located near present Columbia Park on the west side of the Deschutes in Bend, this small sawmill provided the wood to build the two larger firms, Brooks-Scanlon and Shevlin-Hixon; tractors moved the lumber over board roadways. Built in 1910, and enlarged in 1911, the mill burned to the ground in 1915, and was not rebuilt (OHS Coll.).

fig. 140

Fig. 140: Large circular saw used to cut lengths of lumber at the Shevlin-Hixon mill in Bend (OHS Coll.).
Fig. 141: Protected by this shed from both winter snow and summer sun, men sorted and graded lumber as it moved from the Brooks-Scanlon mill (OHS Coll.).

Fig. 142: Electric piler brings lumber up and over to man stacking in seasoning yard at the Shevlin-Hixon mill. These hollow stacks often stood 30-feet high (Prentis photo, OHS Coll.).

fig. 141

NO 3 SORTING LUMBER BROOKS - SCANLON MILL BEND ORE.

fig. 142

213

fig. 143

fig. 144

214

fig. 145
fig. 146

Fig. 143: The Shevlin-Hixon and Brooks-Scanlon mills faced each other across the Deschutes River at Bend. This aerial view of the former's operation shows the mill pond and the ramps carrying the logs into the mill. Behind are the seasoning yards, and behind the three smoking stacks can be seen one of the curing buildings (Brubaker photo, OHS Coll.).

Fig. 144: The Shevlin-Hixon mill closed its doors in 1951. By the time of the aerial photo, most of the buildings that had housed that major lumber operation were gone (the mill had occupied the far side of the Deschutes). The Brooks-Scanlon operation still continued, and in June, 1980, it was purchased by Diamond International (©Delano photo).

Fig. 145: A splendid male (note the dark markings on its head) California quail *(Lophortyz californicus)*. These flock-feeding birds range throughout the West, and are common in the Deschutes area (Joseph Van Wormer photo).

Fig. 146: A young golden eagle *(Aquila chrysaetos)* stands guard in its central Oregon nest; that this is an immature bird can be ascertained from the white feathers on its wings. An inhabitant of both the Cascades and the High Desert, this great bird feeds mostly on rodents (Joseph Van Wormer photo).

215

fig. 147

fig. 148

216

fig. 149
fig. 150

Fig. 147: Another Deschutes country inhabitant is this spritely Townsend's solitaire *(Myadestes townsendi),* a bird that is difficult to spot. It spends its summers in the forest and the winters in brushy areas. Part of the thrush family, the Townsend solitaire is often mistaken (at a distance) for a robin. The fly-catching bird nests on the ground (Joseph Van Wormer photo).

Fig. 148: One of the most ubiquitous birds in the High & Mighty country is the black-billed magpie *(Pica pica).* Magpies build extremely large nests, and share with two other species the distinction of being the only North American birds with tails longer than their bodies (Joseph Van Wormer photo).

Fig. 149: Common to the mountains of the Cascades is the Yellow-bellied marmot *(Marmota flaviventris)* (Joseph Van Wormer photo).

Fig. 150: Blacktail jackrabbit *(Lepus californicus).* These animals flourished after the introduction of grain growing in the Deschutes region. Their population grew so rapidly, that community-wide jackrabbit drives were required to rid the landscape of these crop-devouring animals (Joseph Van Wormer photo).

217

fig. 151

218

fig. 152

Fig. 151: Stately elk *(Cervus canaden-sis)* can be found in some of the high-land areas of the Deschutes country (Joseph Van Wormer photo).

Fig. 152: A Mule deer *(Odocoileus hemionus)* (Joseph Van Wormer photo).

fig. 153
fig. 154

fig. 155

220

fig. 156

Fig. 153: Mountain sheep rendered
by Oregon nature artist Harold
Cramer Smith.
Fig. 154: Often sighted in the rimrock
country of central Oregon are pere-
grine falcons *(Falco peregrinus).* One
of the swiftest flyers in North America, it preys on smaller birds (Harold
Cramer Smith).

Fig. 155: *Ursus americanas,* the black
bear, photographed by Joseph Van
Wormer, can be found in the foothills
of the Cascades.
Fig. 156: A group of pronghorn an-
telopes *(Antilocapra americana)*
gracefully run across the high, open
country of the Deschutes region
(Joseph Van Wormer photo).

fig. 157

Fig. 157: The year was 1943, and the influence of the World War II years can be seen with the M.P.'s jeep parked on the main street of Madras. The photo of this section of U.S. Highway 97 (known as "The Dalles-California Highway") was taken from the Madras ration board office (OHS Coll.).

Fig. 158: Today, the popularity of the Deschutes region as a resort or retirement area has brought many mobile homes to the landscape. This early group of trailers, at the Madras Green Spot Trailer Park, housed construction workers laboring on Round Butte Dam (OHS Coll.).

Fig. 159: Opening day for the high lakes fishing season, in May, 1958. Cars, trucks and trailers abound in this morning scene at the Hot Springs campground at East Lake. The *Oregon Journal* reported that 6,000 anglers filled both Paulina and East lakes that weekend (OHS Coll.).

fig. 158

fig. 159

223

fig. 160

fig. 161

fig. 162

Fig. 160: One of the most striking resorts in Oregon is Kah-Nee-Ta, owned by the Confederated Tribes of the Warm Springs Reservation (OHS Coll.).

Fig. 161: Mountain View Lodge at Sunriver, a highly successful and popular resort development south of Bend. With its own airstrip, golf course, amphitheater, and other recreational facilities, and its access to the great central Oregon outdoors, Sunriver attracts persons from all over America to the Deschutes country (Edmund Lee photo, OHS Coll.).

Fig. 162: In 1964 the *Oregon Journal* stated: "Wood-shingled roofs with wide overhang lend distinctive air to new buildings of Central Oregon College, blending with ponderosa pine and juniper trees on 160-acre Bend site and keeping out direct rays that sweep across from the scenic Cascades range to the west." The building shown here is the Library (Lindsay photo, OHS Coll.).

fig. 163

Fig. 163: Built in the mid-1950s by
the Bend Chamber of Commerce for
a Hollywood movie company, this log
fort stood near Benham Falls. It was
eventually torn down, but the structure was used by a number of television and motion picture organizations
(OHS Coll.).

fig. 164

Fig. 164: Bend, about 1905. At left
facing Wall Street are city hall (false
front), and The Bend Mercantile
Company—a Salem paper wrote in
1904 that it was "the largest business
firm in Bend and the first to be
started in that city." And in 1903 the
Bend Bulletin stated: "This will be
the most modern store and the most
complete stock of goods on the Deschutes river and Prineville prices will
rule" (24 July). Early version of the
Pilot Butte Inn stands in the foreground (OHS Coll.).

fig. 165

fig. 166

228

Freight and Express
arriving in
Bend, Ore

fig. 167

Scene in Bend Ore

Fig. 165: During Bend's 1909 Fourth of July celebration, horse races were run along the main street. Eager bettors and bystanders crane to see the results (OHS Coll.).

Fig. 166: Two modes of transportation park in front of the Bend post office, a six-horse, three-wagon rig, and a pioneer automobile (OHS Coll.).

Fig. 167: It is not known what the exact occasion was in this 1910 photograph, possibly the auto caravan of Louis Hill at the Pilot Butte Inn. But an occasion it was, for there were flags, an expectant crowd and a band (OHS Coll.).

229

fig. 168

Fig. 168: Bond Street, Bend, probably in the late 1910s. First National Bank building is the brick structure on the right. There were many restaurants; the Electric Lunch served chili con carne, and the Royal Cafe occupied the left end of the street, and, over the door of the building at the left, is the simple admonition—"Eat" (OHS Coll.).

Fig. 169: Long a distinctive architectural feature of Bend, the Pilot Butte Inn was dedicated in 1917, and leveled in 1973. A number of structures used the name, but this one was the best remembered (OHS Coll.).

Fig. 170: This interior view shows the Pilot Butte Inn's lobby, with its large stone fireplace and other early 20th-century amenities.

fig. 169

fig. 170

231

fig. 171

Fig. 171: American flags fly in this view of Bend's Wall Street, 1939. Bend was preparing to welcome engineering troops to nearby Camp Abbot. The *Oregon Journal* noted: "Bend residents have organized USO services, arranged housing, taken steps to provide adequate food supplies, and arranged transportation facilities for the soldiers coming to camp" (OHS Coll.).

Fig. 172: Bend and its important forest hinterlands and magnificent mountains can be seen in this 1960s air photo (Dept. of Trans., OHS Coll.).

fig. 172

233

fig. 173

Fig. 173: Two young women sit and
enjoy this rustic gazebo along the
shores of the Deschutes in Bend (OHS
Coll.).

5

DESCHUTES COUNTRY PINE LOGGING

Timber and transportation. Those were the two interlocked ingredients of central Oregon's developing economic base in the 20th century, together making possible enterprises that brought wealth to some and jobs to thousands.

The timber was ponderosa pine, an estimated 26 billion board feet of it,[1] in open forests on flat or gently sloping ground, waiting, seemingly, for someone to come and cut it. But getting to the trees was only a relatively easy first step; getting the trees—or more precisely the lumber made from them—to market was the difficulty. Central Oregon in 1900 was virtually isolated from the rest of the nation, including other parts of Oregon, as far as volume commercial transportation was concerned, and the exploitation of *Pinus ponderosa* would have to wait for a railroad.

The ponderosa pine is one of nature's striking trees. To a traveler crossing the Cascade Range from west to east, its distinctive appearance marks the descent into the arid country of the central Oregon plateau, with the ponderosa zone appearing a little below the true firs. Mature trees, 150 to 200 years old, grow to heights of 125 to 200 feet, with a diameter of two to five feet, and are easily recognized by their cinnamon bark formed in large elongated scale-like plates. The bark is black on younger trees.

Philip Cogswell, Jr.

The staple of central Oregon's lumber economy, the ponderosa pine has the greatest range of any commercially important tree in America and is logged in all western states. Its white to straw-colored wood is one of the soft-textured pine woods and is considered one of the most versatile woods produced in America, especially for fabricating into millwork (such as moulding and door and window frames), furniture and finished lumber. The tree was reported by the Lewis and Clark Expedition in 1805 and named by famed botanist David Douglas, whose own name was attached to the Douglas fir.

Even before the completion of a railroad to Bend in 1911 made large-scale lumber production commercially practical in central Oregon, the value of the region's pine forests had been recognized by potential mill operators and timber speculators willing to gamble on values increasing. By the mid-1890s, chunks of what had been public domain timberland were passing into private hands, a process that would come to a climax a decade later.

Details of how hundreds of thousands of acres of timberland were obtained by private interests are vague, and the information that has been passed down reflects a confusing variety of names, shifting ownerships and trades. It appears, however, that there were several methods by which timberland moved from public to private ownership, some completely legal and aboveboard, others ranging from questionable to deliberate fraud. Three-quarters of a century later, some present-day owners are vague as to the origins of their holdings, although within the timber industry it is generally maintained that shady deals played a relatively minor role in timber acquisitions with ouside estimates ascribing a higher percentage to fraudulent actions.

On September 28, 1893, at the urging of concerned organizations, President Grover Cleveland withdrew from the public domain what is now basically part of the Deschutes National Forest west of the Deschutes River.[2] The creation of what was then called the Cascade Range Forest Reserve gave the state of Oregon the right to claim lands outside of the reserve as an indemnity for sections 16 and 36 in each township within the reserve. The Act of Statehood had granted those sections to the state for school use.[3]

Those indemnity lands were then sold to private individuals. Robert Sawyer, owner of the *Bend Bulletin,* mentions some 56,000 acres being obtained by four firms—three buying 16,000 acres each and the fourth about 8,400—and indicates there were other acquisitions as well. Thousands of acres also had been granted by the federal government to encourage wagon road construction.

Other timberland had been legally obtained by settlers under various land laws intended to spur settlement and development of the West, including the Homestead Law of 1862 and especially the Timber and Stone Act of 1878. Some of these lands were later purchased by timber interests. The Timber and Stone Act, however, had what could be charitably referred to as a checkered history. Its key provision allowed settlers to purchase 160 acres of non-mineral land for $2.50 an acre in order to obtain timber and stone they needed for their ranches or farms.

In its early years, few settlers took advantage of the law because they needed little timber or stone they could not find otherwise, but as central Oregon's timber began to look commercially attractive, a timberland rush broke out in 1902 and droves of "entrymen," interested not in settling and improving but in filing and selling, came to the region from around the country, many having their way paid by the timber interests. At times, with the collusion of federal authorities, they conveniently ignored provisions of the law preventing transfer of title, turning their acquisitions over to their sponsors or other speculators. This activity continued until July 31, 1903, when President Theodore Roosevelt withdrew timberlands in the Deschutes area from entry under the Timber and Stone Act. In 1905, federal forest lands were placed under the jurisdiction of the Department of Agriculture, and in 1906, the region's first national forests were created.

Before they passed into obscurity, however, the Timber and Stone Act frauds, along with other simimlar fraudulent acquisition of timber in the Pacific Northwest, brought national attention to the region and provoked some inconclusive trials. The beneficiaries, however, emerged with their land, if not with unblemished reputations.

In retrospect, 75 years later, it is difficult to even guess what percentage of the land that entered private ownership did so by means of fraud.

Accounts indicate "hundreds" of persons came to the area expressly to take out timber claims. If there were 1,000 fraudulent claims of 160 acres each, that would account for 160,000 acres, a substantial portion certainly, but not, it appears, the majority of the privately owned timber.

The period 1902-07 was characterized by efforts of major investors, buying timberland wherever the price was acceptable. These individuals, partnerships and firms accumulated holdings measured in the tens of thousands of acres. Sawyer lists S. O. Johnson and associates, who comprised the Deschutes Lumber Co., ending up with scattered holdings of 60,000 acres. F. W. Gilchrist of Michigan, whose family would later start a mill and a town south of Bend, also began buying timberland about 1902, ending up with 85,000 acres. The Irvine Family Investment Co. obtained about 20,000 acres in 1905 from A. T. Bliss. Competition increased about 1906, with T. H. Shevlin (whose firm would start a huge mill in Bend 10 years later), Mueller Land & Timber Co., Scanlon Gipson Lumber Co. (forerunner of Brooks-Scanlon), Alworth-Washburn Co. and others, all seeking holdings.

Success, however, was not assured. Those early investors were gambling on the future; some went bankrupt, unable to recover their investments in an era when timberland could be bought but not commercially logged because of the lack of a railroad to carry the lumber to market. Accounts of transactions after 1900, in fact, sometimes give as the reason for an action—sudden logging, sale of land or establishment of a mill—the need to begin recovering on the investment in timber.

Much of the purchasing by speculators stopped with the financial panic of 1907-08, but the Bend Timber Co. bought the Irvine holdings and added another 15,000 acres, later selling to Shevlin-Hixon.

After land was purchased, another problem remained. Investors had bought lands when and where they could and often ended up with holdings scattered over a large area. Thus, the process began of land exchanges in order to consolidate holdings into economically usable units. A key figure in this process was John E. Ryan, part-owner and agent of the Deschutes Lumber Co., who in 1908 began working on an exchange plan that was accepted by owners in 1913. With that agreement and other exchanges blocking up ownerships, all that remained was for something

238

to be done with all that timber, but before that could be accomplished, somebody had to do something about a railroad.

It is difficult to realize now how isolated Bend was at the turn of the century. The only access was by stage, wagon or horseback either over the rugged Santiam Pass or across the desert. In 1908, for instance, S. O. Johnson traveling from Portland to Bend, went by train to Shaniko, took a stage to Prineville and stayed overnight. The next day he forded the Crooked River, and then proceeded on to Bend. More direct routes were blocked to wheeled vehicles by the deep river canyons and mountain slopes.[4]

Various efforts had been made to find a railroad route to the Bend area. In 1855, Henry L. Abbot and Robert S. Williamson of the Army Topographic Corps had explored the Deschutes country in search of a practical Pacific railroad route. They found the natural barriers "almost impassible" and offered little hope of the region ever developing.[5]

In 1871, plans were formulated to approach the region from a different direction—over the Santiam Pass. Colonel T. Egenton Hogg wanted to make Yaquina Bay Oregon's major port, envisioning as part of the plan an east-west railroad. He obtained control of the Willamette Valley and Cascade Mountain Wagon Road, using land-grants to float bonds in the East. Some railroad construction—mostly by Chinese laborers—was conducted in the Santiam Pass before the effort was abandoned.[6]

Finally, after several other ventures died in the planning stage, the Oregon Trunk Line was organized in Nevada on February 24, 1906. The route it planned to take, and for which it obtained a state charter, was from The Dalles up the Columbia River to the mouth of the Deschutes and then up the Deschutes and Willow Creek to Madras.[7]

The Oregon Trunk still was only a paper plan—like several planned central Oregon railroads before it—when John F. Stevens arrived in Portland and bought its stock and charter.[8] Stevens, one of America's most prominent engineers and a key figure in the construction of the Panama Canal, was representing James J. Hill, who controlled the Northern Pacific and Great Northern railroads. Hill, one of America's great railroad developers, was locked in fierce battle with Edward H. Harriman of the Union Pacific and Southern Pacific lines and had turned his eye towards

239

central Oregon in search of a route to the pine timber and agricultural lands and, incidentally, to match the Southern Pacific's western Oregon route from the Columbia to California.

Hill had dispatched Stevens with a well-funded checkbook to the region in 1909, and the engineer proceeded to make deal after deal with ranchers whose lands were needed for a railroad right-of-way.[9] Along with acquiring the Oregon Trunk, Hill also acquired the rights of the Central Oregon Railroad Co., which had plotted a route from Madras to Bend, including a crossing site over the Crooked River.

The announcement of Hill's plan for central Oregon prompted quick action by Harriman, and suddenly not one but two railroads were on their way up the Deschutes Canyon. Harriman obtained a charter for what he called the DesChutes Railroad (as the name was commonly spelled then), and gangs of workers began work on the two competing lines.

Thus, a fascinated Northwest was treated to the site of Harriman forces pushing rails up the east bank of the Deschutes while the Hill forces moved along the west bank. It was the last of the great railroad construction wars and also one of the last major railroad jobs done primarily by hand labor.[10] As the construction crews, comprising hundreds of men each, blasted and dug their way along, they also skirmished with each other, trying through physical harassment and by laying first claim to vital stretches to delay the opposition. Shots were reported fired back and forth, and reports also indicate such maneuvers as blowing up the opposition's powder supply, but it is possible the violence has been overemphasized in the interest of drama.

In the Warm Springs area, only one route through the canyon offered itself, and federal authorities solved the conflict by enforcing what was known as the Canyon Act, requiring the two lines to agree to joint use of an 11-mile stretch between North Junction and South Junction.

That agreement, signed on May 17, 1910, was expanded to give the Harriman line, which had ended at Culver, joint use of tracks the Oregon Trunk had been laying between Madras and Bend, and the DesChutes Co. through the next three decades gradually abandoned its hard-fought route in favor of sharing trackage with Oregon Trunk.

240

On October 5, 1911, James J. Hill came to Bend and drove the golden spike marking the completion of the route. Harriman had died the year before, bringing to an end the bitter personal rivalry and probably paving the way for the joint-usage agreements that had brought the abatement of the construction war. The death of his main competitor may also have been a factor in Hill's decision not to continue south to California with his line. Indeed, it was not until 1928, 12 years after Hill's death, that the extension through Klamath Falls to Bieber, California, and a link to the Western Pacific's line to San Francisco was achieved.

In retrospect, this collision of the two giants of American railroading appears to have been wasteful and unnecessary, involving personal pride as much as competitive advantage. But it did have one beneficial result: once a railroad began moving toward Bend, it moved along rapidly.

On May 10, 1915, the *Bend Bulletin* carried the announcement the region had been awaiting since the completion of the railroad: "Shevlin-Hixon Company Will Build in Bend." News accounts went on to say that the Minnesota-based company would locate its mill on the west bank of the Deschutes River, would process 80 million board feet of timber and employ about 500 men at an average wage of $3.00 per day.

Like the railroads, however, the big mills, when they came to Bend, came in pairs. On August 18, another banner headline announced: "The Brooks-Scanlon Will Build Here At Once." That company, also from Minnesota, would build a mill, almost a duplicate of the Shevlin-Hixon facility, on the east bank of the Deschutes. Bend would never be the same.

In 1910, the federal census listed 536 people in Bend with another 616 in "Deschutes," just to the north. By 1920, however, after the two big mills had begun operation, the Bend population had boomed to 5,414, a growth rate of about 1,000 percent and said to be the greatest percentage growth of any American city in that decade.[11]

It is intriguing to reflect on how decisions made in Minnesota affected Bend. It was in St. Paul that James J. Hill had his headquartes when he decided the time had come to build a railroad to Bend, and it was in Minnesota that both big mill owners were headquartered when they decided to process central Oregon timber. While the Minnesota connection might have been coincidence, it was characteristic of western states that the development of their natural resources would depend largely on the investment of eastern interests, which also receive a great deal of the profits.

Shevlin-Hixon and Brooks-Scanlon were not the first mills in the pine country, although they were and remained by far the largest. Timber had been cut into lumber for local use by a variety of small mills, generally situated close to the timber and shipping only a short distance. Early mills included the Mailing Mill on Willow Creek and the Durham Mill on Trout Creek as well as other small steam-powered mills.[12]

In Bend itself, the Pilot Butte Development Co. started what was called the Drake Mill on the Deschutes in 1901, making lumber for local consumption. John Steidl started the Steidl & Reed sawmill in 1903, but it was destroyed by fire in 1908.[13] Logs for these mills had been cut just south of Bend and were hauled to the mills stacked on horse-drawn wagons, some with massive iron wheels. Contemporary accounts indicate the Shevlin-Hixon site was donated by the Bend Co., which may have taken over one of the earlier mill sites.

Despite the earlier mills, it was the Brooks-Scanlon and Shevlin-Hixon operations that were to mark the development of the timber-oriented economy of central Oregon.

The Shevlin-Hixon operation was headed by Thomas L. Shevlin of Minneapolis, whose family had extensive timber interests in Minnesota when the decision was made to build a mill in Oregon. Shevlin, who had taken over the management of the family enterprises on the death of his father, T.H. Shevlin, in 1912, was nationally known as "Tom Shevlin of Yale" for his ability as a college football player.

"Considered to be one of the greatest ends that ever played foot ball, he was more than once selected by Walter Camp as an all-American star," the *Bend Bulletin* commented (May 12, 1915). "No one who ever saw him play will forget the ease with which he broke up interference, nor the incredible speed with which for a man of his weight, he went down the field at the kick-off or under a punt."

242   Shevlin's abilities were considered to have carried over into the lumber business, and the *Bulletin* reported: "Those who have had an opportunity

to observe his development in the lumber business assert that his grasp of the problems and his knowledge of its conditions will serve to place him at the head of the industry in the United States."[14]

That was not to be, however. On December 29, 1915, Tom Shevlin of Yale died of pneumonia in Minneapolis, only 32 years old, but the mill he had decided to locate in Bend was already under construction and due to begin operation shortly.

For the Bend enterprise, the Shevlin interests had been combined with financing from Frank P. Hixon, a La Crosse, Wisconsin, banker, who had been frequently involved with the Shevlin operations. On Tom Shevlin's death, Hixon became president of the firm and T. A. McCann, a cousin of Shevlin's, became manager of the company's western operations.[15]

The Brooks-Scanlon operation also was based in Minnesota and also was a family enterprise. The firm was incorporated in 1901 in Minneapolis, but had its origins in the decision 40 years earlier of Dr. Sheldon Brooks to build a grain elevator in Minneiska, Minnesota. Sheldon Brooks died in 1883, but his three sons, Lester, Dwight and Anson, operating as a partnership called Brooks Brothers, continued the family enterprise, by 1900 owning 30 grain elevators and lumber yards and taking an increasing interest in the lumber side of the business.

In 1893, Dwight Brooks, traveling to Brainerd, Minnesota, met M. J. "Joe" Scanlon, already at age 31 a figure in Minnesota timber circles. The two men decided to combine in a joint enterprise, and a year later, H. E. Gipson, another lumberman, joined the group and the Scanlon-Gipson Lumber Co. was formed, buying a mill at Cass Lake, Minnesota, in 1898. In 1901, the firm name was changed to Brooks-Scanlon Lumber Co.

Lester Brooks died in 1906, and Dwight Brooks, a conservative and shrewd businessman, and Joe Scanlon, a bold and imaginative one, were the major figures in the firm until their deaths in 1930, although Anson Brooks was considered a balancing influence.[16]

By the time Brooks-Scanlon announced it would build in Bend, the company had already built a large mill in Cloquet, Minnesota, and was planning what would be one of the world's largest paper mills in British

243

Columbia. Later, it would expand to Montana, the South and into Cuba.

Before deciding to build their Bend mills, both companies had first made sure they would have an adequate timber supply and had been working diligently for years to accumulate their holdings.

Shevlin, by the time its mill opened in 1916, had obtained about 200,000 acres of timber, generally to the south of Bend, in deals going back several years.[17] The *Bend Bulletin* translated this into two billion board feet and said that amount would last 25 years at a cutting rate of eighty million feet a year. The mill's production would more than double that amount and new purchases would be made, but the *Bulletin*'s guess on the duration of the mill turned out to be fairly accurate; it lasted about 34 years.

Tom Shevlin, himself, had worked for six months in the Bend area in 1906, which apparently stimulated his interest in the region and led to efforts through the next decade to obtain timber there. The Shevlin family had purchased timber in its own name in the area, and preparatory to building its mill, the firm purchased 35,000 acres of timberland from the Bend Co. Earlier that year, it had purchased the Deschutes Lumber Co. holdings south of Bend that S. O. Johnson and his associates had bought in the early 1900s from the A. J. Dwyer Land Co., which was in bankruptcy court.[18]

Joe Scanlon also had been a visitor to the Bend area in 1898, and had begun obtaining timber holdings then, 17 years before the decision would be announced to build a mill there. By the turn of the century, he had obtained 32,000 acres in two 16,000-acre tracts, and through the years the firm would continue increasing its holdings.

This far-sighted purchase of timber, far from current operations, marked many of the lumber manufacturers at the turn of the century. With their pattern of operating in one area until the timber was exhausted, they were always on the lookout for the next place to go, or even the place after the next place. It was central Oregon's fortune that it was to a degree the last place possible, and sensible operators eventually recognized that sustained-yield operations were necessary for continuation of their businesses.

244

The Shevlin-Hixon and Brooks-Scanlon mills were very similar facilities, facing each other across the common millpond behind a dam across the Deschutes River. The Shevlin-Hixon facility was the first to get under construction, with the dam and railroad spurs the first items of work. On June 2, 1915, the *Bulletin* observed that the pace of construction was "gladdening to all beholders."

On that date, less than a month after the Shevlin-Hixon announcement when the mill project was still in its early stages and before Brooks-Scanlon had even announced its project, the *Bulletin* took stock of developments, happily reporting that "the actual starting of work for the Shevlin-Hixon saw mill has caused a revival of business activity in Bend extending into all branches. Stores are being leased, real estate is changing hands, merchants are putting in new stocks. The impetus is being felt everywhere." The manager of the local power company reported installing 15 new electric meters the week before, and the phone company reported 15 new phone orders. (The article does not say if they were the same customers.)

Bend businessmen obviously knew what was good for their economy. They had, after all, subscribed more than $8,000—$1,000 more than was needed—to buy river property for Shevlin-Hixon, a forerunner of modern civic efforts to encourage new business by helping provide land.

The *Bulletin* also noted in passing the starting up of another sawmill in the Bend area. A Mr. Griffin started a mill east of Bend with a contract from Shevlin-Hixon to supply 20,000 ties for the firm's logging railroad as well as structural lumber. His mill employed 20 men, apparently the first millworkers actually to gain jobs from the Shevlin-Hixon project.[19]

Construction of the Brooks-Scanlon mill began early in October, 1915, with about 120 men working on the project. Logging operations began later that year in anticipation of the mill openings.

On March 3, 1916, the Shevlin-Hixon mill began operations, with the *Bulletin* proclaiming:

The dream, Bend, the sawmill and lumbering center of Central Oregon is now an actuality. . . . After years of "watchful waiting" by men who were possessed with faith that one day saws would

245

be humming and that the vast area of Deschutes timber would be cut and manufactured at Bend, they have today to take a 10-minute walk from the center of town to see that realization of their dreams.[20]

The Brooks-Scanlon mill cut its first board on April 22, 1916.

What kind of mills were these? Well, they were large, among the biggest pine mills in the country, and considered the most modern, although not radically different from their predecessors. Even today, their statistics are impressive. The Shevlin-Hixon facility, built by the experienced sawmill-building firm of Dion and Horscotte, had buildings covering 7.54 acres with the layout and equipment including an office, barn, pump house, engine and power house, sawmill building, machine shop, water tank, stacker, dry kiln, unstacker, planer, sash factory, box factory, two dry sheds, two locomotives, fifty logging cars, two skidders and one locomotive gear train. One dry shed covered 78,368 square feet, the mill's largest building, and the sawmill itself measured 54 by 180 feet.

The sawmill operated on two 10-hour shifts, with each shift having a capacity of 150,000 board feet of lumber a day. Some 65 percent of the cut was manufactured into sash, windows, box material or finished lumber, and some 35,000 lath would be manufactured daily as a by-product. The mill itself was steam operated, with the planer and auxiliary machinery electric powered.[21]

The Brooks-Scanlon mill operated much the same way, although initially it was a slightly smaller operation. Its sawmill was 54 by 150 feet.[22] Brooks-Scanlon apparently did not have a sash factory at first.

Once they began operation, the mills soon began to expand. Shevlin-Hixon constructed a "twin mill" to boost its sawmill capacity by one-third to about 110 million board feet a year, with the new facility starting operation October 5, 1916. Brooks-Scanlon added a second sawmill in Bend, "Mill B," upstream from the first, in 1923, giving it a capacity of 200 million board feet a year. That same year, Shevlin-Hixon added a third mill unit, increasing its cutting capacity by another 50 percent.[23]

The initial opening of the two big mills had apparently created something of a labor shortage in Bend, with each operation employing several hundred men. The *Bulletin* reported on September 27, 1916,

246

With the labor situation at the [Shevlin-Hixon] *mill now becoming brighter no difficulty in obtaining mill hands and loggers is expected. The situation which was acute a few weeks ago is much better, according to foremen of various parts of the plant. Men, who have been engaged on homesteads and in the harvest fields for several months, are now turning to steadier work for the fall and winter months, and it is expected that all the men necessary to run the plant to its capacity will be available.*

Employment by Shevlin-Hixon in the fall of 1916 was in the neighborhood of 600 men, or about Bend's total population only six years before. Of these, about 400 apparently were employed in the logging operations while the remainder worked at the plant site. These figures, however, are not exact, based on contemporary and imprecise newspaper articles. The Brooks-Scanlon operation probably employed about the same number. The impact on the Bend area, of course, was magnified several times by stores and other service businesses that accommodated the expanding economic base. Other wood products firms, such as a sash factory, also were founded.

Truly, if the coming of the railroad made Bend's transformation into a thriving city possible, it was the arrival of Shevlin-Hixon and Brooks-Scanlon that actually caused that transformation to take place.

The logging techniques used in the ponderosa pine country of central Oregon evolved over the precious century as the timber industry moved around the nation, seeking new trees and adapting to changing terrain. And over the coming decades after 1916, forest harvest and management practices would change even more.

Transporting logs to mills was one of the early problems of logging. The commercial timber industry had started in the early 1800s in Maine and New England floating logs on local rivers. Between 1840 and 1860, the industry shifted to the lake states, seeking Midwest timber and markets. The industry moved into the pine forests of the South and areas in the Northwest close to water between 1870 and 1880. And in 1881, John Dolbeer in Eureka, California, invented the donkey engine, making large-scale western logging economically advantageous.[24]

In central Oregon, the scarcity of rivers and the relatively flat, open terrain made railroads the obvious means of carrying logs from forest to mills for those with enough financial resources to build the railroads. Even as they were constructing their first mills, Brooks-Scanlon and Shevlin-Hixon were also laying their rails into the forests. Their logging operations began, in fact, before the mills were completed, so a backlog of logs would be on hand when mill operations began.

The technique of logging railroad construction had evolved from early systems built without technical engineering to utilization of fairly sophisticated technology. By the mid-1920s, some western universities were offering special courses on logging engineering and were granting degrees in the field.

Basically, a logging railroad consisted of a main line (which could be dozens of miles long) between the mill and the area of logging operations, with branches and spurs running to specific logging sites. The main line, costing as much as $50,000 a mile in the 1920s, would be the best engineered, longest lasting and most substantial, with the spurs, by contrast, laid down along routes that may well have been located virtually by eye by the logging superintendent. The most common rail in use weighed 60 pounds per yard and generally was "re-lay" rail—used rail purchased from standard railroads upgrading their trackage. Some main lines could be 50 miles long.

The construction of the spurs was a rapid process, and just as quick was their removal when the logging at a particular site was completed. Log bridges were used over creeks and gullies. The logs themselves were carried on flatcars that basically consisted of two "trucks" held together by a metal body or a wooden spar.[25]

While the railroad was the key to removing logs in the early days of central Oregon's pine logging, many men and skills were involved in the process of transforming a growing tree into a log on a railroad car.

The logging process might be considered to have started with the cruiser, a skilled timber expert who surveyed the standing trees and estimated the volume and quality of timber in a tract. He also determined the boundaries of the track with which he was concerned, measuring with compass and chain from known surveying points. Cruisers had their own distinctive marks with which they marked the boundary trees. The cruisers' reports were used to determine prices for timber tracts as they were bought and sold as well as for predicting the expectable volume of saw-logs when a logging site was laid out.

When a logging operation actually started, the logging superintendent, better known as the logging boss, was in charge, laying out the route of railroad spurs, deciding what trees would actually be cut and generally supervising the operations. One logging boss might be in charge of several adjacent sites or "sides."

The fallers cut the trees with ax and crosscut, sometimes referred to as a "misery whip." Working on contract, they were paid according to the amount they cut, and in at least some cases did not work fixed shifts. In the central Oregon forests, the trees were cut from ground level, without the high-climbers that first removed the upper parts of the tree in the Douglas fir forests west of the Cascades.

Once a tree was felled, it was bucked into 16-foot lengths by the fallers, the limbs removed, and then it was taken to the railroad loading area, which could be several thousand feet away.

The machine used to carry the logs was a remarkable-looking device variously called the Michigan wheel, Wisconsin wheel, big wheel, or most frequently, high wheel. As its different names indicate, the most noticeable features was the pair of wheels, 10 or 12 feet in diameter. Logs, usually in bundles called "turns," were suspended below the axle joining the wheels.

Logs were lifted—either by one end or completely off the ground—by an ingenious mechanism that typified the lever and gear arrangements farmers and loggers used to lift heavy weights in the days before more sophisticated lifting machines.

A sliding tongue extended forward from the wheel axle and a long lever struck upward toward the rear from a "wildcat" winch arrangement, with a cable connecting tongue to lever. With the tongue pushed back toward the wheels, loops were passed under the turn of logs. When horses began pulling, the tongue moved forward pulling down the lever which in turn cranked the wildcat enough to hoist at least one end off the ground. Old photographs indicate the entire bundle frequently was suspended under the high wheels.

The logs were then hauled or skidded to the loading site, where another marvelous machine—the McGiffert Loader—hoisted them onto the railroad flatcars. Unlike the high wheels, which had been developed to make the most of horse power, the McGiffert Loader made use of steam power. There were many models and improvements through the several decades the McGiffert Loader dominated the scene, but its basic character remained the same. Developed in the early 1900s, it looked something like a railroad steam crane on stilts, with a long boom used to hoist the logs. The loader could be moved from place to place on railroad wheels, but once it was in location, those wheels were lifted and the loader perched over the rails on long legs, its midsection high enough for strings of empty flatcars to be backed underneath. The loader or a locomotive would pull the cars from behind the loader one by one, positioning them under the boom so a load of logs could be hoisted on. Then, the string of cars would be advanced and the process would be repeated.

This brief description does not do justice to the impression the loader must have created, with its heavy metal bulk, its assembly of gears and drive shafts and its belching smoke and steam clouds from wood-fed fires. Adding their own local flair were the hook tenders, the men who rode the load of logs through the air to unfasten the lines once they were aboard.

Through the decades, many technological improvements came to the woods. The high wheels gained steel wheels and more sophisticated hoisting devices. They continued in use behind crawler tractors, when those machines came to the woods, but gradually evolved into the modern logging arch, with the lifting done by a tractor-mounted winch.

The McGiffert Loader continued to be improved, and from its basic concept, the Ledgerwood Skidder was developed. This was basically a McGiffert Loader with a vertical spar pole attached that could be used for yarding logs to the loading site, in some instances making the use of the high wheels unnecessary.[26]

On October 20, 1922, the *Bend Bulletin* reported that one of the most familiar logging aids was on the way out: "Horses, so long considered essential to the type of logging carried on in the pine forests of Central Oregon, are to vanish from that industry. . .as a result of the successful

250

use of the caterpillar tractor, it was indicated today by J. H. Meister, logging superintendent for the Shevlin-Hixon Co.," the paper said. It was an accurate prediction.

The company had been trying a gasoline-powered crawler tractor for two weeks, the paper added, and while Meister said the experiment was not complete, "he did declare. . .that the caterpillar can do anything that horses can do in the woods, and do it better. One tractor can do the work of three teams. . . . It can be used in any situation where horses can be used." The article added that the tractor "hauls bigger loads than horses formerly did, and hauls them easier and faster."

The gasoline tractors were followed in the 1930s and 1940s by diesel models, and while the high wheels were used behind them for a considerable period, they eventually disappeared as the attached logging arch was developed. In many cases, the tractor winch itself was used to lift the logs just clear enough that their ends did not dig into the dirt.

Another innovation began gaining some use in the 1930s—the powered saw. Various types of patented devices aimed at cutting trees faster and easier than the hand-operated crosscut saw had been developed, but were not universally accepted, in part because of their weight. One early cutter was basically a machine-powered crosscut blade.

The crosscut saw continued in general use, at least by some logging operations, until the chain saw came into its own in the late 1940s. In the Gilchrist operations, for instance, fallers began using chain saws about 1950.[27]

One of the celebrated byproducts of the logging railroad era was the often publicized town of Shevlin, which wandered about Deschutes, Lake and Klamath counties, moving every few years to be close to Shevlin-Hixon's logging operations. Shevlin was made to be moved. Its buildings—houses, stores, school, church and offices—were built in sections narrow enough to fit on railroad cars and mounted on skids. When moving day came, tractors towed the sections to a siding where they were lifted onto flatcars and carried to a new site, where the location of each building had been planned ahead of time.

Shevlin's moves attracted amused newspaper articles about the portable town, including the problems the shifts caused postal authorities,

251

voting registrars and mapmakers. In its heyday, Shevlin had a population of about 600, with about 150 homes, a church, post office, and school for about 60 children. The town had been brought to Oregon from Minnesota in 1921 and was originally located in Deschutes County. Not all of its moves may have been recorded, but it evidently moved into Lake County and then back to southern Deschutes County. In 1942, it moved to the Summit Stage area in Klamath County and in 1947, to a site near Chemult, 40 miles away. In 1952, its new owners, Brooks-Scanlon, moved it another 40 miles to a site south of Gilchrist. At the end of 1955, with the logging railroad era coming to an end, Shevlin met its demise, the post office was closed, its remaining families were moved to permanent homes, and the portable city was abandoned.

"Railroad logging rapidly is going out of style, and loggers have become family men who like to stay put," the *Oregonian* editorialized on January 8, 1956. "Shevlin was a symbol of an era now past in the timber industry, and its disappearance was inevitable. But it was fun to have this lively community here in Oregon, even if we never could be quite sure where it was, and we are sorry Shevlin is to be expunged forever from the Postal Guide." (Brooks-Scanlon ran its last trainload of logs in December, 1956.)

Shevlin, of course, was not the only logging camp, perhaps just the most unusual. But its character, with church, school and post office, does indicate an interesting characteristic of the central Oregon logger and millworker: he tended to be much more of a family man than the transient and rowdy contemporary west of the Cascades. Many central Oregon loggers and millworkers had been unsuccessful homesteaders, which might be one reason they tended to be more settled.

Along with the transition in logging machinery, the forests of central Oregon saw an equally, perhaps even more important change in logging practices. In the early days of central Oregon's timber industry, clearcutting, the harvest of all usable trees within an area, was common, with operations moving on after cutting through one location. In a larger sense, that technique is what brought the industry to Bend; central Oregon was the next place to go after the forests of New England, the Great Lake states and the South were depleted.

252

But from central Oregon, there was no place else to go in the United States, and in the 1940s the industry moved toward what is known as selective cutting—harvesting designated mature trees while leaving younger ones to reach their full growth potential. New state conservation laws also began regulating logging practices.

The trend toward selective cutting was aided in the 1940s by the improvement of log trucks, which, operating over relatively inexpensive logging roads, reduced the pressure for the centralized kind of logging the economics of railroad logging required. An additional benefit to the conservation of trees was the opening up of access to an owner's entire forest via logging roads, making it easier to control fires, fight insects and inventory the forest. The tree farm concept gained wide use, and by 1949, 842,717 acres in eastern Oregon were in certified tree farms, with the number growing to 1,091,387 by 1952.[28]

A companion trend, aiding the move toward sustained-yield management of private forests, was the change in the national forests from forest preserves to timber producers. The national forests had been created originally to stop what was perceived as the depredation by private interests and to protect some timber from private acquisition. The first step toward commercial timber management was an exchange policy, whereby private firms could trade their cutover land to the U.S. Forest Service in exchange for cutting rights in national forests. By about 1950, however, that policy had been abandoned and a system of selling tracts of timber by auction had been instituted.

As firms competed for timber, however, there was considerable friction between the Forest Service and private firms, with frequent complaints that not enough federal timber was being sold and that the cost of buying it was too high. Nevertheless, companies turned increasingly to the national forests for their timber—many relying almost entirely on federal forest sales—even if they complained about prices and policies as they did so.

Brooks-Scanlon and Shevlin-Hixon dominated the ponderosa pine industry in central Oregon, but by the mid-1930s, some other timber owners were starting their own mill operations around Bend. In some cases, stock companies and private individuals had purchased timber as an investment, but suffered as the Depression reduced the demand for lumber, some finding themselves land-rich but capital-poor. Liquidation of the timber was the obvious recourse, with mills operating near the timber stands, trucking the rough-cut lumber to Bend for reprocessing or shipment. In addition, other timber-related firms, making specialty products for instance, were in operation, adding their payrolls to the economy. Some small mills were established in the Sisters area.

In the shifting ownerships and partnerships were opportunities for individual entrepreneurs, and figures such as Sam Johnson (son of timber buying S. O. Johnson), C. E. Dant, Phil Dahl, Bert Peterson (Dahl's father-in-law) and Robert Wilson were there to take advantage of them. But Johnson estimated that the various small mills did not have a total production as great as one shift at Brooks-Scanlon or Shevlin-Hixon.

Mills also were started at Redmond, Madras and the Warm Springs Reservation, with the latter two eventually being acquired and combined by the Confederated Tribes of the Warm Springs Reservation.

As Brooks-Scanlon and Shevlin-Hixon had moved into Bend, the city of Prineville, with its approximately 1,000 residents, decided its problem in obtaining lumber mills was the same as Bend's had been. Prineville rested near the Ochoco forest lands, but had no railroad to haul the processed lumber to market. So, since the railroad lines were not interested in building to Prineville, Prineville decided to build its own railroad.

On March 28, 1916, city residents voted to establish the City of Prineville Railroad and bond themselves $100,000 for its construction. Eventually, the bonded indebtedness was to reach $385,000 and the actual cost much more, but the railroad, with 19 miles of track to the Oregon Trunk Railroad's Bend-The Dalles line, was completed in 1918.

The benefits of its railroad, however, came to Prineville somewhat more slowly than to Bend. Sawmills did not arrive for two decades, and the city defaulted on the bond interest and then refinanced its faltering railroad, which was beginning to look like a classic example of civic wishful thinking.

Finally, however, the mills did come. The Alexander-Yawkey mill, the city's first major mill, began operations in 1937 followed the next year by the Ochoco Lumber Co. A smaller mill, Pine Products Co., had started in 1936. Alexander-Yawkey, after an ownership exchange, eventually liquidated its timber holdings and closed, but Ochoco Lumber and Pine Products continued operation.

The history of Ochoco Lumber Co. gives some clues to the nature of the pine industry generally. It originated when investors in the Ochoco Timber Co. decided something had to be done to begin recovering some revenue from the 90,000 acres the company owned in the Ochoco region. The timber company was heavily financed and deeply in debt, with creditors demanding payment. Ochoco Timber had been formed in 1922 as an outgrowth of the Rogers Lumber Co., which had acquired military wagon road timber allotments.

The problem the company faced was the discovery in 1927 that it would cost so much to build a logging railroad into the Ochocos that there would be nothing left to finance construction of a mill. Thus, the timber sat for another 10 years while bond and note holders became increasingly restless and the Depression kept timber prices down. That also gave time for log trucks to be developed to make logging railroads unnecessary.

In 1937, the Ochoco Lumber Co. was formed with ownership divided among operating officers of the new firm and owners of the timber company, which had about 45,000 acres of timber left after refinancing their venture. In 1938, the mill was placed in operation and began cutting the timber company's holding under a 30-year contract. In 1946, Ochoco Lumber bought Ochoco Timber, and the same year the lumber mill began buying timber from the Ochoco National Forest. The firm gradually shifted the emphasis in log acquisition from its own lands to federally owned timber, using its holdings mostly as a backstop. This was a common trend after World War II all over central Oregon. The company's markets also changed. Originally, much of its production was shipped to "cut-up mills" along the Mississippi River to be made into moulding or other finished products, but increasingly similar enterprises were started in central Oregon and began buying its supply of local pine.

Also in Prineville, John Hudspeth, an entrepreneur from Oklahoma, established a mill in the early 1940s as part of his developing pine lumber and ranching empire. Later, Louisiana-Pacific Corp. and Consolidated

255

Pine would come to the city as well, giving the Prineville area a total annual potential production of about 135 million board feet of lumber.[30]

Hudspeth, a native of Arkansas, had come to Oregon with a load of portable sawmill equipment and started a small pine mill at Mitchell, meanwhile buying as much land as he could. Eventually, he was to accumulate more than 1.3 million acres for his timber and ranching operations, with major mills in John Day and Colorado as well as Prineville, making him one of the larger pine lumber producers.[31]

For the city of Prineville and its hard-pressed railroad, the developing timber business in the late 1930s finally fulfilled the expectations the civic visionaries had held out two decades earlier when the railroad construction was approved. The railroad began making money off shipments of pine lumber, began paying off its indebtedness and survived some financial setbacks after World War II, when a strike and a fire at the Alexander-Yawkey mill temporarily slowed shipments. By the late 1940s, it was returning money to city coffers, dramatically lowering the city tax rate to one of the lowest levels of any municipality in the Northwest; for a while, in fact, Prineville had no municipal tax levy.

Pine was the big revenue producer for the railroad. In 1949, the railroad handled 8,203 loaded cars of which 6,649 were pine,[32] the others primarily agricultural commodities. About the same time, the railroad switched to diesel equipment—replacing its two steam locomotives—for its twice-a-day train run from Prineville to the mainline junction. In 1950, the railroad shipped out 7,936 cars of timber to help supply the post-war housing construction, and the city—with four large and eight smaller mills in the vicinity—laid undocumented claim to being the largest shipping center for pine lumber in the United States.[33]

Thus, while it went through some worrisome times before its builders' expectations were fulfilled, the Prineville railroad ended up as a double-edged asset, not only making the area's timber industry possible but making a profit for the city as well.

While other central Oregon towns waited for the arrival of the timber industry, one came with it. Gilchrist, about 45 miles south of Bend, started and remained a company town, operated in conjunction with the Gilchrist Timber Co.'s mill there.

The Gilchrist mill began operating in 1938, but its Oregon origins went back 36 years earlier when Michigan lumberman Frank William Gilchrist began purchasing timberland in the La Pine area between Bend and Klamath Falls. Gilchrist was looking ahead; Michigan timber was running out, and he was reserving supplies for the future. First, the Gilchrist company would operate a mill in Laurel, Mississippi, but Gilchrist's timber buyer Frank Dushau kept coming to La Pine to increase holdings in the area.

By 1937, the mill at Laurel was out of timber, and it was time to begin cutting the 85,000 acres that had been accumulated in Oregon, and F. W. Gilchrist, grandson of Frank William of Michigan, came to Oregon to start a new mill.

Once again, however, as in Bend and Prineville, there was need for a railroad to get the processed lumber to market. Gilchrist solved this problem by building a short line, the Klamath Northern Railroad, 11 miles to link with the new Southern Pacific line that ran from Eugene over the Cascade Range (the Natron Cutoff) to Klamath Falls. Also in 1937, a dam across the Little Deschutes River formed the millpond, and the site was cleared for the mill that would be completed the following year. Coming with Gilchrist from Laurel were 25 or 30 persons, mostly supervisory personnel, who lived in the company town along with many of the firm's 250 other employees.

For its first dozen years of operation, Gilchrist logged only on its own land, clearcutting until about 1943 and then moving to a system of selective cutting. In the early 1950s, it began buying Forest Service timber, and within a few years was buying as much federal timber as it was cutting on company lands. After about 1970, about 80 percent of the firm's timber was from federal land, with Gilchrist's own timberland being managed on a sustained-yield basis. Like other medium-sized mills (average annual production 40-50 million board feet), Gilchrist did not use logging railroads, relying on crawler tractors and trucks to move the logs through the woods.[34]

From the beginning of central Oregon's pine industry, competition in sales of finished products has appeared to take a back seat to competition for available timber. This was especially true of Bend's two giants;

almost from their beginnings in 1916, it had been wondered how long Brooks-Scanlon and Shevlin-Hixon could sustain their enormous production. At their peak, with several head rigs and triple shifts, the firms were cutting a total of about 500 million board feet a year, with work forces of nearly 1,000 persons each. Obviously, the closure of either mill would be a severe economic blow.

Pessimists had only to look at other parts of the country—New England, the Great Lake states, the South—to see the inevitable consequences of over-cutting in mill closures, although the South was eventually to achieve a renewal of lumber activity with a third growth of pine. Even with federal timber becoming available after World War II, supply problems remained, with an allowable cut in the Deschutes National Forest of 138 million board feet not matching either mill's production.[35]

It had long been anticipated that one of the two big pine mills eventually would have to close in order to maintain a stable timber supply for the other, and from the 1930s on, the threat of such a closure worried investors and restricted development in Bend because of the fears of the economic setback a mill closure would bring.[36]

On November 21, 1950, the long-expected and feared announcement came. Shevlin-Hixon sold its entire central Oregon holdings—timber, mills and equipment—to Brooks-Scanlon, with the Shevlin-Hixon operation to be ended and about 850 persons to lose their jobs.

The formal announcement of the sale noted that for several years both companies had become increasingly concerned about the impact that would be felt when one or both ceased operations because of the lack of timber. It also said that because of heavy cutting to meet war and post-war demands, Shevlin-Hixon faced exhaustion of its timber reserves within about three years. The purchase price was not revealed, but revenue stamps indicate it reached several million dollars.

Shevlin-Hixon cut its final trees on December 9, 1950, in northern Klamath County. On December 23, 73-year-old J. N. Mahoney, who had been employed by the firm since 1914, tears streaming down his face according to newspaper account, stepped into the sawyer's box and moved the last log through the mill he had watched go into operation 34 years before. A blast on the mill whistle signalled that the company had ended production.[37] In early March, 1951, the last load of lumber was shipped from the mill site.

For Shevlin-Hixon, the closure of the Bend mill marked the end of an empire that once spread from the Minnesota woods to the South, into Canada and Oregon. The company dissolved after a half century in the lumber business.[38] For Brooks-Scanlon, the purchase meant the continuation of operation and the expansion of its operating base.

For Bend, the loss of the Shevlin-Hixon mill was an economic setback, but one the city withstood more easily than had been expected as an increase in tourist travel and presence of other wood products firms helped ease the job loss. Timber and transportation had given the city an economic base that even the loss of one of its biggest payrolls could not permanently damage.

In June, 1980, Brooks-Scanlon—still owning 230,000 acres of timberland and employing 1,000 persons—ceased to exist as an independent corporation, merging with the giant Diamond International Corporation to become one of Diamond's operating divisions. The $103 million transaction was one of the largest in Oregon's corporate history.

DESCHUTES COUNTRY: RECENT TIMES

The Deschutes country, or that portion of it which lies roughly 2,500 feet or more above sea level, has for many years occupied an unusual place in the thoughts of Oregonians. It is where, judging from their comments, most of them would like to live, or to visit frequently and for extended periods.

That is the first and strongest impression gained by a new resident of the area. Friends from other parts of the state are likely to congratulate him. "I'd like to live there myself," the friend is likely to say, "if I thought I could make a living. Maybe I'll move there when I'm ready to retire."

Oregonians are no more given to this type of idle talk than anyone else. But an inordinate number of them make statements like that about the Deschutes country, extending from Madras to Bend and beyond on the south, west to Camp Sherman and east to Prineville.

A surprising number of them do move to that small-yet-large part of the state which lies in the Deschutes River's upper watershed on the immediate east side of the Cascade summit. Or they vacation there regularly. Or they acquire property for vacation campsites, or buy or build a "second home" in one of the proliferation of real estate developments that have covered the area during the past 20 years.

Robert Chandler

Today's part-year resident often considers himself part of something new. He sees the development of the second home as something unique in recent years. But the Deschutes country has housed part-time residents for more years than we have recorded its history. The cave dwellers at Fort Rock 9,000 years ago were not, strictly speaking, a part of the history of the Deschutes region, since Fort Rock is not in the Deschutes River's watershed. But the findings in those caves suggest that the earliest families in this region of harsh winters were visitors, not full-time residents.

The pre-Lewis and Clark Indians who frequented the upper Deschutes country in the summer and early fall had a well-established pattern, and were the first regularly to use the high country as a second home. They came to hunt for deer and to collect roots and berries. When the fall nights grew cold they returned to their winter homes along the Columbia River near the Dalles and the river's rich salmon runs.

The first recorded white visitors to the area used its natural resources similarly, trappers and explorers connected with the Northwest's fur trade. They were followed by graziers, who used the free forest and desert range for cattle, sheep and horses.

Not too much later came the vacationers and part-time residents. The period between the late spring wheat harvest and fall planting was vacation time for Oregon's wheat ranchers. So many of them came regularly to the banks of the Metolius River in what was to become Jefferson County that the principal settlement in the area acquired the name of Camp Sherman, after Sherman County where they and their families spent the rest of the year.

Even then some residents thought that for the quantity of available resources, the area was becoming overpopulated. (From today's perspective the problem seems not to have been great; Crook County, which then included what was to become Crook, Jefferson and Deschutes counties, contained fewer than 4,000 persons at the turn of the century.) The land resource used at the time, uncultivated animal forage, was certainly severely limited.

Expressions of concern about overpopulation were few in those days; they have multiplied manyfold since. The 1978 elections were the first in which serious contenders for local public office sought voter support for strong no-growth policies.

The recent substantial criticism of the area's growth has been expressed simplistically: Is the entire area to be covered with roofs and asphalt? Are there soon to be so many new residents that earlier arrivals and visitors will lose the magnificent isolation that attracted the attention of at least some of them?

No doubt some of the isolation is gone, and more will go in the years ahead. This seems likely to happen to small towns and cities everywhere, as young persons return to the countryside their parents and grandparents left for larger cities a generation or two ago.

But since 1970, it has been happening to the central part of Oregon at a faster rate than any other section of the state. Growth rates for both permanent and part-time residents have outstripped every prediction, reasonable or absurd.

Is the concern that the Deschutes country will become wall-to-wall with people justifiable? It is widespread, as anyone who talks to any number of people can tell you. But is this likely to happen? By some definitions it already has happened, of course. Families that bought five acres for a vacation home a few years ago seldom gave much thought to the idea that someone else might buy the adjoining five acres. Those who early on purchased a lot at Sunriver or Black Butte Ranch, or one of the less posh developments, have been in some cases disappointed because others have bought and built upon adjacent lots.

But if those persons who wished for isolation had realized how strong was that old "I'd like to live there myself, someday" feeling, they could not have realistically expected to find it. And contrary to the belief of some, most new and part-time residents of the area are Oregonians, not from some Los Angeles or San Diego suburb.

Those who come for any reason other than the pursuit of solitude have little reason to fear the effects of an increase in population. More than 80 percent of the land in Deschutes County, for example, is in public ownership and almost certainly will remain so. Crook and Jefferson counties had only about one resident for each 160 acres at the time of the

1970 census, and like Deschutes have huge quantities of their areas in public ownership.

And, those who think the recent spate of growth will continue for an indefinite period probably are wrong, else by the time the 2010 census figures are gathered, the three counties in Deschutes country would contain half of the state's population.

The story of these three counties' population growth is one of boomers and promoters, of rapid growth alternating with somnolence, even decline. There is no reason to believe this pattern will not be repeated in the years to come.

The boomers and promoters were not among the earliest arrivals, of course. No irrigation developer accompanied Ogden or Wyeth. No subdivision signs sprang up immediately in the tracks of Frémont and Sheridan. Not until the early days of the present century can we record the arrival of those who saw a marketable resource in trees, water and scenery.

The catalyst that allowed the first promoters to operate effectively was the arrival of the railroad in Bend, in 1911. The railroad brought with it, for the first time, a larger-than-local market for lumber and farm products. Combined with low-priced land, the railroad made the area irresistible to farm pioneers.

Towns were platted with abandon. Maps drawn then showed water from the Deschutes River and its tributaries irrigating almost every square foot of the area. Alexander M. Drake, who platted Bend, even established a park on the banks of the Deschutes River—three-fourths of a century later, it still delights residents and visitors.

And the promoters promoted. George Palmer Putnam, who later was to return east to his family's publishing business, wrote from Bend for anyone who would publish his writings, declaring that the soil was good, the water cheap, the markets nearby. America's Last Frontier was in the Deschutes country waiting for the taking.

Putnam was practical as well as visionary. He spent much of his time in Salem, where he successfully lobbied to split off Oregon's two last-formed counties, Deschutes and Jefferson, from the vast area that, prior to 1914, was Crook County.

His desires to see the country grow, and in particular to see Deschutes County formed, were not without self-interest. A major source of revenue for small newspapers of the day were land notices, published in the county seat newspaper as part of the homesteading process. The formation of Deschutes County, with Bend as its county seat, alone nearly guaranteed the continued financial health of Putnam's *Bend Bulletin*.

The rapid growth of the area's population (relative to earlier figures) in what was roughly the second quarter of the 20th century was due for the most part to increasing use of the area's natural resources. As was the case in most of the Pacific Northwest, large amounts of government-owned stumpage became available for sale. During that time Bend, with two major sawmills—Brooks-Scanlon, Inc. and the Shevlin-Hixon Company—milled more pine lumber than any city in the world. There were half a dozen smaller mills in and near Sisters. Timber harvests in the Ochoco National Forest led to a boom in Prineville, at least in part made possible because the city owned a railroad, enabling it to ship products to main transcontinental lines.

Timber, and the cutting and milling of it, brought the first large influx of new residents to the area. By 1950, however, the primary manufacture of lumber had reached a mature stage, and, as mills increased production in the face of largely static supplies of raw materials, it became obvious some mills would close in the years ahead.

First to go was the Shevlin-Hixon Company, which sold its central Oregon operations to Brooks-Scanlon. The immediate effect on Bend, headquarters for both companies, was devastating. Half its basic industrial payroll vanished overnight, due to a decision made in Minneapolis, which few Bend-area residents had realized was imminent.

There had been warnings, of course. A former chief of the U.S. Forest Service, testifying before a congressional committee studying a sustained-yield unit act, predicted that Bend would become a "timber ghost town," a statement that drew little praise from Deschutes country residents.

The immediate effect of the closure of one of the two big mills in Bend was to halt population growth of the city and its immediate surrounding area. But something came along, as always appears to happen, to take the edge off the shock.

That was the growth of the lumber re-manufacturing industry, the business of making little pieces of wood out of larger ones, and of making large ones out of small ones. Plywood and veneer plants were established in Redmond and Madras. Moulding plants operated in Bend, Redmond and Prineville. A particle board plant was built in Bend.

Between them they picked up the employment slack, and rather quickly. The demand placed on local sawmills increased. By the end of the third quarter of the century some sawmills occasionally hauled logs from distances of up to 200 miles to have on hand sufficient raw materials.

The other main development of the mid-century was the completion of water storage facilities on the Deschutes and Crooked rivers, and the consequent opening of large acreages for the production of irrigated crops. Large dryland wheat ranches in the Madras area were turned into family-sized farms for the production of grass seed, potatoes, mint and alfalfa.

The fall potato crop attracted large numbers of migratory workers. Even then there were not enough hands to complete the harvests. Schools took mid-fall vacations so youngsters could assist. There were also plenty of summer jobs in the hayfields.

And then the agricultural revolution of the 1960s hit the Deschutes country as it did everywhere else in the United States. Changes in processing practices did away with the jobs in the hay and potato fields. Often it became uneconomic to operate small farms; owners sold out to neighbors and left, or turned to part-time farming, their incomes augmented by jobs in basic or service industries in nearby towns.

Farming in the area had been difficult at best from the earliest times. With limited rainfall and a short growing season, dryland farmers were at the mercy of the weather. The development of water resources was not easy, particularly around Bend where rock outcroppings and loose soil made it difficult to distribute water. The change in some types of farming meant the Deschutes country no longer could compete. Commercial dairies, once a major source of income to the area, disappeared by 1975.

But still the new residents came.

266 The earlier generation already on hand was baffled by some of the new arrivals: Some of the men had longer hair than many of the women.

Some of them settled in mini-communes, half-a-dozen couples in a large old house or two smaller ones. Many participated in a variety of alternative lifestyles.

They came, too, without visible means of support, they did not appear in response to a labor shortage in the high country; unemployment rates remained steady, and among the state's highest, for several years. They came without jobs, but with faith that eventually they would find or create gainful employment.

And their faith was justified somehow. Sometimes there seemed to be as many real estate salesmen as loggers. The national trend toward growth of service industry employment was evident locally: there were more motel maids than cowboys.

Some of the new arrivals took up crafts, with varying degrees of success. The women who made curtains were matched by men who took up furniture making. It seemed that for everyone who worked in a lumber mill there was someone offering to build a house, or part of one. Some came with poorly developed ideas and few skills. But some gained reputation and clients from all over the West Coast, like one young man who developed a thriving business building roll-top desks.

Some came to retire, and the over-65 population of the Deschutes country increased more quickly than that of the state or nation as a whole. Some who came to retire found themselves bored, or under-financed for their hoped-for leisure. These retirees took up a variety of activities. Furniture refinishers proliferated, as did repairmen and tinkerers. Some found themselves taking up new endeavors, and some of those endeavors grew to be full-time-plus careers.

But the majority of the newcomers followed the usual line of activities. The number of doctors on the staff of the Bend hospital increased by a factor of six over the 25 years between 1953 and 1978. The number of restaurants, franchised and independent, grew by a similar factor during the same years. The number of lawyers grew more rapidly than legal activity in the high country's court system.

The newcomers were not all professionals or entrepreneurs. Some, through necessity or choice, engaged in a variety of manual or service jobs. They did so with little regard, it seemed, to their backgrounds, which

267

varied as much as their appearance. Holders of Ph.D. degrees and high school dropouts both undertook a variety of manual labor.

Local government swelled in response to foreseen or imagined needs, as it did elsewhere in the state. The federal bureaucracy grew as rapidly in the Deschutes country as it did anywhere in the nation.

And though casual visitors may not have noticed it, the newcomers engaged in a wide variety of leisure-time activities. The number of golf holes available to residents and visitors more than tripled between 1960 and 1970. The number of tennis courts increased by a larger percentage. Residents who once looked askance at walkers grew accustomed to seeing runners along the streets and roads and in the parks.

The continued development of the ski area on The Bachelor (often incorrectly called Mt. Bachelor or Bachelor Butte) attracted students to the fledgling Central Oregon Community College as well as short-term visitors to the resorts. Motels, once nearly empty from November until April, filled up on winter weekends as skiers arrived. Local residents also took up skiing with a vengeance.

During the summer, residents and visitors used public lands for camping. Light trucks became a favored method of transportation, many of them equipped with extra tops to afford camping accommodations ranging from modest to luxurious. Vacationers also crowded natural and man-made lakes. Fishermen and water skiers, neither too willingly, shared the water. Canoers and speedboat drivers kept a wary eye out for one another. Many pick-up trucks and station wagons came equipped with four-wheel drive. During summer weekends their owners prowled the forest and desert. During the winter the desert remained a favorite, and substantial number of vehicles hauled trailers that carried snowmobiles.

The high-powered off-road vehicles, plus the boats capable of speeds in excess of 25 miles per hour, plus the snowmobiles, brought on the first major recreation-user conflicts on the vast quantity of public lands in the Deschutes country. The hunter, rockhound, birdwatcher or naturalist was irked when his activity was disturbed by an off-road vehicle, roaring and spitting out dust and smoke as it bounced up a hill. The fisherman enjoying a lazy afternoon on a lake was angered when a fast boat rocked him, or a propeller cut his line. The cross-country skier, seeking solitude on the edges of a wilderness area, hated to hear a snowmobile approaching, sounding like a chain saw or motorboat gone crazy.

Not all of those irked or angered were residents; a number were casual or regular visitors. Some, and a few organizations to which they belonged, became decidedly unpopular as they attempted to reduce activities to which they objected. Two major Oregon political figures found their margins slipping in the high country when they took up the cudgels against off-road wheeled vehicles and snowmobiles. Presumably their losses in the Deschutes country were offset by their gains in Portland and its suburbs, in Salem and in Eugene.

The newcomers for whom were developed the major resorts, from Kah-Nee-Ta on the Warm Springs Indian Reservation to Sunriver, and for whom were built the growing numbers of second homes, from Black Butte Ranch to A-frames beside a ditch where water flowed only part of the year, caused the second large boom in the high country's history to date.

The second boom was unlike the first in one major respect. The first fed off the development of natural resources, timber, water, farmlands and grazing lands. The second fed off construction of new facilities— mostly residences—and the growth of service industries.

There were as many experts on the extent of the second boom as there were speculators on the origins of the new permanent or part-time residents and their activities once they arrived. Without the sobering influence of an annual official census, dozens of guesses were published each year on the number of the new arrivals.

Their arrival was obvious. Old establishments grew, and new ones sprang up. School population, particularly in Bend, Sisters and Redmond, grew rapidly, when all across the nation it leveled off or declined. Traffic lights sprouted from the corners, in an attempt to create at least some flow along major thoroughfares. Aircraft passengers arriving after dark were amazed at the number of yard lights gleaming from dusk to dawn in areas where 20 years ago no one had lived.

Some foresaw boom-without-end, an increase in population until the area's privately owned land was filled with homes and the air with smoke produced by their occupants' possessions. Some who predicted such

269

growth wore rosy glasses; others wore the blackest tints available. For there was less and less agreement on the value of growth. Once they themselves were on board, some apparently thought, it was time to pull up the gangplank. This view ran directly counter to those of individuals in a variety of activities who felt their own continued prosperity depended upon a constantly increasing population. Central Oregonians are no different than other persons in one respect; for a lot of them their most sensitive nerve is the one directly under their pocketbook.

Many guessers put recent growth at a rate that if extrapolated would double the population of Deschutes County each six or seven years. More conservative estimates still put the increase at a rate that would double the population each twelve to fifteen years. But no matter which of these estimates of recent population increase one accepts, the area's growth seems unlikely to continue indefinitely at this rapid rate.

More likely, there will be a slowdown at some time in the fairly near future, a slowdown which will allow the area to catch up on local construction; the building of things like streets and schools has lagged behind population growth in the past few years. (The start of the slowdown seemed apparent in various 1979-80 indices.)

It is beyond belief that the bubble of expansion of the last decade can continue indefinitely, simply because there are not enough marketable resources to sustain this kind of growth. Most recently it has fed on construction; for it to continue, it must have some basic industrial foundation.

Such a foundation is going to be difficult to establish. Additional water supplies for agriculture or major industries can only be developed through an extensive and expensive conservation program, which would require the lining of miles and miles of leaky ditches with concrete. For an area that produces crops at the low end of the current range of monetary values such conservation programs are too expensive. High-value crops never will become common in the high country; the climate is too severe for avocados.

Nor is the major forest resource—contained in the Deschutes and Ochoco national forests and on the Warm Springs Indian Reservation—capable of much expansion. Large infusions of funds for silvicultural prac-

270

tices would increase the yields of those forests. No national administration seems likely to propose such budgets, however, and no Congress appears likely to approve them. Present output from the area's lumber mills, then, is likely to remain stable, or even decline, in the years ahead. A cutback in log production is more likely to mean fewer, rather than more or larger, sawmills.

It is no more likely that the amount of lumber going to the area's re-manufacturing plants will increase. Mills in the Deschutes country already are unable fully to supply the demand of local secondary manufacturing plants. As old-growth timber continues to be cut more rapidly than it grows, availability of the kind of stock desired by re-manufacturers is more likely to decrease than increase.

There are other industrial plants in the area that are not dependent for raw materials on the products of the high country's farms and forests, and not dependent upon the area's small but growing population for their market. But their number is not likely to increase rapidly. Only those whose final product is relatively expensive can afford to haul raw materials across mountain ranges for manufacture and send finished goods back across the same ranges to markets.

That does not mean, however, that the Deschutes country will not remain a pleasant place to live, one which many Oregonians keep in the backs of their minds as an eventual residence. Most of the qualities that have attracted people to the eastern slope of the Cascades will continue to exist. With each passing year this isolation that has been both the attraction to some and a drawback to others becomes less of a reality. While most social amenities—from water systems to education systems to medical care—now are present, those not immediately at hand are available a few hours away.

That means the high country will continue to be what present and would-be residents and regular visitors most desire. The air is clean, and climatic conditions refresh it constantly. The mountains are still visible in the mornings, with their white caps sticking up into the clouds or the blue sky. The open spaces will remain, although not as open and free of the signs of mankind as they were 50 or fewer years ago. The magnificent forests still will be there, for those who make a living from them as well as for those who simply want to be in them or look at them or listen to the wind sighing through the pines. The high country will survive and will continue to attract man, even if in surviving it undergoes a more-than-gradual change.

NOTES

INTRODUCTION

1. U.S., Congress, State Executive Document 78, *Reports of Explorations and Surveys to Ascertain the Most Practicable and Economical Route for a Railroad from the Mississippi River to the Pacific Ocean* (commonly cited as *Pacific Railroad Reports*), vol. 6, pt. 2, pp. 40-41, 32nd Cong., 2nd sess., 1854-55 (Serial 763).

2. Essie Maguire's original letters are located in the A. R. Bowman Memorial Museum (Prineville), and have been transcribed by Irene Helms and Donna Clark. They will be published by the Oregon Historical Society.

PIONEERS OF DESCHUTES COUNTRY

1. John Gray, "Trip Across the Cascades, 1859," in *Oregon Democrat* (Albany), 10 January 1860.

2. *Before the Indian Claims Commission* (Docket No. 198), *The Confederated Tribes of the Warm Springs Reservation in Oregon* v. *The United States of America,* "Petitioner's Proposed Findings of Fact and Conclusions of Law—Value and Brief," pp. 76, 78, 79; Keith and Donna Clark, eds., *Daring Donald McKay, or The Last War Trail of the Modocs* (Portland, 1971), pp. 4, 5, 22, 23, 116.

3.　Diary of John F. Noble, 18-19 May 1864, OHS Mss. 1000. John M. Drake wrote in his diary, 6 June 1864: "Poor old fellow: he has fought his last fight, and now sleeps his last sleep. He was the noblest Indian I ever knew, and approached something near the ideal of the Indian character." See Priscilla Knuth, ed., "Cavalry in the Indian Country, 1864," *Oregon Historical Quarterly* (hereafter, *OHQ*) 65 (1964), pp. 48-49; also *An Illustrated History of Central Oregon* (Spokane, 1905), p. 703. (Hereafter cited as *HCO*.)

4.　John Charles Frémont, *Memoirs of My Life* (Chicago, 1886), pp. 287, 410, 411, 413, 424; Zephyrin Englhardt, *Santa Barbara Mission* (San Francisco, 1923), pp. 272-75.

5.　*HCO*, pp. 710, 713.

6.　Treaty with the Tribes of Middle Oregon, 1855, in Charles J. Kappler, comp., *Indian Affairs, Laws and Treaties,* vol. 2 (Washington, D.C., 1904), p. 714.

7.　Hamil to Warm Springs Indian Agent William Logan, 30 June 1862, in *Report of the Commissioner of Indian Affairs for the Year 1862* (Washington, D.C., G.P.O., 1863), pp. 291-92.

8.　Reaves to Huntington, 30 October 1865, and Letter no. 83, 6 December 1865, in Oregon Superintendency of Indian Affairs (hereafter cited as OSIA) Records, 1847-73, Letters Received, National Archives Microfilm 2 (hereafter, NA M-2), roll 22.

9.　Warm Springs Indian Agent John Smith to Huntington, 31 December 1866, in OSIA Records, Letters Received, NA M-2, roll 23.

10.　Oregon Superintendent of Indian Affairs A. B. Meacham to Maj. Gen. George Crook, 1 May 1870, in OSIA Records, Letters Sent, NA M-2, roll 10.

11.　Indian Census Rolls, 1888-1940, NA M-595, roll 635. Early census reports list his name as Kwi-uh-pum-ma, but in 1890 it is given as Lee Quehpama.

12.　Luther S. Cressman (Dept. of Anthropology, University of Oregon) to authors, 19 May 1971, states that "13,200 radiocarbon years ago is the correct date for the earliest occupation of Fort Rock Cave" (authors' file).

13.　Three such excavations: Melvin W. Knickerbocker at Sisters, 1910, at depth of eight feet, a cache of large, perfect spear points; Carl Ladewig at Bend, 1911, at three feet, a cache of arrowheads, spear heads, and other cutting implements; Mr. and Mrs. Joe Werner at Bend, 1925-26, at over five feet, about ten fine obsidian points and some broken ones. *Deschutes Pioneers' Gazette* (Bend), 19 January 1973; January, 1977.

14. E. E. Rich, ed., *Peter Skene Ogden's Snake Country Journals, 1824-25 and 1825-26,* Hudson's Bay Record Society Publication no. 13 (London, 1950), p. 101.

15. F. G. Young, ed., "The Correspondence and Journals of Captain Nathaniel J. Wyeth, 1831-6," *Sources of the History of Oregon,* vol. 1 (Eugene, 1899), p. 243.

16. John Minto, "From Youth to Age as an American," *OHQ* 9 (1908), p. 157. In 1868-70, Edwin W. Follett with John and James Simms hunted and trapped the Deschutes River area from a base cabin they built "where the river makes a sharp bend to the west" (Bend). In all they took 700 beaver, 500 deer, 4 timber wolves, and "some" fishers, foxes and martins. "It was a great disappointment to me to have to leave the mild Deschutes Valley and come back to the long cold Winters of Michigan. The three Winters spent on the Deschutes were mild, the deepest snow being eight inches and it lasted only a week. None of us were sick a moment. The river was very steady and filled with splendid trout. Game of all kinds was plentiful. We all greatly enjoyed the time," Follett wrote from Olivet, Michigan, in later years. The furs, however, stored with French Brothers at The Dalles, were destroyed by fire in 1871, with $525 loss. *Bend Bulletin,* 22 June 1910.

17. John C. Frémont, *Report of the Exploring Expedition to the* Rocky Mountains (Washington, D.C., 1845), p. 200 (entry for 30 November).

18. Charles Preuss, *Exploring with Frémont,* trans. and ed. Erwin G. and Elisabeth K. Gudde (Norman, Oklahoma, 1958), p. 101.

19. W. A. Goulder, *Reminiscences of a Pioneer* (Boise, 1909), p. 126.

20. Leah Collins Menefee and Lowell Tiller, "Cutoff Fever," pt. 4, *OHQ* 78 (1977), p. 247.

21. Menefee and Tiller, "Cutoff Fever," pt. 4, p. 245.

22. Benjamin F. Owen, *My Trip Across the Plains, March 31, 1853-Oct. 28, 1853* (Eugene, 1959), p. 38.

23. Menefee and Tiller, "Cutoff Fever," pt. 6, *OHQ* 79 (1978), p. 19.

24. Menefee and Tiller, "Cutoff Fever," pt. 4, p. 241.

25. James Field, "Crossing the Plains" (journal entry for 23 September 1845), *Willamette Farmer* (Portland), 1 August 1879.

26. Bailey to Lucy P. Griffith, 20 September 1849, OHS Mss. 1508 (manuscript copy of letter).

27. Diary of Samuel Parker, 1845 (entry for 21 September) (copy at OHS). For the story of these immigrants, see Keith Clark and Lowell Tiller, *Terrible Trail: The Meek*

Cutoff, 1845 (Caldwell, Idaho, 1966).

28. Prospecting diary, 15 September 1858, OHS Mss. 732.

29. Leslie M. Scott, "The Pioneer Stimulus of Gold," *OHQ* 18 (1917), pp. 147-53; Lewis A. McArthur, *Oregon Geographic Names* (4th ed., revised and enlarged by Lewis L. McArthur, Portland, 1974), pp. 120, 330. (Hereafter cited as *OGN.*)

30. George Barnes, 1887, in *HCO*, p. 704; also *Bend Bulletin,* 5 August 1922 (reprinted from an 1887 edition of *Prineville News*).

31. Lewis A. McArthur, "Reminiscences of John Y. Todd," *OHQ* 30 (1929), pp. 70-73; A. L. Veazie, "Address at the Dedication of a Monument to the Pioneers of Crook County, August 7, 1938" *OHQ* 39 (1938), p. 374; *The Bend Press,* 1 June 1922.

32. *HCO,* pp. 704-705; see also pp. 700, 703, 781, 782.

33. *HCO,* pp. 704, 706, *Bend Bulletin,* 19 August 1922.

34. *HCO,* pp. 700-701.

35. *HCO,* p. 701; H. K. Hines, *An Illustrated History of the State of Oregon* (Chicago, 1893), pp. 1062-63. Hines gives 1858 as the date for Abram's entry to central Oregon, but between 1868 and 1872 Hackleman settled on Camp Creek. See also Veazie, "Address at the Dedication," *OHQ* 39 (1938), p. 381.

36. *Bend Bulletin,* 8 July 1922.

37. Fred Lockley, "Impressions and Observations of the Journal Man," *Oregon Journal* (Portland), 30 November 1938; also *Bend Bulletin,* 8 July 1922.

38. *Bend Bulletin,* 12 October 1922.

39. Keith Clark interview with Claude Vandevert, 30 September 1970, Central Oregon Community College (Bend) (hereafter COCC) Library Oral History Tape no. 40.

40. John Sisemore obituary, *Bend Bulletin,* 7 December 1910; also Linsy Sisemore, ed., *History of Klamath County, Oregon* (Klamath Falls, 1941), p. 214.

41. *Crook County News* (Prineville) ("Pioneer Edition"), 4 August 1939.

42. Ibid.

43. Kessler Cannon interview with W. E. Claypool, COCC Library Oral History Tape no. 35. Cannon recorded interviews for Bend Radio KBND during 1953.

44. Kessler Cannon interview with John Fryrear, COCC Library Oral History Tape no. 38.

45. A. W. Boyce, "Deep Snow

Takes Heavy Toll of Sheep in Early Day Winter," *Crook County News,* 4 August 1939.

46. *Central Oregon Shopper* (Prineville) ("Old Timers Edition"), 4 August 1949.

47. Keith and Donna Clark, "William McKay's Journal, 1866-67: Indian Scouts, Part I," *OHQ* 79 (1978), p. 167.

48. *HCO,* p. 705, also *Bend Bulletin,* 19 August 1922.

49. Editorial, *Bend Bulletin,* 22 December 1960; Phil Brogan, *East of the Cascades* (Portland, 1964), pp. 111-13.

50. *HCO,* pp. 719, 754, 759, 761, 762, 773, 783; McArthur, *OGN,* p. 461.

51. *Central Oregonian* (Prineville), 11 October 1934.

52. *Redmond Spokesman* (50th anniversary ed.), 22 August 1955.

53. Ibid.

54. *HCO,* p. 786; Hazel Foster, "Biographical Sketches for Prineville Centennial, 1968": Knox Huston (copy in authors' file).

55. *HCO,* pp. 789, 791; *Bend Bulletin,* 5 July 1916.

56. Brogan, *East of the Cascades,* pp. 122-27; George F. Brimlow, *Harney County, Oregon, and Its Range Land* (Portland, 1951), p. 234; Howard McKinley Corning, *Dictionary of Oregon History* (Portland, 1956), p. 37.

57. Interview with Cleon and Wanda Clark, Redmond, Oregon. See also Charles Conkling, E. R. Jackman and John Scharff, *Steens Mountain* (Caldwell, Idaho, 1968), pp. 149, 152.

58. Fisher Logan, COCC Library Oral History Tape no. 29; Corning, *Dictionary of Oregon History,* p. 37.

59. The reader may wish to compare this version with another in Conkling, Jackman and Scharff, *Steens Mountain,* p. 153, and Brimlow, *Harney County, Oregon, and Its Range Land,* p. 234.

60. Brogan, *East of the Cascades,* pp. 126-27; Corning, *Dictionary of Oregon History,* p. 37.

61. Personal interview with Ellis Edgington, Sisters.

62. Clark and Tiller, *Terrible Trail,* pp. 97, 230; Jack R. Brandt (Sweet Home, Oregon) to authors, 12 June 1968.

63. *Central Oregonian,* 6 March 1972 (reprinted from *Sunday Oregonian,* 19 March 1939); *Oregonian,* 31 October 1866; William Parsons and W. S. Shiach, *An Illustrated History of Umatilla and Morrow Counties* (Spokane, 1902), p. 257.

64. *Central Oregonian*, 6 March 1972; *Oregonian*, 19 March 1939. According to Blakely, Long later went to Washington, "kept telling a young tenderfoot he was going to take his ranch away from him. The fellow waited behind a door one day and blowed him to hell."

65. Joel Davis, "Hank Vaughan's Last Ride," *Pendleton East Oregonian*, 7 May 1977. Accounts vary— some relate that the horse slipped and fell. Vaughan died two weeks after the fall on 15 June.

66. *HCO*, pp. 710-12; Jim Blakely interview, *Central Oregon Shopper*, 4 August 1949 (reprinted from *Sunday Oregonian*, 14 November 1948). Blakely was told by one witness, Leo Fried, that the killers were not masked and were vigilantes.

67. "The Citizens Protective Union" was commonly known as the "Moonshiners." *HCO*, p. 711. Other sources for the paragraph are: *Central Oregon Shopper*, 4 August 1949, p. 3; Hazel Foster, "Biographical Sketches": Isaac Ketchum and David Stewart (copies in authors' file); *HCO*, pp. 701, 772, 793.

68. *Central Oregon Shopper*, 4 August 1949; *HCO*, p. 701.

69. *Central Oregonian*, 6 March 1972.

70. Ibid.; *Central Oregon Shopper*, 4 August 1949.

71. *Central Oregon Shopper*, 4 August 1949.

72. Kessler Cannon interview with Prince Staats, COCC Library Oral History Tape no. 38.

73. *HCO*, p. 713.

74. A. H. Hodgson, *Ochoco National Forest History* (Ochoco National Forest Headquarters, Prineville, 1913).

75. Ibid.

76. *HCO*, pp. 719, 720.

77. *HCO*, p. 719.

78. *Crook County News*, 4 August 1939.

79. *HCO*, pp. 720-21.

80. *Bend Bulletin*, 16 December 1916.

81. Cannon interview with Staats, COCC Library Oral History Tape no. 38.

82. Clark interview with Vandevert, COCC Library Oral History Tape no. 40.

83. *HCO*, pp. 724, 778. The plat consisted of 17 full and 5 half blocks. See also interview with Mrs. L. M. Hodges (*Central Oregonian*, 23 August 1934) in which she states that Monroe Hodges "traded Barney Prine a pony and $25 for a squat-

ter's right and a small hut made of juniper logs and covered with willows and ryegrass"; also, *Central Oregonian,* 9 September 1934.

84. Hazel Foster, "Biographical Sketches": Benjamin F. Allen (copy in authors' file). An earlier resident (1868) was James M. Allen, a member of the lost Meek party, who built the first flour mill in Prineville in 1875. Sons also in Crook County (then Wasco County) were Andy M., John and Albert. The latter was also with the 1845 party. See Clark and Tiller, *Terrible Trail,* pp. 28, 169-70; *HCO* pp. 240, 724, 764.

85. Fred Lockley interview with Prine, *Oregon Journal,* 31 March 1927.

86. Ibid.; Herbert B. Nelson and Preston E. Onstad, eds., *A Webfoot Volunteer, The Diary of William M. Hilleary, 1864-1866* (Corvallis, 1965), p. 37.

87. *HCO,* pp. 723-24. Barney left Prineville in 1870, moved up to Weston where he became city marshal. From there he went to Lapwai and operated a blacksmith shop for nearly 20 years. Lockley, *Oregon Journal,* 31 March 1927.

88. Veazie, "Address at the Dedication, *OHQ* 39 (1938) p. 382.

89. Ibid. William Heisler was first postmaster of Prine, established 13 April 1871. The post office name was changed to Prineville on 23 De-cember 1872. McArthur, *OGN,* pp. 251, 602. The Til Glaze story is in *Central Oregonian,* 27 September 1934.

90. *Central Oregonian,* 27 September 1934; *Bend Bulletin,* 2 September 1920, 9 September 1920, 16 June 1953 and 28 November 1917.

91. Sources of the paragraph, in order: McArthur, *OGN,* p. 30; *Laidlaw Chronicle,* 27 June 1908; *Bend Bulletin,* 20 January 1921, 15 May 1903 (advertisement) and 15 March 1972 (Frances Juris interview with Winifred Cline Jordan); *Redmond Spokesman,* 15 October 1942.

92. *Central Oregonian,* 30 August 1934; *HCO,* p. 754; John Dierdorff, *How Edison's Lamp Helped Light the West* (Portland, 1974), p. 7. Steve Yancey served as Crook County sheriff 1924-28.

93. *Redmond Spokesman,* 22 August 1955 (see also advertisement, p. 2).

94. B. Elizabeth Ward, *Redmond Rose of the Desert* (Redmond, 1975), p. 1; *Bend Bulletin,* 24 June 1904 and 20 October 1905; *Redmond Spokesman,* 7 March 1912; McArthur, *OGN,* p. 611.

95. Howard W. Turner, "Madras," in *Jefferson County Reminiscences* (Portland, 1957), pp. 115, 118, 122.

96. McArthur, *OGN,* p. 553; *HCO,* pp. 796-97; *Bend Bulletin,* 11 June 1929.

97. *Bend Bulletin,* 15 April 1904, 20 July 1926 and 15 March 1972; the *Redmond Spokesman* (15 October 1942) gives 1889 as year of Cline's arrival in Prineville. See McArthur, *OGN,* p. 162.

98. *Bend Bulletin,* 4 October 1924 and 17 February 1927; Brogan, *East of the Cascades,* pp. 174-75, 177.

99. *Bend Bulletin,* 17 February 1930 and 22 June 1910.

100. Tillie Wilson and Alice Scott, *That Was Yesterday* (Redmond, Oregon, 1976), pp. 5, 6.

101. *HCO,* p. 701.

102. *Central Oregonian,* 26 July 1934; *HCO* p. 792.

103. Carey W. Foster (article for *Central Oregonian,* early 1950s), Hazel Foster scrapbook (Prineville) (typed copy in authors' files).

104. Wanda Buslach, "William Henry Snook" (paper in authors' files).

105. *Bend Bulletin* ("Golden Jubilee Edition"), 16 June 1953.

106. Statement from daughter (Mrs. John Berning) (in authors' files); C.J. Rademacher, "History of Medicine in Central Oregon" (typed copy in authors' file). Dr. Edwards began practice in Bend during 1902.

107. Urling C. Coe, *Frontier Doctor* (New York, 1939), p. 2.

108. Ibid. pp. 70-73.

109. Cannon interview with Staats, COCC Library Oral History Tape no. 38.

110. *Bend Bulletin,* 31 July 1903.

111. Kessler Cannon interview with N. P. Smith, COCC Library Oral History Tape no. 42.

112. O. K. Burrell, *Gold in the Woodpile* (Eugene, 1967), pp. 255, 256.

113. Kessler Cannon interview with S. E. Roberts, COCC Library Oral History Tape no. 44; Phil F. Brogan, "He Arrived from Shaniko Just 50 Years Ago Today," *Bend Bulletin,* 20 January 1960.

114. *Bend Bulletin,* 9 September 1914.

115. *Bend Bulletin,* 19 November 1924; "Early Days—Central Oregon" (Pacific Northwest Bell, Portland) (copy in authors' file). See also *Bend Bulletin,* 24 November 1924 and 19 August 1904.

116. Cannon interview with Smith, COCC Library Oral History Tape no. 42.

117. Jim Crowell, "G. P. Helped Shape Frontier Community," *Bend Bulletin* ("West '76" edition), 26 March 1976.

118. Paper, "Early History," from records of Robert W. Sawyer, COCC Library vertical file; *Bend Bulletin*, 14 October 1904 and 8 August 1951; Wilson and Scott, *That Was Yesterday*, p. 42.

119. Dedication ceremony was 10 July 1971, according to U.S. Forest Service records (Bend). Sam Johnson represented central Oregon in the state legislature for 14 years, retiring in 1978. He is currently serving as mayor of Redmond. Becky Johnson has served many years on the state board of higher education and on various state education committees.

120. Charles Porfily, son of Crook County pioneer stockman Ralph Porfily.

121. *HCO*, p. 746; Jerry Dale Deats, "A History of Education in the Public Schools of Deschutes County Before 1925" (thesis, Eastern Oregon College, 1964) (copy in authors' file). See pp. 10, 8, 23, 24, 26, 29.

122. Statement from author's mother (in authors' files).

123. Mrs. Koenig, an early teacher east of Madras, told this to Dorothy Moore Nelson. *Deschutes Pioneers' Gazette*, January, 1976.

124. *HCO*, p. 746.

125. Wallis Nash, *A Lawyer's Life on Two Continents* (Boston, 1919), p. 142.

126. Water right from Willow Creek to irrigate 16.6 acres of land by Charles W. Palmehn. "Findings and Order of Determination Before the State Engineer of Oregon, 1924-25: Deschutes River," p. 12 (on file, Deschutes County Courthouse, Bend).

127. Deschutes Valley Land and Investment Company pamphlet (Portland, 1910), pp. 1, 38.

128. Allen Johnson, ed., *Dictionary of American Biography*, vol. 3 (New York, 1928), p. 489.

129. *Oregonian*, 18 November 1894.

130. *HCO*, p. 717; *Oregon Compiled Laws* (annotated), vol. 8 (Bancroft-Whitney, 1940), pp. 101-102.

131. "Findings and Order of Determination before the State Engineer of Oregon, 1924-25: Deschutes River," p. 27.

132. C. C. Hutchinson to Binger Hermann, 10 October 1901 (copy in authors' file) (original Hutchinson letters in Central Oregon Irrigation files, Redmond). Also see *Bend Bulletin*, 19 May 1909.

133. *HCO*, p. 713.

134. F. F. Henshaw, John H. Lewis and E. J. McCaustland, "Water Rights and Appropriation," *Deschutes River, Oregon and its Utilization* (Washington, D.C., 1914), U.S.

Geological Survey Water-Supply Paper 344, p. 149.

135. Hutchinson to Hermann, 10 October 1901; *HCO,* p. 717.

136. Hutchinson to Malcolm A. Moody, 10 October 1901 (copy in authors' file).

137. Editorial, *Bend Bulletin,* 27 March 1903.

138. *HCO,* pp. 718, 804.

139. Deschutes Valley Land and Investment Company pamphlet, pp. 3, 4.

140. *Bend Bulletin,* 18 November 1904 and 23 September 1904.

141. *Bend Bulletin,* 23 September 1904, 30 September 1904 and 7 October 1904.

142. *Bend Bulletin,* 17 March 1905.

143. *Bend Bulletin,* 24 August 1906.

144. *Bend Bulletin,* 15 December 1905.

145. *Redmond Spokesman,* 22 August 1955; information from Cleon Clark, Redmond.

146. "Deschutes Project," Jefferson County Extension Service Bulletin, p. 2 (copy in authors' file). The first water was available during 1946-47 for 17,000 acres; not until 1949 were the remaining 32,000 acres watered.

147. *Bend Bulletin,* 23 September 1904.

148. *Bend Bulletin,* 3 June 1904, 10 June 1904 and 27 April 1972.

149. *Bend Bulletin,* 19 August 1904.

150. Crane Prairie Reservoir, completed in 1922, covers an area of about seven square miles and stores 55,330 acre feet. Wickiup Reservoir, begun in 1939 as a CCC reclamation project, was completed in 1949, and stores 200,000 acre feet. "Crane Prairie Reservoir Capacity Table," Bureau of Reclamation (November 1971), p. 1 (copy on file at Watermaster's office, Deschutes County Courthouse); *Bend Bulletin,* 30 July 1940; McArthur, *OGN,* p. 188; "North Unit Irrigation Project," Jefferson County Extension Service Bulletin, p. 2 (copy in authors' file); *Redmond Spokesman,* 16 June 1938 and 13 April 1939.

151. U.S., Congress, Senate Document 1097 (Carey Act Projects, 1913), p. 16. The other six projects were: two Central Oregon Irrigation companies, Deschutes Land Company, Deschutes Land Board, Deschutes Irrigation and Power, and the Columbia Southern Project. See *State Desert Land Board Reports, 1910-1923* (state printer, Salem, Oregon), 1923 report, pp. 4, 5; 1913 report, p. 3. *HCO,* pp. 717-20, lists the

Oregon Irrigation Co., Pilot Butte Development Co., Columbia Southern Irrigation Co., Central Oregon Irrigation Co., Squaw Creek Irrigation Co., Buck Mountain Irrigation Co., and Deschutes Irrigation and Power Co., between 1901 and 1905.

152. Quotations in this paragraph are from the *Redmond Spokesman*, 22 August 1955.

153. *Bend Bulletin*, 7 December 1906, 21 December 1906 and 10 May 1907.

154. *State Land Board Reports Relative to Desert Land, 1901-1908* (state printer, Salem), p. 36.

155. *State Desert Land Board Reports, 1909-1923*, 1913 report, p. 3; also "Findings and Order of Determination Before the State Engineer of Oregon: Deschutes River," p. 43.

156. Elsie Allen, "Tumalo Irrigation Project: An Episode in Irrigation Development," pp. 1-12 (copy in authors' file).

157. *Bend Bulletin*, 14 December 1906.

158. Allen, "Tumalo Irrigation Project," p. 6.

159. *Bend Bulletin*, 12 April 1907 and 5 December 1936.

160. O. Laurgaard, *Project Engineer's Final Report to the Desert Land Board* (Laidlaw, Oregon, 1914), p. 4.

161. *State Desert Land Board Reports, 1909-1923*, 1917 report, p. 4; personal conversations with author's aunt, Freda McDaniel, and author's father, R. L. Clark.

162. *State Desert Land Board Reports, 1909-1923*, 1919 Report, p. 5.

163. *Bend Bulletin*, 27 April 1972.

164. *Bend Bulletin*, 8 September 1915.

165. Ibid.

166. *Bend Bulletin*, 9 February 1916 and 21 June 1916.

167. Cecil Moore (1905 pioneer, Agency Plains) in *Deschutes Pioneers' Gazette*, January, 1978.

168. Leslie M. Scott, "The Yaquina Railroad," *OHQ* 16 (1915), pp. 228-29.

169. *Deschutes Pioneers' Gazette*, 18 January 1975.

170. Ibid.

171. In local terminology, an area west of the Deschutes River and south of the Metolius, including homestead communities of Geneva and Grandview.

172. Isaiah Bowman, *The Pioneer Fringe* (New York, 1931), p. 109.

173. Ibid., p. 94.

174. Ibid., p. 98.

175. *Deschutes Pioneers' Gazette,* 18 January 1975.

176. *Bend Bulletin,* 1 April 1914.

177. E. R. Jackman and R. A. Long, *The Oregon Desert* (Caldwell, Idaho, 1971), pp. 44, 63.

178. *Jefferson County Reminiscences,* pp. 197, 249, 260, 299, 300; *Redmond Spokesman,* 19 February 1920; conversations with homesteaders.

179. *Bend Bulletin,* 16 December 1916.

180. *Bend Bulletin,* 20 January 1948.

181. *Bend Bulletin,* 11 August 1951 and 16 August 1951.

182. *Redmond Spokesman,* 22 August 1955; Harry Heising, "Grandview, Camp Sherman and Metolius River," *Jefferson County Reminiscences,* pp. 217-19.

183. *Bend Bulletin,* 31 August 1910.

184. *Deschutes Pioneers' Gazette,* 18 January 1975.

185. "High Desert Homesteaders' Dream," *Sunday Oregon Journal,* 20 November 1960.

186. Bowman, *The Pioneer Fringe,* p. 93.

187. *Redmond Spokesman,* 22 August 1955.

188. Ibid.

189. Henry Schumacher in *Redmond Spokesman,* 22 August 1955.

190. *Crook County News,* 4 August 1939.

191. *Redmond Spokesman,* 22 August 1955.

192. Ibid.

193. *Central Oregon Shopper* ("Old Timers Edition"), 4 August 1949.

194. Kessler Cannon interview with Elizabeth Bogue, COCC Library Oral History Tape no. 42.

195. *Redmond Spokesman,* 22 August 1955.

196. Ibid.

197. Ibid.

198. Ibid.

199. *Bend Bulletin,* 3 February 1977.

200. Kessler Cannon interview with Mrs. Gus Stadig, COCC Library Oral History Tape no. 37.

201. Personal interview with Cochran, Prineville, July, 1978.

202. Kessler Cannon interview with "Klondike Kate" Van Duren, COCC Library Oral History Tape no. 5.

DESCHUTES COUNTRY GEOGRAPHY

1. Lewis A. McArthur, *Oregon Geographic Names* (4th ed., revised and enlarged by Lewis L. McArthur, Portland, 1974), p. 217.

2. Phil F. Brogan, *East of the Cascades* (Portland, 1964), p. 14ff.

3. John D. Beaulieu, *Geologic Hazards of Parts of Northern Hood River, Wasco, and Sherman Counties, Oregon,* Oregon Dept. of Geology and Mineral Industries (Portland, 1977), p. 44.

4. William G. Loy et al, *Atlas of Oregon* (Eugene, 1976), p. 108.

5. Loy, *Atlas of Oregon,* p. 136.

6. Raymond R. Hatton, *Bend Country Weather and Climate* (Redmond, 1973), pp. 7, 39-44; also Pacific Northwest River Basin Commission, *Climatological Handbook, Columbia Basin States,* vols. 1 & 2 (Vancouver, 1968-69).

7. Jerry F. Franklin and C. T. Dyrness, *Natural Vegetation of Oregon and Washington,* U.S.D.A. Forest Service General Technical Bulletin PNW-8 (Portland, 1973), pp. 160-92.

8. Center for Population Research and Census, *Population Estimates of Counties and Incorporated Places of Oregon* (Portland, 1977), pp. 1-4. (See also previous annual reports.)

9. *Oregon Blue Book, 1977-78* (Salem), p. 260.

10. Loy, *Atlas of Oregon,* p. 20.

11. Sheldon D. Ericksen, *Occupance of the Upper Deschutes Basin, Oregon,* Geography Research Paper No. 32, University of Chicago (1953), pp. 121-26.

12. U.S. Dept. of Commerce, Bureau of the Census, *Census of Agriculture for 1974, Oregon* (Washington, D.C., 1977), tables for Deschutes County.

13. Raymond R. Hatton, "The Impact of Tourism on Central Oregon" (M.A. thesis, University of Oregon, 1969), pp. 160-69.

1.   Keith Clark in "Travelers at the Deschutes, 1813?" *Oregon Historical Quarterly* (hereafter cited as *OHQ*) 77 (1976), pp. 79-81, suggests that Donald McKenzie or Pacific Fur Company men may have reached the Deschutes in 1813.

2.   Because it entered the Columbia River near falls in that river.

3.   Carl I. Wheat, *Mapping the Trans-Mississippi West,* vol. 2 (San Francisco, 1958), pp. 146, 162. The Hudson's Bay Company sent its maps to Arrowsmith, including information from Peter Skene Ogden and others, perhaps Tom McKay.

4.   U.S., Congress, Senate Document 470, 25th Cong., 2nd sess., 1837-38 (Serial 318).

5.   See Keith Clark and Lowell Tiller, *Terrible Trail: The Meek Cutoff, 1845* (Caldwell, Idaho, 1966); and Leah Collins Menefee and Lowell Tiller, "Cutoff Fever," pts. 1-6, *OHQ* 77:4-79:1 (1976-78).

6.   Records of the Office of Indian Affairs, Record Group 75, no. 1702, National Archives, Washington, D.C. (hereafter cited as RG, NA). (Photostat in Richardson Collection, IV-82, OHS, copy printed in Ralph M. Shane, "Early Explorers Through Warm Springs Reservation Area," *OHQ* 51 (1950), p. 288.

7.   Annotated ms. map on paper, 1855, RG 75, no. 234, NA.

8.   See Menefee and Tiller, "Cutoff Fever," pt. 2, *OHQ* 78 (1977), pp. 45-51; also Stanley S. Spaid, "Life of General Joel Palmer," *OHQ* 55 (1954), pp. 313-18.

9.   U.S., Congress, Senate Executive Document 78 (hereafter, SED), *Reports of Explorations and Surveys to Ascertain the Most Practicable and Economical Route for a Railroad from the Mississippi River to the Pacific Ocean* (commonly cited as *Pacific Railroad Reports,* hereafter cited as *PRR*), vol. 6, pt. 1, 32nd Cong., 2nd sess., 1852-53, p. 75. Lewis A. McArthur's *Oregon Geographic Names* (4th ed., revised and enlarged by Lewis L. McArthur, Portland, 1974) indicates that Whychus Creek, which Williamson says is a Deschutes tributary (*PRR*, vol. 6, pt. 1, p. 78) is Squaw Creek, flowing in Deschutes and Jefferson counties. The party was near Camp S on the Why-chus, marked on the published map.

10.   *PRR*, vol. 6, pt. 1, p. 85.

11.   Background on fort and city

growth appears in Priscilla Knuth, *"Picturesque" Frontier: The Army's Fort Dalles* (Portland, 1967), pp. 2-3. Among orders forbidding settlement east of the Deschutes, see Special Order no. 87, from Brig. Gen. N. S. Clarke, commanding the Department of the Pacific, in U.S., Congress, House Executive Document 112 (hereafter HED), Indian Affairs in Oregon and Washington Territory, 35th Cong., 1st sess., 1857-58, p. 2 (Serial 958). General Wool issued such an order in 1856 (see Knuth, *"Picturesque" Frontier,* p. 31n96).

12. Though the treaty creating the Warm Springs Reservation was made in 1855, the tribes that made it at that time were living mostly along the Columbia, and probably hunting in the reservation area (Shane, "Early Explorers," p. 280). The treaty was not ratified by Congress until 1859, but the Indians were on and off the reservation before that time. On Snake raids on the reservation, see Shane, "Early Explorers," p. 280; Keith and Donna Clark, "William McKay's Journal, 1866-67," *OHQ* 79 (1978), pp. 125-26; James Arneson, "Property Concepts of 19th Century Indians," *OHQ* 81 (1980), pp. 397-98.

13. U.S., Congress, SED 34, 36th Cong., 1st sess., 1859-60 (Serial 1031). Or U.S., Congress, HED 65 ("Affairs in Oregon"), 36th Cong., 1st sess., 1859-60, particularly pp. 133, 156, 208ff ("Affairs in Oregon" also contains the preliminary material of late 1858, with reports from Joel Palmer, Robert Newell and Louis Scholl).

14. Former Fort Dalles "supervising architect" Scholl also figured in the 1860 Army expedition into southeastern Oregon. His background included Oregon Trail experience to California and back to Salt Lake, work with the Army from Salt Lake to southern Oregon in 1854, following which he drew the "official" maps for Col. E. J. Steptoe's expedition from Salt Lake to the Pacific Coast. For biographical data on Scholl see Knuth, *"Picuresque" Frontier,* p. 34n.

15. Wallen to Capt. A. Pleasonton (Harney's adjutant), 12 June 1859, RG 393, NA (Dept. of Columbia, Letters Received, Box 3, W116).

16. Wallen to Pleasonton, 1 July 1859, op. cit., W122. Scholl and Wallen gathered everything about the country they could find, from Army maps (which would have material derived from Frémont in the 1840s) to information as recent as a report from Dr. Fitch of the Warm Springs Agency. Fitch had gone with some reservation Indians on a raid on the Snakes "within the past three weeks," Wallen commented in a letter of June 5. (Ibid., W108.) Both Scholl and Wallen (and the other sub-expeditions like Bonnycastle's) had parties of Indians of the country—including Paulina and We-ow-we-wah, who had been captured ear-

lier that spring when they raided the Warm Springs Reservation, and were taken to the guardhouse at Fort Dalles. Somewhere along the way with the Wallen expedition the two Snake or Paiute leaders 'left' or escaped. See Erminie Wheeler-Voegelin, "The Northern Paiute of Central Oregon," pt. 2, *Ethnohistory* 2 (1955), pp. 242, 260; Scholl's notation on a letter to him from Rufus Ingalls dated 5 June 1859 (Scholl Papers, OHS Mss. 311); Maury-Drake Papers, Yale University Library, microfilm roll 2 (Fort Dalles Guard Reports, 1859) (copy at OHS); Agent A.P. Dennison to Oregon Indian Superintendent J.W. Nesmith, 18 April 1859, National Archives Microcopy 2, roll 17 (Oregon Superintendency of Indian Affairs, Letters Received, Jan. 3-Dec. 30, 1859).

17.   Quoted in Harney to Asst. Adjutant General, 1 August 1859, in "Affairs in Oregon," p. 208.

18.   That is, to the "Free Emigrant Road." "Affairs in Oregon," p. 208.

19.   See Robert C. Clark, "Harney Basin Exploration, 1826-60," *OHQ* 33 (1932), pp. 112-13; and Priscilla Knuth, ed., "Cavalry in the Indian Country, 1864," *OHQ* 65 (1964), p. 51n80.

20.   U.S., Congress, SED 1, 37th Cong., 2nd sess., 1861-62, p. 531 (Serial 1118).

21.   Ibid., pp. 531-32.

22.   Ibid., p. 532.

23.   Steen to Pleasonton, 21 June 1860, RG 393, NA (Dept. of Columbia, Letters Received, Box 5, S42). The miners lost 70 horses—which might have encouraged the subsequent (and much less fruitful) attack on Captain Smith's Army party. *Oregon Statesman* (Salem) reported on 10 July 1860 that "gold in considerable quantities has been found on tributaries of the Des Chutes."

24.   Col. Justus Steinberger, 1st Washington Territory Infantry, then commanding the Oregon military district, complained from Fort Vancouver to Department of the Pacific headquarters, San Francisco, on 11 June 1862, that "all the records of the former Department of Oregon up to 21st January 1861 and to the time when it was merged into the Department of the Pacific, were ordered to be sent to San Francisco and I am informed are now at department headquarters. Among them are many reports from officers commanding expeditions to the country east of the Cascades Mountains. . . . Much valuable information is contained in these records that it will be difficult if not impossible to obtain at the present time here." See U.S., Congress, House Document 59 (*War of the Rebellion*, series I, vol. 50, pt. 1, Washington, D.C., 1897), 55th Cong., 1st sess., p. 1132 (Serial 3571).

25.   For Drake's identification of

Scholl see note 29 below. Scholl comments in a notation on a letter of General Alvord, 5 March 1864 (OHS Mss. 330) that he was never paid for making the map. On Scholl, Cayuse George and Indian George see Knuth, "Cavalry in the Indian Country," pp. 5n2, 23n40, 61-62.

26. Bowen, born in Pennsylvania, at age 29 enlisted in Jacksonville, Oregon, 30 November 1861, as a private. By mid-1862 he was regimental quartermaster sergeant, and was transferred to the regimental staff, then discharged for the purpose of accepting a second lieutenancy. He was finally mustered out 6 June 1866. Salem, Oregon State Archives, Adjutant General's Papers, Inventory 59-36, Item M.6-A; Inventory 60-28, Items 5b. (1), (3), (7), (9). (As cited by Marshall Hanft to P. Knuth, 8 June 1961.)

27. Bowen to Drake, 19 July 1864 (typed copy in John M. Drake Collection, OHS Mss. 80).

28. Such as Indian Springs, Pleasonton's Butte, Harney Lake, Spring Valley, Barren Valley, et cetera. The 1864 Bowen map is at OHS, the 1865 at the Oregon State Archives. While Bowen's name does not appear on the latter, it does appear on the 1864 map (of identical outlines and scale) at OHS.

29. Knuth, "Cavalry in the Indian Country," p. 61. Perhaps Bowen referred to the map Drake had from Scholl after the 1864 campaign to add some material to his. There is an earlier map, probably dated in 1863-64, which may have been drawn or traced by Bowen, titled "Genl Alvords Map of Eastn Oregon & Western Idaho." Records of the Office of the Chief Engineers, RG 77, U.S. 324, no. 39, NA. It includes the then new Fort Lapwai and Idaho material pertinent to district military operations of 1862-63. For central Oregon it includes locations identified as Deschutes, Hay Stack, Black Hollow, Cross Hollow, Antelope Valley and Muddy, on a route from Fort Dalles to the Canyon City and Idaho mining area.

30. They add more to southeastern Oregon. See Knuth, "Cavalry in the Indian Country," p. 25n42.

31. U.S., Congress, SED 1 (Report of the Secretary of the Interior) 37th Cong., 2nd sess., 1861-62, p. 470 (Serial 1117). The Willamette meridian had been run east across the Cascades as far as the Umatilla by late 1859. SED 2 (Report of the Secretary of the Interior), 36th Cong., 1st sess., 1860-61, p. 189 (Serial 1023).

32. A. B. Carter to W. W. Chapman, 18 March 1860, from Lebanon, Record Group 94, Sand Point Federal Records Center, Seattle (Misc. Letters Received). The Army had some communication within a particular branch, at least. Lt. Joseph Dixon, who went with Steen in 1860, wrote Pleasonton on 30 April 1860, that Lt. R. S. Williamson (of

the Pacific Railroad exploration) had told him that the route along the Willamette Middle Fork, crossing the Cascades south of Diamond Peak, "and from thence to the head waters of the Des Chutes near a small mountain lake," was "practicable for a wagon road, but it would require a great deal of labour to cut a road through the heavy timber on the mountains, especially on the western side." Williamson told him that people in Eugene "often remarked," when he was there the winter of 1859-60, that there was another practicable wagon route from there to the summit "following up the dividing ridge between the middle and McKenzie's Forks. . .and he also informed me [Dixon] from his personal knowledge that the eastern side of the Cascade range could be ascended or descended at either of the above named places without much trouble." Dixon to Pleasonton, 30 April 1860, Records of United States Army Commands, RG 98, NA (Dept. of Columbia, Letters Received, Box 4, D10).

33.   Chapman sent a copy of the Diagram of Oregon to Harney with the letter. RG 98, NA (Dept. of Columbia, Letters Received, Box 4, C8).

34.   U.S., Congress, SED 1, 37th Cong., 2nd sess., 1861-62, p. 530 (Serial 1117) (1861 Oregon Surveyor General's report, acc. doc. no. 13).

35.   Published in U.S., Congress, HED 1, vol. 5 (maps), 37th Cong., 3rd sess., 1861-62 (Serial 1120).

36.   Wheat, *Mapping the Trans-Mississippi West*, vol. 5, pt. 1, p. 51.

37.   1861 is published in U.S., Congress, SED 1, 36th Cong., 2nd sess., 1860-61; 1863 is in HED 1, 38th Cong., 1st sess., 1863-64 (and has been reprinted by OHS); and OHS has a photostat of 1865 (no. 364) from RG 75, NA.

38.   U.S., Congress, SED 124 ("Forfeiture of Oregon Lands"), 50th Cong., 1st sess., 1887-88, pp. 137-42 (Serial 2510).

39.   U.S., Congress, House Report 332, 46th Cong., 3rd sess., 1880-81, pp. 27, 40-41, 5 (Serial 1982); and U.S., Congress, HED 131, 49th Cong., 1st sess., 1885-86 pp. 27, 40-41 (Serial 2399). The total length of the road was 448.7 miles, providing 861,504 acres of land for the company, of which by 1886, it had patented 548,749.53. Up to 19 June 1876, 107,893 acres were patented; in 1879, 437,997.7 acres were selected but not yet patented (House Report 332, p. 2). The secretary of the interior in 1881 recommended resumption by the U.S. government of WV&CM grant lands, which it was decided, had to be done by judicial proceeding. It was concluded that the wagon roads "have never been built as designed, that the lines of these roads, as located, have in no single instance been followed by anything fairly approximating construction; that to a great extent such roads as exist in the general course of the located routes and have been

attempted to be adopted as parts of them, are the only roads of practicable use on the lines, and that these were not constructed by the wagon-road companies. . .but either by some other companies, or by the counties in which they lie" (SED 124, op. cit., pp. 4-5). Nevertheless, because the grants had been sold, ultimate court decisions did not return the land to the federal government. See note 56 below.

40.   SED 124, op. cit., pp. 142, 143, 145.

41.   House Report 332, op. cit., p. 24.

42.   See Keith and Donna Clark, "William McKay's Journal"; also Erminie Wheeler-Voegelin, "The Northern Paiute," pts. 1-2, *Ethnohistory* 2 (1955). Actual interest in a road east across the mountains from Lebanon-Albany went back to the early 1850s (see Menefee and Tiller, "Cutoff Fever") and was expressed in 1860 to Harney. The WV&CM Wagon Road Co. was organized in 1863-64 by "citizens of Linn County. . .chiefly farmers and stock-raisers, desiring to secure direct communication with Eastern Oregon as a range for their surplus cattle, sheep and horses." (HED 131, op. cit., p. 13.) It was a joint stock company, and when "first organized and the work of building the road was commenced, no idea of such a grant was entertained, and the company proceeded for a time upon the supposition that the road could be built from their own resources. . . . In the meantime their subscriptions of money and labor were exhausted, and in the year 1866 a land grant was obtained." (Ibid.) Other pertinent material includes: petition to Gov. Addison C. Gibbs from Linn County people (sent by the governor to Col. Geo. B. Currey) asking for military protection for the Deschutes country and the road; Currey's response to Gibbs, dated Ft. Vancouver, 3 August 1865, in Gibbs Collection, OHS Mss. 685; *Salem Daily Record*, 31 August 1867, a letter from "E", dated 26 August, Lebanon, describing the company which would start from that place on 10 September, "to settle and locate claims in Ochoco valley, bordering on Crooked river, east of the Cascade mountains, through which the Lebanon wagon road runs, leading from Albany. . . . [Capt. J. A. White] desires all persons who wish to obtain claims and settle in a new country, to join his company." The same paper on 12 September 1867, reports that Sam Headrick, who had just returned from examining the WV&CM road from Lebanon to the Deschutes (101 miles), "preparatory to its acceptance by the Governor on behalf of the State," had "found it to be a good passable wagon road, and has so reported it. Several companies were met crossing the mountains to seek for homes in some of the fertile valleys beyond."

43.   Supplemental report to accompany report of Oregon surveyor general for year ending 30 June 1868,

dated 15 September 1868, to commissioner of General Land Office (typed copy from University of Oregon transcription).

44. For background see Richard A. Bartlett, *Great Surveys of the American West* (Norman, Oklahoma, 1962, also 1980 reprint), pp. 336-38; William H. Goetzmann, "The Wheeler Surveys and the Decline of Army Surveys in the West," in *The American West, An Appraisal,* ed. Robert G. Ferris (Santa Fe, 1963), pp. 37-47.

45. Unfortunately for those interested in the maps, only part of the Wheeler Survey records survived, very few for Oregon. See C. E. Dewing, "The Wheeler Survey Records: A Study in Archival Anomaly," *American Archivist* 27 (1964).

46. Appendix B, Symons Report, 31 March 1879, p. 2193, in documents accompanying the *Report of the Secretary of War, Message and Documents,* vol. 2, pt. 3 (Washington, D.C., 1879) (Appendixes to the Report of the Chief of Engineers).

47. They called it Davis Lake (ibid., p. 2196), which McArthur's *Oregon Geographic Names* states was named just about that time for a Prineville stockman, formerly of Linn County, who ran stock in the area.

292

48. Symons report, op. cit., pp. 2196, 2197.

49. The Columbia Southern Railway, built to aid shipment of wheat and wool from the east side of the Deschutes in Sherman County, was begun in 1897, and completed through Moro at the end of 1898, and to Grass Valley and Shaniko by spring of 1900. West of the Deschutes in Wasco County the Great Southern Railway, begun in 1904 to do the same job, was completed to Dufur in 1905 and a few years later reached its greatest extent of 41 miles south at Friend. See John F. Due and Giles French, *Rails to the Mid-Columbia Wheatlands* (Washington, D.C., 1979), pp. 45-51, 215-37.

50. *Oregon Journal,* 29 May 1910.

51. On 10 May 1910, the *Journal* reported that railroad contractors were "flocking into Bend," anticipating work on the Oregon Trunk extension south. On the same page was the report of Bend residents rising before dawn to "catch the first glimpse of Halley's comet. The first early risers a week ago saw but a small portion of the tail, but toward the last of the week and early this week the vastness of the tail's expanse became apparent and plainly visible to the naked eye." Central Oregon skies had cleared to give "probably the best view of the comet in any place in the state. The lightness of the atmosphere is also conducive to a remarkably clear view of the heavenly visitor."

52. Background on the Hill-Harri-

man battle appears in Due and French, *Rails to the Mid-Columbia Wheatlands,* p. 99ff.

53.   At Madras on 7 May Hill enjoyed a lunch prepared "by the ladies of the town" (*Oregon Journal,* 8 May 1910). He saw Redmond, Laidlaw and Prineville, and in Bend on 9 May, standing in an auto, advised residents to prepare for "scores" of new people. "The advertising campaign to be given Central Oregon will be no infantile affair. Mr. Hill said that from the Atlantic to the Pacific people who heretofore have known little or nothing of this wonderful, productive country are to learn of it intimately. . . .   He expressed great pleasure at the beauty of Bend and surrounding country" (*Journal,* 9 May 1910). See also *Journal,* 3 May, 5 May, 11 May, 12 May 1910.

54.   Hanley's own account of the 1910 trip appears in *Feelin' Fine! Bill Hanley's Book,* ed. Anne Shannon Monroe (Garden City, N.Y., 1930), p. 161ff.

55.   *Oregon Journal,* 11 May 1910.

56.   *Oregon Journal,* 13 May 1910. For a summary of the wagon road land-grant situation and some effects, see Due and French, pp. 37-39.

57.   *Oregon Journal,* 29 May 1910. The American Automobile Association was formed in 1902, the Portland Automobile Club in 1905 and the Oregon State Motor Association in 1917, according to information from the Portland AAA office.

58.   *Oregon Journal,* 29 May 1910. Due and French, pp. 107-11, supply background on early automobiles in the lower Deschutes country.

59.   *Portland Telegram,* 23 May 1910. Benson was prominent in Columbia River highway affairs, and a few years later was a member of the state highway commission.

[There is no definitive published history of central Oregon's pine lumber industry. The material in this chapter came largely from newspaper articles and from interviews with persons either involved in the industry or who have studied aspects of the developing history. Helpful were files of the Western Wood Products Association (successor to the Western Pine Association) and information supplied by Brooks-Scanlon, Inc.]

1.   Phil Brogan, *East of the Cascades* (Portland, 1964), p. 246. (This book is especially helpful in providing a narrative of events in central Oregon.)

2.   Brogan, *East of the Cascades,* p. 249.

3.   Notes on timber acquisition prepared by Robert Sawyer.

4.   Samuel Johnson interview, 1978.

5.   Brogan, *East of the Cascades,* p. 236.

6.   Brogan, *East of the Cascades,* p. 237.

7.   Brogan, *East of the Cascades,* pp. 198, 238.

8.   Stewart Holbrook, *Age of the Moguls* (Garden City, N.Y., 1953), p. 198.

9.   Albro Martin, *James J. Hill and the Opening of the Northwest* (New York, 1976), p. 567.

10.   Holbrook, *Age of the Moguls,* p. 200; Brogan, *East of the Cascades,* p. 242.

11.   Article by Jim Crowell, *Bend Bulletin* (undated promotional issue).

12.   Information from Ward Tonfeldt, Central Oregon Community College.

13.   *Bend Bulletin,* 20 May 1976.

14.   *Bend Bulletin,* 12 May 1915.

15.   *Bend Bulletin,* 12 May 1915.

16.   Article by Jim Crowell, *Bend Bulletin* (undated promotional issue).

17.   Brogan, *East of the Cascades,* p. 253.

18.   *Bend Bulletin,* 12 May 1915.

19.   *Bend Bulletin,* 9 June 1915.

20.   *Bend Bulletin,* 22 March 1916.

21.   *Bend Bulletin,* 29 March 1916.

22. *Bend Bulletin*, undated excerpt, ca. 13 September 1916.

23. Article by Jim Crowell, *Bend Bulletin* (undated promotional issue); also issue of 2 March 1923.

24. Timber industry chronology prepared and provided by Ward Tonfeldt.

25. Walter J. Ryan, "Logging Railroads," American Society of Civil Engineers Transactions, 14 July 1926 (Symposium on the Logging and Lumbering Interests of the Pacific Northwest).

26. Information on logging techniques from Ward Tonfeldt.

27. Charles Shotts (Gilchrist Timber Co.) interview.

28. Western Pine Association (now Western Wood Products Association), Forest Conservation Committee minutes, 11 August 1942-22 February 1949.

29. Samuel Johnson interview.

30. Stuart J. Shelk (Ochoco Lumber Co.) interview.

31. Series by Gerry Pratt, *Oregonian*, 10-12 August 1958.

32. *Oregonian*, 8 January 1950.

33. *Oregonian*, 29 April 1951.

34. Charles Shotts interview.

35. Brogan, *East of the Cascades*, p. 256.

36. Article by Phil Brogan, *Oregonian*, 13 January 1952.

37. *Oregonian*, 31 December 1950.

38. Article by Phil Brogan, *Oregonian*, 4 March 1951.

INDEX

[Italicized numbers indicate illustrations]

297

301

305

306

308

COLOPHON

This collection of selected essays, *High & Mighty*, was composed by Sandy K. Westbrook in the roman typeface Sabon. The display typography, Peter, was set by Spartan Typographers. Artline Printers of Beaverton, Oregon, printed this study about the Deschutes country of central Oregon. The clothbound copies were bound by Lincoln & Allen of Portland. The text paper is 60-lb. Simpson Vellum Offset. The paperbound copies are covered with l8-pt. Feedcote.

Yeomen service was performed by a great number of persons—typesetters, artists, processers, printers and suppliers—on this "High & Mighty" effort. To them goes the appreciation of the Publications Department of the Oregon Historical Society.

Ably assisted by Colleen Campbell and Tracy Ann Robinson, the design was created and production was handled by Bruce Taylor Hamilton.